BLACK STUDENT ACHIEVEMENT

HOW MUCH DO FAMILY AND SCHOOL REALLY MATTER?

William A. Sampson

A SCARECROWEDUCATION BOOK

The Scarecrow Press, Inc.
Lanham, Maryland, and London
2002

A SCARECROWEDUCATION BOOK

Published in the United States of America
by Scarecrow Press, Inc.
A Member of the Rowman & Littlefield Publishing Group
4720 Boston Way, Lanham, Maryland 20706
www.scarecroweducation.com

4 Pleydell Gardens, Folkestone
Kent CT20 2DN, England

British Library Cataloguing in Publication Information Available

Library of Congress Cataloging-in-Publication Data

Sampson, William A., 1946–
    Black student achievement : how much do family and school really matter? / William
A. Sampson.
        p. cm.
    Includes bibliographical references and index.
    ISBN 0-8108-4402-8 (alk. paper) ISBN 0-8108-4295-5 (pbk. : alk. paper)
        1. African Americans—Education—Illinois—Evanston—Case studies. 2. Poor—
    Education—Illinois—Evanston—Case studies. 3. Home and school—Illinois—
    Evanston—Case studies. 4. Academic achievement—Illinois—Evanston—Case
    studies. 5. Educational surveys—Illinois—Evanston. I. Title.

LC2803.E93 S26 2002
371.829'96073—dc21
                                                                        2002020080

♾™ The paper used in this publication meets the minimum requirements of
American National Standard for Information Sciences—Permanence of Paper
for Printed Library Materials, ANSI/NISO Z39.48-1992.
Manufactured in the United States of America.

CONTENTS

PREFACE

While America's long-running discussion regarding the quality of urban education in general and the education of poor nonwhites in particular is certainly sincere and often impassioned, it is in a sense disingenuous. This is because the debate centers almost exclusively on schools and school policy. While it makes sense for school policymakers to focus on school-based initiatives given their vested interests, it has done little to improve education, particularly that of poor nonwhites. School policymakers' focus on school-related policies allows them to argue that they are indeed working on the problems and at the same time protect their turf—schools.

Without doubt, changes can be made in schools that can make an enormous difference in the quality of the education offered to those who most need our help. We could reduce class sizes to fifteen to seventeen students per class. We could make certain that every child had a good preschool education. We know from previous research that both of these policies can have a great impact on the quality of education. We also know that each is highly unlikely given the very high financial cost. In fact, school superintendents take credit for reducing class size from thirty to twenty-eight when there is really little chance that this reduction will significantly improve the quality of the education offered in their schools. The reduction does, however, allow them to suggest that they are working to improve schools. The schools don't get improved, but teachers are happy, and parents feel that something is being done.

I wanted to study the possibility that another direction, a different focus, might be in order. The work of Reginald Clark, Doris Entwisle, James Comer, F. Furstenberg, and J. Bempechat suggested that direction, and reflections on my own background and family life underscored my choice. As I saw the situation, "raising the bar" for teachers and students—that is, higher expectations reflected in increased testing and changes in teacher certification—has little chance of bringing about significant improvements in the quality of the education offered to poor non-white students. Neither do curriculum changes, vouchers, charter schools, changes in school governance, nor school uniforms. These are all school-based policies discussed by educational policymakers who focus on schools in part because that is all that they know and in part because that is all they can easily control.

There is, however, little empirical evidence to suggest that any of these changes will significantly help. This is not to say that school-based changes cannot help. If students do not have adequately trained or motivated teachers, if they lack textbooks or a safe school environment, they have little chance to do well in school. But students who have parents who are involved in the educational experience are, by definition, different kinds of students from those who do not, and my suspicion is that these familial differences, and not the educational changes themselves, will account for much of the difference, if any, in school success experienced by these students.

I wanted to focus on the possibility that family-based changes can have a significant impact on the quality of the education achieved by poor non-white students. I have come to believe that students who are not sent to school prepared to learn have far less chance of doing well in school no matter what is going on in the school, and the research reported in this book was designed to test this belief. If I am correct, then the school reform movement is pretty far off base, focusing as it does almost exclusively on schools, when it may well be that the emphasis should in fact be on families and homes.

To test this belief I placed observers in the homes of twelve poor black families selected for me by a highly respected community social service agency in Evanston, Illinois, for seven to eight weeks to record the home environment and family dynamics of the students. All of the students are poor, all are black, all live in roughly the same neighborhood. Nine attend the same school district (indeed, six go to the same school), and three attend the local high school. Four of the twelve had poor school grades, three had average grades, and five had high grades. I wanted to examine the possibility that differences in family dynamics and/or home environment account for the differences in school performance, for if I am correct, and the data suggest that I may well be, then perhaps the nation should begin to look into the possibility that much of the discussion regarding changes in school policy to improve the education offered to poor nonwhites is off base. Perhaps the focus should shift from schools to families.

This is not an easy shift, given that in America the family is sacrosanct. If, however, we continue down the current path, I do not see much improvement on the horizon for poor nonwhites. I began to think about this issue years ago, well before I became an academician. I grew up a poor black student in the ghetto of Milwaukee, and as my life progressed I wondered often why it was that my sisters and I did so well in school while others—in the same neighborhood, in the same schools, with the same family income—did badly. Why was it that one on the next block could become a law professor and one of my best friends across the street a taxicab driver without a diploma? How did I manage to get three degrees and a friend on my block got none? The neighborhood and the neighborhood schools produced doctors, lawyers, professors, and teachers, but they also produced drug addicts and high-school dropouts. It clearly wasn't the neighborhood or the schools. They were, after all, the same. It wasn't race or poverty, for they were also the same. Was it family?

That is the question that I posed for the research reported in this book, and that is the question educational policymakers need to address. This research suggests the answer is that the family is crucial in the attempt to improve the education offered to poor nonwhites, and educational policy must change to take this fact into account. The book tells us precisely how the family plays out its role and therefore precisely how policy needs to shift.

This work would not have been possible without the initial guidance and questions posed by my mother, Dorris J. Sampson. I thank her much not just for the family environment but for our discussions about it over the years. I must also thank the DePaul University students who volunteered to be trained and to do the observations that made the research possible. They put enormous effort into this work and were very professional and supportive all the way. Thank you, Charles Collins, Kim Conlon, Jordan Davis, Jasmine Harris, Amanda Ladas, Jane Lee, Wyllys Mann, Helen Mesoloras, Twjuana Robinson, Adam Tupper, Brian Walsh, and Rahilla Zafar. I would also like to thank the staff of Family Focus, especially Delores Holmes and Kim Estell-Ross, without whose assistance this work could not have been done.

THE PROBLEM

For over thirty years now, America has agonized over and struggled with what has been seen as the failure of our public schools, particularly those in urban areas, to adequately educate our children. While we talk and write about education generally, the underlying, and occasionally open, focus is on urban, poor, nonwhite students. While of course not all of these children perform badly and not all suburban, nonpoor, or white students do well, our primary concern continues to be the unsatisfactory performance of poor nonwhite youngsters. As James Traub (2000) so powerfully put it, "Though over the past 35 years we have poured billions of dollars into inner-city schools, and though we have fiddled with practically everything you could think to fiddle with, we have done almost nothing to raise the trajectory of ghetto children" (52). Traub raises two important issues here. First, our focus has been on the lack of education of the poor, and second, we have attempted (and are attempting) all manner of solutions, none of which seem to work very well. Some reformers focus on preschool education, others on educational vouchers. Some want charter schools; others believe that a longer school day or school year will bring about significant change. Some think that we need better teachers; some believe that student uniforms will turn the tide. Many have called for smaller class size. Some think that parental control of schools is the answer. Still others want higher academic standards. While we have poured billions of dollars into all of these efforts, the problem remains. It is my position that we are by and large wasting a great deal of money because we are looking at the wrong "solutions." How do I know this? Simple. None have worked.

There are, however, two possible exceptions to this rather bold assertion: class size and preschool education. Even Myron Lieberman (1993), a staunch opponent of any education "solution" that is not a function of market forces, acknowledges, in a backhanded way, that reduced class size may well have a positive impact on education. He correctly points out, however, that in order to be really effective, the reductions would have to be significant. Indeed, the ideal class size appears to be between fifteen and seventeen students per class. However, as Lieberman rightly concludes, "the costs would be prohibitive" (264).

Take Chicago, for example. The Chicago school system currently spends just over $3 billion per year to inadequately educate about half a million students. The average class size is about thirty pupils. In order to reduce the class size to the point where we might see significant improvements based on these reductions, Chicago would have to spend some $9 billion per year, and this does not include the cost of building the additional classrooms, many of which would not be needed twenty years down the line due to population changes. These costs certainly appear "prohibitive."

As Zigler and Styfco (1993) have shown, Head Start does indeed work if the effort is properly extended. Schweinhart et al. (1993) also show very promising outcomes for preschool efforts, as do Campbell and Ramey (1995). But preschool programs are also quite expensive. So while we have tried all sorts of efforts to improve our urban education programs, the two that seem to work, preschool and significant class size reductions, are probably too expensive in the long run. Though I am certain that many would suggest that no amount of money is too much given what is at risk, I am equally certain that once race and politics are factored into the equation, we will have to look elsewhere for an answer.

Over the past twelve or fifteen years, more and more scholars have looked to the family as an answer. Of course, the family is certainly not a new research topic or variable in the study of student achievement. The difference is that more and more research is focusing on why and how some poor children manage to do well in the schools while others living in similar circumstances, often in the same neighborhood and attending the same schools, do badly. Given racial and ethnic housing segregation, race and ethnicity are not the answer. Poverty is by definition (and research design) not the answer, and by design, differences among school systems are not the answer. While there may well be a host of other possibilities, the most compelling variables involve the family; as Reginald Clark (1983) puts it, we now see the "families as educators" (9). I agree with Clark that "it is the family members' *beliefs, activities,* and overall *cultural style* that produce the requisite mental structures for effective and desirable behavior during classroom lessons" (1). In other words, if we want to better educate poor minority students, we should look to the family. I believe that this is the case for all students but, for reasons we will see later, it is typically not a big issue for middle-income families, whether white or nonwhite. This book explores why and how some poor black children, most from the same neighborhood, attending the same suburban Chicago school system, do well in school and others, with what on the surface appears to be the same characteristics, do badly.

Poverty is not the answer. The children are all poor. Race is not the answer. They are all black. The school system is not the answer. They all attend the same system. Indeed, a number attend the same school. Neighborhood is not the answer. Almost all live within several blocks of each other. I believe that family is the answer, but the question is: What is it about the family?

Like Clark (1983), I reject the beliefs based on earlier research that various "personnel and role properties"—such as family size, parental marital status, parental employment status, child's position in birth order, and the like—determine the success of the child in the educational system. I am not suggesting that these characteristics are not important in the life of the child. It is, however, simply not clear that they play a significant role in the educational life of the student. Too many poor minority students do too well for this to be the case. The important question is *why?*

As Janine Bempechat (1998) correctly states, "Unfortunately, we know surprisingly little about the factors that contribute to [good students'] high achievement" (2). Many poor minority youngsters do well in the same schools that we think are failing. Others in those schools do unsatisfactorily. Again, the question is why? If we can determine how some do well while others who appear to be quite similar do badly, then we may well be in a position to begin to solve this vexing problem of the failure of many schools to adequately educate poor minority students.

STUDYING SUCCESS

I am not, of course, the first to study the educational success of poor minority students. Clark 1983; Bempechat 1998; Furstenberg et al. 1999; Entwisle, Alexander, and Olson 1997; and Harrington and Boardman 1997 have all recently examined the issue of how poor minority individuals have managed to do well in our society as well as, to some degree, the impact of the family on the educational success of those who made it (and those who did not). Not all of this research focused mainly on education or on children. Harrington and Boardman, for example, are concerned with adult success and explore the relationship between family and education only as that relationship affects that success. Furstenberg et al. are in fact interested in adolescents, as am I, but they focus on "the interface between the family and community that influences the course of adolescent development for disadvantaged youth" (7). They are actually more concerned with the influence of the neighborhood on success than on parenting, though they do pay considerable attention to the latter. They question how young people can be successful under "unfavorable conditions" (6), and their success paradigm includes the role of the family and the educational process. The focus of my research is almost exclusively on why some poor minority youngsters are successful in school and others are not and the role of the family in this issue.

Entwisle, Alexander, and Olson (1997) are interested in why some children get more out of schooling than others. Like me, they focus on the middle school years and find the family only part of the process of getting more out of schooling. In fact, they pay considerably more attention to the educational process than do I. They are also more concerned with the traditional family variables such as the occupation and education of parents, family size, job loss, and the like, though they do study parents' attitudes and activities related to schooling. It is basically only these last two variables that are directly relevant to my work.

Bempechat (1998) focuses on fifth- and sixth-grade black, Latino, Indochinese, and white children in poor neighborhoods in the Boston area, and she also pays considerable attention to the role of the family in the efforts of these children to beat the odds. Like all of the others mentioned earlier, she used survey research to collect her data. She interviewed over a thousand children and no parents. Thus, what we know about the parents and the family all comes from the responses to questions by ten- and twelve-year-old students.

Furstenberg et al. (1999) also used questionnaires to gather data from the almost five hundred families they studied, though they interviewed both parents and children, as did Reginald Clark (1983), though his work is based on interviews with a total of ten families with twelfth-grade students. Like Furstenberg et al., Clark also obtained data from observations over a period of time, though Clark actually participated in some of the activities of the families, while those collecting data for the Furstenberg work did not. I will present more detail on the methods of various recent research on the role of the family in the success of poor minority children in chapter 2. The point I wish to make here is that there have been several recent studies on the ways in which "black youth are 'educationally' prepared by their families" (Clark 1983, 19), and this work is welcome because heretofore such research has been "sketchy." Blau and Duncan 1967; Coleman et al. 1966; and Jencks et al. 1972 all study the influence of the family on academic test scores, social status, and/or other educational outcomes. They each find that family does indeed have a significant impact on the education and social status of individuals. The problem is that they define "family" in ways that I (and others such as Clark, Bempechat, Furstenberg et al., and Entwisle et al.) think are far too superficial. The education and occupation of parents, the skill level of parents, the number of children in the family, whether there is a television, vacuum cleaner, or record player in the home, the educational expectations of the parents in the family—all may well be important in predicting the educational success and/or quality of life of young people. They are, however, no substitute for knowledge of the more complicated processes of family dynamics and interaction studied in some of the more recent works.

The problem, of course, is that these interactions, these values, this behavior that so clearly define families are difficult to measure and extremely difficult to quantify. The earlier pioneering works on family and success were all quantitative, and the various family variables had to be measured in such a way that they could be quantified. How do we quantify discipline or self-control or structure or family culture? Oh, sure, we can do it. But will the numbers have much meaning? I do not think so.

While the family is perhaps the most studied of all institutions, there is relatively little work that seeks to link what goes on in families to educational success or failure, and the bulk of that work is relatively recent. What's more, most of the work on family influences on the success of children deals with white families. While there is certainly nothing wrong with this, our schools are currently struggling to find ways to adequately educate poor nonwhite children. It would seem that we need more work to help us determine just how we might accomplish this.

Over the years I have casually asked many successful blacks whether they grew up poor and how they became successful. I have long been intrigued by this issue, perhaps in part because I was a poor black youngster who grew up to do fairly well, while reading and hearing that this did not happen too often. Since I knew that it could happen, I wanted to determine why and how.

To a person, these formerly poor and now successful blacks emphasized the role of their families in their success. What's more, their family lives were remarkably similar. There was a great deal of discipline and a lot of structure and order in their homes. The children were expected to do well and were taught to think highly of themselves and their accomplishments. They were expected to assume responsibility for their actions and were allowed few explanations for failure. They had to demonstrate constraint and control and think always of the future. These were precisely the characteristics of my family upbringing, and these are, to a significant degree, the characteristics of the middle class— not the middle-income class, the middle class.

I believe that the values, beliefs, and behavior that we generally associate with the traditional social-class variables of income, education, and occupation are clearly not unique to those with certain income-based characteristics. In other words, those with better education, higher incomes, and higher-ranking occupations have no corner on the market of high self-esteem, discipline, internal control, and the ability to delay gratification. If they did, few would get out of poverty in America. Social class should be seen not simply as related to the easily measurable variables of education, occupation, and income, but also—perhaps alternatively—as a function of those more complicated and certainly more difficult to measure variables such as internal control and self-esteem.

My position, based in part on my discussions with many successful blacks and in part on my study of social class, is that many poor blacks are middle class and lower income, and since public schools are middle-class institutions (Comer 1993), those who are middle-class students should perform better than those who are not. While it is increasingly difficult for poor blacks to maintain this class position given the continuing changes in poor black neighborhoods, many manage to do so, and I believe that the children of these families do well in school if given the opportunity.

FRAMING THE ISSUES

Clearly, our educational system is at or near a crisis stage. Our big cities have dropout rates near 40 percent. Our big businesses spend billions of dollars educating workers who should have been educated by our schools. Our school expenditures go up with little significant effect. As I indicated earlier, the most popular attempts at solving the problem have shown little positive result, and the differences that any of these efforts would appear to make are likely to be the result mainly of self-selection. That is, parents who do not believe that the local public school can or will properly educate their children manage to do the necessary homework and then the required fieldwork to locate an alternative that they believe will do the job. That alternative may be a charter school, or a parochial school, or a voucher. But if that parent has the values, the discipline, the sense of control required to go through this process, then that parent is, by definition, quite different from the parent who simply sends his or her children down the street to the local school. I contend that it is these differences that really determine the success of the child, and it is these differences that we must identify in detail if we are to really make a difference in our educational system. It is these differences that this research was designed to identify.

This is not simply a case of some parents being more interested in their children's education than others, or at least not on the surface. As Lareau (1989) shows us, poor and minority parents are indeed interested in the education of their children. Interest may well be important, but is it enough? How does it get translated into values or beliefs or actions that have a positive impact on educational success? Or how do the values and beliefs influence the interest? If Clark (1983); Bempechat (1998); Furstenberg et al. (1999); Entwisle, Alexander, and Olson (1997); and I are correct, then the family is at least one of the keys to solving our educational problems and finding answers to these questions.

As I have indicated before, for some time now the nation has looked to a number of "solutions" to the problem of education. We have looked to vouchers, charter schools, longer school days or school years, and higher standards (among other less-discussed reforms). It is my belief, based largely on the analysis of my data and the work of those listed above, that these reforms are off base. We need to focus on changes in some families. As we will see later, however, this is not at all easy. The alternative, though, is to continue to spend time, money, and effort on reforms that have little chance of helping us to properly educate poor minority students.

Vouchers have caught the attention of many policymakers, media representatives, and parents recently. The idea has, however, been around for some time. Milton Friedman (1962) sparked a great deal of interest in the concept in the 1960s. Essentially, vouchers allow public financial support for students to attend virtually any school—public, private, or parochial—that their parents select. The idea is that schools other than the typical public schools tend to do a better job of educating students, and therefore students who are otherwise locked into poorly performing public schools should have the opportunity to attend such schools.

Supporters of vouchers argue that this concept brings choice, and therefore market forces, to bear on education. The belief is, of course, that market forces involve competition and this leads to improvement. There are only two problems with the idea. One, it makes no sense logically, and two, there is little empirical evidence to suggest that it works. As Berliner and Biddle (1995) point out, voucher programs would require additional bureaucracy, result in increased inequality between the haves and the have-nots, and shift money from those who need it most to those who need it the least. Further, what is to happen to those who cannot or do not receive these rather small vouchers? If the thoughtful and aggressive parents receive vouchers and send their children out of the local schools, that ultimately leaves only the most needy students and their parents. This is likely to make for an even worse school. As Myron Lieberman (1993), a rather astute observer, points out, voucher systems are not really competitive or market systems, and it is not clear just what would happen to the public schools after those who could leave have done so. Do we close the schools up? Unlikely. So schools that do unsatisfactorily, attended mainly by students who do badly, would still operate. What have we accomplished?

We might help the education of a few, but as Berliner and Biddle (1995) correctly indicate, what we have primarily accomplished is the diversion of tax dollars to middle- and upper-income parents and neighborhoods. This does not help many poor minority parents, even though many conservatives are trying to suggest that these are the people they really want to help. Certainly, many poor parents want to get their children out of neighborhoods with high crime rates, poor transportation, and poor city services. I find it interesting, however, that many of these same conservative observers who opposed civil rights for minority citizens, integration, and now often oppose affirmative action for minorities, seem to want to support educational help through vouchers for poor minority students. It appears that many of them have not been very concerned with the well-being of these people for years. Why now? One could argue that they are not. This is basically camouflage for their attempt to help middle- and upper-income parents.

Let us not rely on logic and politics alone. What about the evidence? Vouchers have been tried in Australia and France. According to Berliner and Biddle (1995), in both cases they have led to "greater inequalities in education" (179) and have done little to help students who remain in the schools doing the worst. This is precisely what will happen in America and what has already happened in Philadelphia. According to Lieberman (1993), assessing one of the larger voucher plans in the country: "Not surprisingly, there is no evidence that the Milwaukee public schools have changed since the voucher plan became operative" (13). So vouchers do not seem to be the solution. There is very little empirical evidence to suggest that vouchers improve public education, and they will most certainly exacerbate economic inequality.

Charter schools are another form of choice, a much more recently suggested reform than vouchers. They are basically public schools that operate with a charter from the state that allows them to function relatively independently from the local board of education. Therefore they are largely free to emphasize whatever they wish and teach almost however they choose. The idea seems to be that many public schools serving poor minority students are doing very unsatisfactorily because the wrong things are taught in the wrong manner, and bureaucracy prevents significant changes. Charter schools avoid that bureaucracy and can therefore make the changes. Since there are few charter schools that have been is existence more than a few years, it is too early to determine their success.

However, Michael Winerip of the *New York Times* writes: "In the course of visiting charters, I spoke to hundreds of parents. What distinguishes them is their motivation. They are out hunting something extra for their children" (1998, 47). Again, self-selection. Parents who do the research and thinking necessary to determine that their children would be better off in a specific charter school are quite likely to be the kind of parents who would send their children to school prepared to learn. The children in these families are very likely to do well in almost any school—unless people in the school are trying to prevent it. So even if the charter schools appear to be effective, we must try to separate the parental effects from the school effects. It is the same conundrum that we saw with vouchers.

Furthermore, what do we do with those students who do not receive a voucher or attend a charter school? What do we do with those left behind? For financial, logistical, and political reasons, not every student can have a choice. Indeed, most cannot. Do we ignore these students?

Another suggested reform is longer school days and/or longer school years. The thinking appears to be that students can learn more if they have more time in a classroom. Berliner and Biddle (1995) question this. Indeed, they write, "we know of no strong evidence indicating that student achievement will rise if the school year is lengthened" (185). They cite the work of Nancy Karweit (1976) in support of this position. Furthermore, if teachers are to be in class longer, they will have to be trained and retrained to use the extra time in a useful way. This will not be an easy effort, nor will it be easy to come up with the additional money to pay the teachers for the additional time. I am not trying to suggest that improving the education of poor minority students will be easy at all. But we must consider the downside of every effort to do so, including the suggestions that my data lead me to make.

Some educational observers have suggested higher standards for teachers, students, and administrators, and few would object to this on the surface. But what do we do with those who fail to meet the standards? Do we fire the teachers? Do we hold back the students? If so, for how long? Do we expel them? If it takes three years for one to meet the standards and we hold him or her back, will he or she want to go to the next grade two years older than the others in the class? If not, will he or she drop out?

Given that most suggest that we use tests to determine whether teachers and students meet the standards, it is quite possible that teachers will teach the tests rather than needed material or how to learn. This is just what Gilles, Geletta, and Daniels (1994) found in Missouri when that state developed an accountability program designed to raise and test for standards. So it is not clear that this is the answer either.

Other reforms have been proposed, ranging from major curriculum changes to privatizing public education. Each has its supporters and its detractors, each has its limitations, and some have certain strengths. None alone shows signs of helping to significantly improve the education of poor minority students. The purpose of this book is not to examine each of these reforms. Others can do a better job of this than can I. It is my goal to explore the possibility that the family is the key to such reform. I wanted to touch on the most popular of the reforms to show that either they do not seem to solve our problem or the economic or political price is too high. Major reductions in class size and sound preschool programs would seem to make a difference, but at costs that we may well not be prepared to pay. Furthermore, what do we do with those students already in school who would not benefit from preschool? We cannot simply forget them.

Schools must have competent and motivated teachers. They need adequate space and textbooks. They need concerned administrators and sound curriculums. They need community support and high standards. However, it is my contention that schools can do very little if students are not sent to school prepared to learn, and although this should not be the responsibility of the family alone, it is not really clear that it can happen anywhere else, assuming that children remain with their families. Urban schools have a job to do and they must be prepared to do that job, but they need prepared students if they are to be successful. Without such students, the value of school efforts is unclear.

If the other reforms did indeed work, we would still want to explore the role of the family, for logic suggests that if children go to school prepared to learn, then the educational process should proceed better. Much of this preparation is likely to take place outside of the classroom and within the context of the family. It is not simply for research or empirical reasons I am interested in the family as the source, or at least as one of the main sources, of the problem of the education of poor minority children. I am also interested for policy reasons. If we can determine the source(s) of the problem, then the solutions may well be easier to determine. (Although there will still be policy problems, which I will discuss later.) If the currently debated solutions (vouchers, charter schools, increased time on task, decreased class size, preschool education, and the like) fail to work, are too expensive financially or politically, or will not help enough people, then we must keep searching. That is what I am trying to do. As Furstenberg et al. (1999) put it: "[A] focus on success under unfavorable conditions can provide useful clues about which public policies could be adopted to assist children and families to cope with these conditions, thereby reducing the handicaps imposed on those economically disadvantaged at birth" (6). This is what I would like to help to happen, too.

RESEARCH METHODS

The research methodology of this work owes a great deal to the work of Clark (1983). Both he and I studied individual families in depth, using observational techniques. We both focused on the structures and processes of individual families. We both focused on a single child in each family, and we both used a combination of interviews and observation, though the interviews played a larger role for Clark than for me. My focus was on observation because I believe that if we are to determine just what aspects of family life influence the academic behavior of a child in that family, then we must see all that we can of the behavior of the various members of that family—particularly, though not only, the behavior related to that child. In my opinion only prolonged observations can accomplish this.

As Bempechat (1998) correctly points out, there are essentially three ways that have been used to study the achievement of poor minority students: retrospective studies, ethnographic studies, and large surveys. In a retrospective study (such as Harrington and Boardman 1997), scholars ask successful minority group members to think back to various processes and events that might have influenced their success. The researchers focus on midlife career status and take a long-term retrospective view, using a detailed questionnaire. Their work compares people who grew up poor but did well professionally with those who did well but did not grow up poor (controls). Harrington and Boardman point out that they could have used as controls people who had origins similar to successful people (poor, with parents without high school diplomas). This would have focused their work on "the question of why some people facing negative predictions make it work and some do not" (27). This is precisely what I have studied.

Obviously, retrospective studies face the problem of memory. Still, one of the things that focused my interest on the subject of how some poor blacks do well and others do not was listening to successful blacks who grew up poor describe their childhood and families. The descriptions were remarkably similar, leading me to suspect that certain behavior, thoughts, and values were characteristic of poor black families that produced successful children and then successful adults. Unfortunately, there has been very little empirical evidence, as Bempechat (1998) correctly comments, on the subject.

The second kind of research technique that has been used to study the success of poor minority students is the ethnographic technique, and Bempechat (1998) mentions Clark's work (1983) as an example of this technique, which emphasizes observation of the everyday lives of family members. (While Bempechat seems to support the ethnographic method, she herself uses "an original questionnaire of students' perceptions of their parents' involvement in their schooling" (10). She interviewed over a thousand fifth- and sixth-grade students.) Clark wanted to understand the differences and similarities between the ten families he studied: five with successful students and five with "less successful" students. He used an extensive questionnaire and observations made over two days, though in some cases he exceeded the two days. Most of the data he reports seem based less on the observations and more on the questionnaires. Still, he went with the families to various events, listened to their arguments, and helped "them to buy food and prepare meals" (21).

This technique, too, has its problems. It is not easy to gain the trust of poor families to the extent that they will allow one into their homes for an extended period of time. Many are embarrassed by the appearance of their house or themselves. Many want to imply to the observer that they are not the kind of people their belongings might suggest. Indeed, even if they have nothing to hide, they probably want to be viewed with respect, and poor furnishings and difficult living conditions may cause some to have little self-respect. So some poor people may want to keep strangers out, and others may want to act differently than they normally would. Each condition may be a problem for one interested in empirical data collection. In my case, as I will discuss a bit later, I relied upon a well-known and respected social service agency that has the trust of many poor black residents in the area to make the initial contacts with the families to be studied. Further, since we observed the families over an eight- to ten-week period, I suspect that it would be quite difficult to hide or change behavior over that period of time: a few hours or a few days, maybe, but not for several hours a week for two months.

The third technique is survey research. The surveys typically focus on a variety of subjects related to achievement. Harrington and Boardman (1997) used this technique in their retrospective work with one hundred respondents. They collected data concerning the respondents' background, employment history, educational history, family and community, current family health, and psychological position. Furstenberg et al. 1999 was based on a sample of almost five hundred in Philadelphia. Field-workers observed and conducted "focused interviews" with thirty-five of these families. The Furstenberg work went beyond the educational success of poor minority children. This work focused on a number of variables thought to be related to adolescent success, including education, neighborhood characteristics, parental roles and characteristics, and psychological attributes.

Of course, surveys allow us to probe many different areas in a fairly short period of time and to do so with quite a few respondents. This second characteristic, numbers, gives us more confidence in our findings. On the other hand, surveys are not particularly good at picking up interaction, values, depth, "color," or context. Ethnographic research is better at this because it allows longer looks at behavior and does little to prepackage it. On the other hand, ethnographic research tends to take a great deal of time, and the number of respondents is therefore limited. This makes generalization somewhat problematic. To their credit, Furstenberg and his colleagues attempted both, though their findings clearly are based mainly on the survey results.

After considering the advantages and disadvantages, including cost and time, of the various methods, I decided that long-term observation of the family life of poor minority children promised to give us the best, most accurate, and most usable picture of the characteristics of those families whose children did well in school.

As Bempechat (1998) correctly indicates, we know more about the factors that contribute to the school failure of poor minority children than about why some succeed. I suspect that this has quite a bit to do with the reality that many of these factors are related to the family and the home, both of which many poor families are reluctant to allow observers to closely observe. I know from experience that many will respond to a short questionnaire. However, as Reginald Clark (1983) learned, when it comes to allowing a researcher into the home for a substantial period of time, many are distrustful. As he put it, "Their usual mood was 'What government agency does he work for' or 'I thought you was the police.'" Clark worked with a community service agency and teachers in the neighborhood schools in order to gain entrée.

Once I decided that the place to start was the family (perhaps one of the least-studied institutions when it comes to the educational success—and failure—of poor minority children), I had to decide on a methodology. While my training is in quantitative methods, I decided that if I were to really see the behavior, the values, the struggles, and the interactions in a family that might impact on the educational success of a child, I must be in the home for a prolonged period of time. I was willing to sacrifice generalizability, and I am aware that more work must build on this work in the way in which I have tried to build on the work of Clark (1983) and Furstenberg (1993).

As I have indicated before, Clark (1983) observed ten families, all poor and all black. Furstenberg (1993) interviewed and observed fifteen families, some poor, some working class or lower-middle income. Some of these families were Latino, some white, and some black. He observed these families for almost a year, visiting them once a week or so, and this earlier work led to his 1999 work. Clearly, Furstenberg observed families longer than either Clark or I, and he refers to his sample as a "catch as catch can" one, emphasizing that more of this type of work needs to be done. Furstenberg was not as concerned as Clark or I with the educational success of poor minority students and the role of the family in that success. His focus was the relationship of community and family life among poor people. But given the attention he paid to family life and his methods, his work is important to me and I will refer to this work quite a bit, even though I see several problems with it.

Not only is entry into the home a problem, but one must somehow get the family members' trust, not only to sustain the presence in the home but also to limit the possibility of changed behavior. I wanted not only to see what goes on among family members and to hear discussion and arguments but to see the nuances of behavior and to listen to the tone of voice. I wanted to see what was in the home and to experience the culture of the family. I wanted not simply to hear a parent indicate that he or she supports education (almost all Americans do), but to see what, if anything, was done about that support, how it was done, and when it was done. While I had no magic period of time in mind, I knew that Clark spent time over two days with most of the families he observed and that most of the findings he reported appeared to be based on his interviews. So I decided that if my findings were to be based largely on observations, I needed to observe longer than several hours over two or three days. Furthermore, several hours of observations did not seem sufficient to give me the picture of the families and family lives I needed to determine the characteristics of the families with the successful children. The Furstenberg time frame of close to a year of observations, while desirable and attractive for my purposes, is quite expensive and may have placed a strain on poor families, which are already under quite a bit of pressure. My compromise of observations over seven or eight weeks once or twice a week seemed to work well for my research and for the families involved.

Realizing that many poor families develop a trust for some staff members of social service agencies with which they are connected, I decided early to contact an influential and possibly supportive agency. Since I was also leaning toward observing families within a limited geographic area in order to minimize the role of differences in community on the findings, I decided to collect data in Evanston, Illinois, a rather small, very diverse, and interesting community just north of Chicago. The most important and well-known social service agency in Evanston is Family Focus. I approached the leader of Family Focus with the idea for the research, and she not only agreed to support the work but assigned staff members to work with me. This was critical, because staff members work very closely with poor families in Evanston and have their trust. These relationships afforded us entrée to the homes and families and gave us the initial trust of the families.

Family Focus selected the thirteen families observed in the study. I initially asked the staff to select seven or eight families with a student between the ages of twelve and fourteen doing well in school and seven or eight families with students of the same ages doing badly. I ended up with a total of fifteen families. Thirteen proved cooperative, but there are complete field notes for only twelve; thus I have twelve families in this study. The students were almost equally divided between those doing average, those doing well, and those doing badly. This meant I could do a fair amount of comparing and contrasting, which helps to make a case stronger. I believe that this aids my efforts to ascertain why some poor black children do well in school and others, who seem to be much like them in important ways, do badly. If our society can learn more about this critical issue, then perhaps we can shape educational policies that will really help these students.

I limited the sample to black students so that race or ethnicity would not affect the results. Given that Furstenberg (1993) observed whites, blacks, and Latinos, it is quite possible that some of the differences he finds in the families could be due to differences in race or ethnicity. He fails to explore this possibility, but it is an issue nevertheless. To limit this possibility and this complexity, I focused on blacks. Clearly, this limits the findings to some degree, but it strengthens them as well. It gives more observations with one racial group and provides more confidence in the findings concerning that group. What's more, it builds on Clark's work (1983), which also centered on blacks. Finally, remembering that blacks are disproportionately represented among the urban poor doing unsatisfactorily in school, I would suggest that we need to know as much as possible about those poor blacks who somehow manage to do well.

THE CITY

The diverse suburb of Evanston has two public school systems—one a kindergarten through eighth-grade system, the other a high school system—and the two are closely linked. My original intention was to focus on students in middle school. Given that Evanston has one public school system for the four middle schools, differences in the academic success of the students are unlikely to be the result of differences in schools. Indeed, six of the twelve students in my study attended the same middle school. While schools may certainly vary, and these variations can have significant influence on the success of students, it is less likely in a small school system with fewer schools. Thus, by studying poor black students in Evanston—eleven out of twelve of whom live within seven blocks of one another—I tried to minimize the impact of variables on the success of the students other than family-related variables. I wanted to be more confident that the differences in success are due to differences in families. Can we be certain? Not really. Can we be confident? Yes, particularly given that others have studied the same or similar issues.

Evanston is considered a relatively well-off community, but it has several pockets of poverty. The city has a population of 73,233, with 51,684 whites, 16,749 blacks (of whom 2,134 are West Indian), 3,535 Asians, and 2,289 Hispanics (U.S. Department of Commerce 1990). The median income for whites is $45,606, with 7.3 percent below the poverty line. The median income for blacks is $30,603, with 14.9 percent below the poverty line. The median income for Hispanics is $38,942, with 16.4 percent below the poverty line. Of the 34,484 whites twenty-five or older, 69.4 percent had B.A.s or better. Of the 9,953 blacks twenty-five or older, 16.6 percent had B.A.s or better. Of the 1,841 Asians and Pacific Islanders twenty-five or older, 77.9 percent had B.A.s or better. The percentage was 36.4 percent for Hispanics. For comparison purposes, just north of Evanston in Wilmette the population is 26,530, with 84 blacks and 403 Hispanics. The median household income is $71,274, with 1.2 percent below the poverty line. Clearly, while Evanston is in many ways suburban, it is also quite diverse, both in terms of race and ethnicity and income levels.

Crime statistics in the city are revealing. Police beats 77 and 74, which cover the West Side, are higher than other beats in Evanston in Crime Index crimes, such as robbery, burglary, and assault. I analyzed the monthly crime listings produced and provided by the city's police department from May 1999 to June 2000 and found this to be the case, particularly when compared to the prevalence of these crimes in more affluent, more white neighborhoods/police beats. Furthermore, at my request the Evanston Police Department prepared a comparison of "Part 11" or non–Crime Index crimes, including battery, assault, possession of a deadly weapon, possession of cannabis, possession of other narcotics, disorderly conduct, and the like. While the population of the two police beats on the West Side comprise only 11 percent of the total Evanston population, 44 percent of the battery reports are made in these beats, as are 39 percent of the assault reports and 46 percent of the deadly weapon reports. Forty-two percent of the cannabis reports are made in these two beats, as are 37 percent of the controlled substance reports. Thirty-two percent of the city's juvenile runaway reports occur here, as do 37 percent of the disorderly conduct reports (Evanston Police Department, July 2000).

Clearly, this neighborhood sees a disproportionate amount of crime that might well frighten parents and cause particular concern about the welfare of their children. As the data of my study will show, a number of the parents, particularly of the students doing well, are rather strict when it comes to managing the activities and behavior of the students. While some, such as Clark (1983) and Furstenberg et al. (1999), suggest that this is antithetical to good performances by children, it should be pointed out that the neighborhood in which almost all of the families live is higher in the types of crime that cause fear among residents, which might well lead to a feeling that increased protection is desirable. We should not be surprised to find parents interested in avoiding the exposure of their children to the possibility of these crimes, and we should therefore not be surprised if some of the parents in this neighborhood are more restrictive with their children than we might otherwise anticipate. I would also expect that some parents will be more restrictive than others.

THE SAMPLE

Family Focus defines lower income as ranging from $14,720 for a family of one person to $49,440 for a family of eight, adding $4,960 per year for each additional family member. Of the twelve families, five have incomes of $14,720 or less a year. Two families—one with four members and one with eight—have incomes of $29,600 or less. One family has an income of $19,680 or less with four family members. Two families have incomes of $24,640 or less, one with two family members and one with six family members. One family has an income of $34,560 or less and six family members, and one of $44,480 or less with four family members. None of these families are doing too well financially based on these numbers, though it appears that the latter two might not be considered poor based simply on income. However, the agency Family Focus works primarily with families considered to be poor, and all of the twelve families are involved with Family Focus. So I approached each family as a poor family.

There are three male students studied and nine females. Three of the twelve students are freshmen in Evanston's one high school, eight are in middle school, and one is in fourth grade. They range in age from ten to fourteen years old. Five of the twelve families are headed by a single parent, five have two parents in the home, and two have one parent but the other parent is actively involved in the family. Given that Clark (1983) does not assign much weight to "the issue of family compositional structures" (211) in the learning process for children, I thought that it made sense to pay some attention to this issue. While I am not really as interested in it as was Clark, we can at least determine whether Clark was correct. Neither Furstenberg 1993; Bempechat 1998; nor Entwisle, Alexander, and Olson 1997 seem to focus on this issue at all, though the Entwisle work suggests its importance. This does not make it an insignificant issue, however, and given that Clark's data seem to support his argument regarding family intactness, I decided that I should give it some attention, although it is not my focus.

COLLECTING THE DATA

Once Family Focus introduced me and the twelve observers on my team to the families to be studied, the observers made the initial appointments to meet with the families. All of these observation meetings were to take place when the target student was at home, though in some cases the observer accompanied the student to the store or to other places in the neighborhood, including the Family Focus office. The observers met with the families for two to three hours a day, generally once a week, for six to ten weeks. At the end of each meeting, the observer arranged the next meeting. Of course, the next meeting did not always take place as planned. The lives of poor families are often complicated and stressful. This often required last-minute changes in schedules to which we had to adapt.

The observers were trained to observe almost everything about family life, especially as it pertained to the student being studied. What we really wanted to know is: What are the dimensions of child rearing and family life that positively affect the academic success of poor minority children? Based on my previous discussions with many successful black adults who grew up poor and the work of others, including Clark (1983); Furstenberg et al. (1999); Bempechat (1998); and Harrington and Boardman (1997), I suspected that poor black families that are raising children who are doing well in school are parenting in much the same way as middle-income parents who have academically successful children. They may lack the financial resources, but I expected to find that they have the parenting and familial resources, despite the fact that these are difficult to retain in a poor environment. As Furstenberg et al. put it: "To be sure, parents exhibited a range of competencies, and few scored high on all dimensions of parenting. In this respect, however, we doubt that they differ greatly from parents outside the inner city" (217).

This is a critical point, in my opinion. I see schools as essentially middle-class institutions. So do Lightfoot (1978) and Comer (1993). That is, they are structured in such a way as to work well for the middle class, and they help to train future members of that class for society. They require values, behavior, and attitudes such as self-control, positive self-image, discipline, and the ability to delay gratification if one is to do well. These are typically thought to be middle-class values and beliefs, or, as Comer prefers, "mainstream" attitudes. Think for a moment. Can't most students think of things they would rather be doing on a nice spring day than sitting in a classroom learning algebra? Yet many put off what they would prefer because they believe that the learning experience will pay off later. Like Rodman (1971), I believe that many, perhaps most, poor people have many of the same values and characteristics as middle-income people, and that these help their children to do well in schools, middle-class institutions. While I do not want to launch into a detailed discussion of attitudes, values, and class, at least not at this time, I believe that it is important to underline Furstenberg et al.'s (1999) point that many of the poor parents they observed behaved much like the nonpoor parents they studied. I argue that this may well have a positive impact in schools.

If we suspect that many poor families function much like nonpoor families in their family processes, precisely how do we determine this? A very important assumption that I have made is that Bempechat (1998) is correct when she writes that "barring serious learning difficulties or mental retardation, all young children have the basic intellectual skills and the potential to learn" (2). So it is my position that the students doing well in school are doing so for reasons that have little to do with their intellectual advantages over those doing badly. Other things explain the differences, and I suspected that the family is the key "other thing." In our observations of these families, we wanted to focus on several areas, though it is somewhat difficult to spell out precisely what we wanted to learn given that we did not rely on a questionnaire for most of the data. Unlike Clark (1983); Bempechat (1998); and Furstenberg et al. (1999), I relied on observations for the bulk of our data. Of course, when one relies on observation one has relatively little control over the shape and form of the data because one does not control the behavioral processes. Still, I had some ideas about what I wanted to see and learn and about the data that I felt were needed to answer the critical research question.

The bulk of the observations and data collection centered around:

1. Family structure: number of people in the household, ages, residence
2. Family processes: amount of interaction, type of interaction, parental intervention, discipline (how much and how), responsibilities, division of labor
3. Home environment: space, noise, study arrangements, facilities within the home, books
4. Values and attitudes: self-esteem, importance of education, importance of self-control, expectations
5. Educational processes: homework arrangements, role of parent(s) in the schoolwork of child, value of education to child and parent, grades of child.

The grades are obviously important given that I used them to determine the academic success of the child. While there may be other and even better ways to do this, I decided to use grades. Clearly, my list of the areas around which the observations were centered and the questions that were asked bears some resemblance to that of Reginald Clark (1983). While I have no desire to attempt to replicate his work, it did seem to make sense to build on it. Furthermore, these are the variables/issues that I believe to be critical in any attempt to link family to educational success. As the observations proceeded, data were collected on other issues that seemed to be important. These data will be presented and analyzed as well.

As I have mentioned, there are weaknesses in my approach. The sample is very small, and I could not really ensure that data were collected from each family on the same issues. However, as the sample is almost equally divided between students who are doing well academically and those not doing so well, with three performing at the average or a bit below, we can compare and contrast with some confidence. Other limitations stem from the ethnographic data collection method. Since I believe that it is the best method given the subject, I must live with the weaknesses, but the reader should be clear about them. The best way around these problems is for more work to be done on the topic, using the same technique as Clark 1983; Bempechat 1998; and my own work. I trust that this will happen soon.

I present the data on each family with a chapter devoted to the academically average students, followed by a chapter on the students who are doing well in school, and finally by one on the poor students. The names of the families have, of course, been changed. The subject student was asked to select any first and last name by which he or she wanted to be known in the book. The parents or grandparents are known simply by the last name. Let us now turn our attention to the families and the students.

FAMILY AND THE
AVERAGE STUDENT

PIERRE BAROQUE

James Comer (1993) writes about how those left out of the mainstream often fail to provide their children with the experiences, especially in the social-interactive area, that help them to do well in school. While his research is very important in this field, and very important to my work, he does sometimes write as though almost all poor families are alike. While he uses the term "many" in referring to the poor who lack the experiences to adequately prepare their children for the school milieu, he goes on to write as though the poor are almost monolithic. In this sense he is not much different from Jencks (1991) and others, who seem to group all of the urban poor, particularly the black and Hispanic urban poor, into one category. Well, they do not seem to be writing about Pierre Baroque and his family.

Pierre lives with his mother and one sibling in the Evanston neighborhood in which eleven of the twelve families in the study reside. This neighborhood, the West Side, is historically black and has ranged from middle income to poor. In the past few years it has become more and more working income to poor. Pierre is in the sixth grade and lists as his hobbies reading and crafts. This is interesting and important given the significance of reading to a child's school success (Comer 1993). Ms. Baroque was a teenage mother and indicates that she is a single mother. Pierre's father is involved with the family but does not live in the house. Ms. Baroque works full-time at a local hospital as a scheduler, but the family is considered lower income.

Both Ms. Baroque and Pierre's father completed high school. As is the case for many poor black parents, Ms. Baroque indicates that Pierre's education is "very" important to her, and when asked why, she responded: "So he can succeed in life more." Education is seen as important to many—indeed, most—blacks, regardless of income level. It is often assumed that this is not the case, given that many poor blacks seem to do badly in school. However, value and accomplishment are not the same. A number of poor blacks, like the Baroques, manage somehow to translate value into that accomplishment. The question is how? If we can answer this question, then perhaps we can help others with the same values to do the same.

Ms. Baroque indicates that she does encourage Pierre to do well in school and that she does so by studying with him and by letting him know that it is acceptable to make mistakes as long as he learns from them. As we will see as we present and analyze the data from more families, the characteristic of studying with the child is very important. This issue can become quite complex, however, given that as the child progresses in school and schoolwork becomes progressively more difficult, the parent may well find this harder to do. Still, I found that in a number of the cases in which the student was doing average or well in school, the parent or parents studied with the child. The best explanation for this is probably supplied by Entwisle and Alexander (1996) and Entwisle, Alexander, and Olson (1997). They indicate that parents, regardless of income, can supply the "psychological supports" that all students need to do well in school. While they are writing primarily about students in the elementary grades, I believe that the argument holds for almost all ages below college.

If the student feels a certain amount of interest in and concern for his or her work from the parent, as evidenced by the parent's involvement with the student's work, then the student is more likely to try harder and to feel more confidence. Having a parent say to a student that education is important has become almost expected. But what if the student lives in an environment in which few have done well in school and fewer still have done well in life? What is there to make the exhortation real or meaningful? Parents need to support the schooling of children (Bronfrenbrenner 1991), and for poor parents this is often more difficult, given that they often lack support themselves and that they have so many things to do with so few resources that finding the time and energy to support the student may not be easy. Clearly, Ms. Baroque finds both the time and the energy.

Ms. Baroque visits Pierre's school "five or six times a year." Whether this should be seen as a few times or many times depends largely on the number of times other parents in the sample visit. Be that as it may, as Entwisle, Alexander, and Olson (1997); Comer (1993); and others have pointed out, parental involvement is important to the child's educational success. Many American commentators view parental visits to the school as an important form of involvement. We will see as we continue our analysis whether these visits distinguish at all between those doing well or average and those doing badly. It would seem that this may not be the case, given that students doing badly probably have their parents called to the school more often to discuss their performance, their behavior, or both. Simply going to school may not show the child that the parent seriously cares about his or her education and that he or she should therefore care and take it seriously as well. The purposes of the meetings may be just as important. We will be able to compare the number of visits as we go along. Ms. Baroque feels "good" about her visits to Pierre's school.

When asked, "What, if anything, stands in Pierre's way in terms of getting a good education?" Ms. Baroque indicated that he is "unorganized," that he needs to do a better job of setting priorities. Clearly, she is giving to Pierre the responsibility for his performance and for his future. She did not answer "money" or "race" or "teachers." According to her, Pierre stands in his own way. This suggests she has an appreciation for internal or self-control, and I suspect that Pierre is being raised to believe that he himself controls his actions and his future. It also suggests that Pierre is fully capable of doing well in the view of his mother. This is, of course, important. As Clark (1983) and others (Coleman 1966; Lefcourt 1982) have pointed out, children who feel that they can manage their own affairs, their own "environment," have a better chance of success. Comer (1993) refers to it as "personal control" (304) and suggests that parents or caretakers greatly influence the child in the development of this and other characteristics that may positively influence the child's school success.

Schools are middle-class institutions, or as Comer (1993) puts it, "The school is an instrument of the mainstream culture." He goes on to say: "Children from social networks with similar attitudes, values, and ways to those of the school and the most powerful school people have the best opportunity of meeting the expectations of the school" (305). Schools require and reward behavior and values that the middle class holds high. Behavior and values such as discipline, delayed gratification, anger control, spontaneity, and self-control (or internal control) are not only positively rewarded in schools but needed if one is to do well in schools and in the larger society (Banfield 1970). Students who feel that they themselves control their lives, their destinies, obviously have a better chance of success in school. Their grades are up to them. Their performance is their responsibility. They are then in a position to attempt to influence affairs that they do well (Mele 1995; Harrington and Boardman 1997). This has been seen for some time as a middle-class characteristic, one necessary for middle-class success, and one not seen in too many poor people (Banfield). In fact, we have in the past seen it as one of the many causes of the failure of many of the poor to do better (Glazer and Moynihan 1963; Coleman 1966).

As I indicated earlier, Ms. Baroque's response to the question also suggests that she has fairly high expectations for Pierre. After all, if nothing stands in his way of obtaining a good education, and education is very important to her, it is logical to assume that she expects him to do well. As Entwisle, Alexander, and Olson (1997) indicate, parental expectations and attitudes regarding the child's education are very important in influencing how well the student does. Ms. Baroque does not think that any adult at school or any other child stops Pierre from doing well. It is all up to Pierre, and Pierre himself expects to do well. Indeed, he expects to attend graduate school. Given that Pierre is twelve years old and in the sixth grade, I would say that this is an impressive expectation.

Pierre himself sees no obstacles in his way. I asked each student whether he or she saw any obstacles in the way to educational expectations. Pierre answered no. I also asked whether anyone had tried to stop him from doing well. This question was based on my belief that many poor black students who are doing well in school face pressure from other poor black students to do less well. If the society believes that poor black students will do badly in school settings, then those who do badly have an excuse for failure. It is not their personal failure, their personal responsibility. After all, they are poor and black. This defense is, however, weakened when other poor blacks do well. Comer (1993) has a different explanation, but the result is the same. He believes that academic success is not internalized in many nonmainstream settings. That is, school success is not important to many outside of the middle class. As a result, those who do well will often not only fail to find the necessary support in the family and community but will also face peer group pressure to perform badly.

Pierre indicated that another student who takes the same bus to school often asks whether Pierre has done all of his homework. When Pierre answers yes, the other student "is like, 'Oh, man.'" Pierre sees this as "a competition thing." The other young man does his homework as well, and Pierre does not feel threatened or pressured. So Pierre does not really fit my expectations where peer pressure is concerned. He also does not see race or racial discrimination as something that affects him much. Remember, he lives in an almost all-black neighborhood in an integrated community and attends an integrated school. It would be quite easy to expect that race would be a factor in his life. While it may be that he does not yet see the significance, it may also be the case that Pierre has enough self-confidence that he does not intend to allow factors beyond his control to shape his life if he can help it. When asked who would he be like if he could select one person in the world, he responded that he wanted to be like an uncle because the uncle has a "good job and travels a lot." Pierre does not seem to want to limit himself.

This book is about the impact of the family on the academic success or failure of poor blacks. Yet I have not yet specifically defined success. Given the difficulties in the lives of many of these poor minority families, success is not so easy to determine. With school dropout rates so high in many urban school systems, is remaining in school success? With blacks being arrested at higher rates than whites for all index crimes (Kornblum and Julian 1998), is staying out of jail success? I am interested in a more limited perspective—academic success. Furstenberg et al. (1999) took a broader approach and used "academic competence, self-competence and psychological adjustment, problem behavior, and prosocial involvement" (43). Like me, Clark (1983) was interested in school success or school achievement. He used "student reported grades, and class rank, student reported reading and math achievement scores, teacher's perceptions of child's 'promise,' and student self perception of ability" (25).

While I applaud Furstenberg and his colleagues on their more holistic approach, I am nevertheless concerned only with school performance. Since student-reported grades and perceptions of ability have obvious shortcomings, I chose to use student grades as given on official grade reports from schools. The reports were supplied to Family Focus with the permission of parents or guardians and then relayed to me. Given that we use no real names in this volume, we are protecting the privacy of the grades. While school grades may not be perfect predictors of success in life, they remain the definition of success in school, and I am interested in the role of the family in school performance. I will also refer at times to comments made by teachers on the grade reports concerning the students' attitudes and performance. In most cases I analyzed the students' grades from more than one academic year, and in all cases I had the most recent grades. Thus I was in a position to detect changes in the performance of students over time and to feel confident that my categorization of students as high or low achievers is correct.

My method of determining academic success, while apparently straightforward and simple, is not without complications. If a student has all C grades, is that student successful? Perhaps not when compared to a student with all A's, but when compared to many from poor black communities such a student may indeed be doing well. In fact, while Clark (1983) never really tells us where any specific student falls on his performance index, the aspirations of a number of the students he considers successful do not exactly suggest students who are high performers. One is interested in X-ray technology. Another "has developed few goals for higher education." Another considered auto technology before deciding on college. Again, compared to many poor black students, these may well be the goals of those doing well in school, but when compared to the larger society, they do not suggest high achievers.

So where do I draw the line, especially when we consider the complications of the lives of these children and their families? I decided on a more conservative approach, in large measure because I am not so much concerned with success compared with other poor blacks as with the larger society. We should not have two definitions of success—one for poor blacks and another for nonpoor whites. If we do we may well have two societies forever, and I doubt that many would find this desirable. I realize that Furstenberg et al. (1999) grappled with this issue of two sets of standards as well. They apparently decided on standards for success using what "some may argue is a middle class value" (9). So have I. Thus I defined academic success in terms of high grades and positive remarks from teachers. It was not difficult to decide that a student receiving mainly A's and B's was successful in school. It was not difficult deciding that one receiving mostly D's and F's was not. The problem came with those receiving some C's, some D's, and an occasional B. I decided to classify these students as average, though I understand that some will disagree.

In the case of Pierre, it is a bit more complicated because his grades have changed, gone down, over the last year. In Evanston students below the sixth grade are given check marks on their report cards to indicate "strong performance," "acceptable performance," or "needs improvement." After the fifth grade they are given letter grades. Last year in the fifth grade Pierre's report card showed mostly checks indicating acceptable performance for all three academic quarters. He showed strong performances in several categories of the subject areas communication skills, social studies, math, and science. In fact, by the third marking period his performances were strong in all but one of the six sciences areas. He needed improvement in only a few areas, mainly in social studies and math. Overall, Pierre was a fairly high achiever.

This academic year was, however, a different story. In the seven subject areas—math, language arts, social studies, reading, French, science, and computer technology—he had three D's, three C's, and one B. Not exactly a stellar performance, and quite a bit lower than the previous year. Any number of factors may have caused the drop-off, but I am not trying to explain the grades of each student. I want to understand the role of the family. In the case of Pierre the change in grades, coupled with the few indications from last year that he needed to improve and the comments of his teachers this year, caused me to label him as average. A number of his teachers indicated that he needs to listen better, correct inconsistent work habits, improve self-control, and/or procure the necessary books or materials. This last comment is, of course, especially troubling because it may suggest a lack of funds.

The Observations

Pierre's home is a small two-bedroom house. Pierre and his younger brother share one bedroom. The first time that the observer arrived and Pierre was at home, he was doing his homework. The kitchen table was filled with books and papers belonging to both Pierre and Ms. Baroque. Ms. Baroque, while preparing dinner, asked Pierre what he had for homework. She also asked to see his math textbook and at one point suggested that he needs to be better organized. At another, after looking at Pierre's work, she told him that he needs better organization and to write neatly "so that your teacher can read it." Throughout all of this, Ms. Baroque prepared the younger brother's bath, made certain that he got into the tub (against his wishes), and compelled him to bathe in addition to playing. At one point Pierre asked the observer for help with a homework question. When the observer demurred, Pierre asked his mother, who promptly helped him. At another point Pierre needed help from his mother, and she went to an encyclopedia for information. While she was away from the table, Pierre used the telephone. When Ms. Baroque returned and found that Pierre was on the phone, she yelled at him three times to get off. While he was asking his father the same academic question on the phone, the mother thought that he was not doing his homework, and this was not acceptable. Finally, Ms. Baroque, Pierre, and the brother all looked at the encyclopedia together and answered the question.

Ms. Baroque mentioned math to Pierre several times during the evening and also became upset at the number of loose papers in Pierre's backpack. After telling him, "This is the last time I'm gonna be doing this," she helped to file the papers into folders after properly labeling the folders. Ms. Baroque also discovered an application to the student council in the backpack and asked Pierre about it. Pierre indicated that he was not selected because his application was late. He had still not eaten at 8:15 and was told that his bedtime was 9:00.

Clearly, Ms. Baroque is not only concerned with Pierre's schoolwork but also involved in it. She is not simply telling him that education is important, but showing him how important it is to her by asking about it, helping him with the work, and not allowing other things to come before the schoolwork. She is also teaching discipline. The younger son was not allowed to avoid the bath after whining about it. Pierre was not going to be allowed to use the phone until his work was complete. Finally, she stressed organization several times during the first visit. Discipline, organization, parental involvement: these are all seen as important to a child's success in school (Furstenberg et al. 1999; Entwisle, Alexander, and Olson 1997; Comer 1993) and often seen as lacking in poor minority families. They are not lacking in the Baroque family.

At another visit Pierre was observed sitting down to do his homework almost as soon as he arrived home from Family Focus. He asked his mother for help with a word used in his science work, and she told him to look the word up in the dictionary. Confused by the definition, Pierre asked for more help. After consulting the dictionary herself, Ms. Baroque tried to communicate the meaning of the word. When Pierre used the word incorrectly in a sentence, his mother let him know. He used another word in a sentence that seemed to confuse his mother. She, in fact, used the word incorrectly in an effort to help Pierre. Again, Ms. Baroque is very involved in Pierre's schoolwork, even though it appears that she may have limited ability to help. I suspect that the ability is less important than the effort. It shows Pierre that his mother seriously cares about his education, cares enough to spend her time and energy helping. It also shows that she is helping Pierre to learn how to learn. He uses the dictionary. He uses the encyclopedia. He was seen using a map. He uses confusing words in sentences until he uses them correctly, except when his mother uses them incorrectly.

That evening Ms. Baroque told Pierre that he must go to bed at 8:30 because he had recently been staying up too late and because he had early band practice. Pierre protested, but she would not reconsider. Clearly, Ms. Baroque stresses discipline and self-control. Shouting was not allowed. Whining was not allowed. When Pierre began a protest over the noise of his younger brother with the sounds "ffff . . . ," his mother told him: "Don't say whatever you're about to say." He responded, "I was just going to say freak." "Don't say that," she said sternly. Words considered harsh or crude are not allowed.

It should also be noted that Ms. Baroque asked Pierre about his involvement with the basketball team. So Pierre is involved with the band, wanted to be involved with the student council, and is involved with the basketball team, or would be, were it not for his academic problems. Not only do Pierre and his mother take his schoolwork very seriously, but Pierre is also quite concerned and involved with extracurricular activities, including the school newspaper.

During another visit Ms. Baroque insisted that the house be quiet and orderly. In fact, she emphasized quiet and order numerous times to Pierre during the evening. Ms. Baroque asked during this third observation about Pierre's math and about a required paper on the Holocaust.

The observer visited the Baroque home six times, five times during the week and once during a weekend. Each visit during the week Ms. Baroque asked Pierre about his homework, encouraged him to complete the homework, and worked with him on the schoolwork a number of times. She stressed that schoolwork must be done before anything else, including television, and emphasized discipline for both Pierre and his kindergarten-age brother.

Pierre works on his schoolwork each evening, though some evenings he also works on his extracurricular activities such as the school newspaper. The school-related work comes before everything else—his mother makes certain of this. He spends some two to three hours per weekday on his schoolwork.

Pierre indicated to the observer that he is the best saxophone player in the band. Remember that he also wants to attend graduate school and that he does not see real obstacles to his education. All of this, plus his self-assured and outgoing personality suggests a fair amount of confidence, a fair amount of self-esteem. He is certainly not hiding or avoiding others. He is putting himself forth for a number of school activities. His house is quiet and well organized, and his mother requires discipline—indeed, the observer commented that she seems rather strict. She also works closely with Pierre on his homework and school activities, and Pierre indicates that his family is most important to him in his life. The family interacts well together, though for Pierre, schoolwork comes before other activities such as talking on the telephone, watching television, or even eating dinner. Pierre talks to and plays with his younger brother while he is working until the brother gets in the way. Then either Pierre or his mother or both urge the younger brother to stop bothering him.

When the younger brother had his first homework assignment for kindergarten, Ms. Baroque helped him. Clearly, she is very much concerned and involved with the academic work of her children. On the Saturday during which the family was observed, Pierre made a cake, with a little help from the younger brother, and was told by the mother to empty the trash. She also helped him with the cake. So Ms. Baroque is supportive and affectionate, somewhat strict, and orderly. Pierre is self-confident, serious about his schoolwork and extracurricular activities, close to his family, and cooperative with the family members. The house is quiet and organized. These are the characteristics of successful families pointed out by Furstenberg et al. 1999 and to some extent by Clark 1983. The interaction with others and personal control shown by Pierre are seen as characteristics of successful children by Comer 1993, and the cooperation obtained by Ms. Baroque from both Pierre and the younger, mischievous brother (he is sometimes noisy, sometimes spills food and plays with it, and sometimes bothers Pierre while he is working) is a characteristic of successful families as noted by Furstenberg 1993.

Pierre is not a failure academically, though compared to a number of our students, he is only average. His family appears to be much like those described as successful by other researchers, but his grades do not appear to be as successful as they might be. We should remember that this is a single-parent family, though the father is sometimes involved. This may well place more stress on the mother, since she appears to do all of the family work. As we examine the other families we should be able to cast more light on the relevance of the family structure.

Pierre decides on his extracurricular activities. He has decided to stop playing the violin because "the music sucked." He generally decides on his homework. On the Saturday visit he was dressed differently than during the week. He wore baggy pants and a very large, loose T-shirt. These were new clothes. He obviously has some autonomy, though his mother still seems to make and/or seriously influence the important decisions. I see two of the characteristics mentioned by Furstenberg et al. (1999). First, autonomy is positively correlated with high achievement (see also Lord, Eccles, and McCarthy 1994). Second, they found what they thought might have been too much control among many poor parents with high-achieving children. As they go on to point out, it is often the case that poor neighborhoods require a great deal of control given the negative behavior that one often finds in those areas. Ms. Baroque seems to exert quite a bit of control. She tells Pierre when he will go to bed, she tells him to make certain that he picks up after himself, she tells the brother to be quiet very often, and she also tells the brother to use the pillows from the bed for a bed he has made on the floor rather than the pillows from the couch. She tells Pierre when and how to organize. The strictness and discipline seem to overrule the autonomy, though Pierre has some.

Ms. Baroque may well be preparing Pierre for a difficult neighborhood and for control over his life as he moves on academically. In many ways this appears to be a regular middle-class family. There is confidence, creativity, internal control, quiet, and organization. Pierre and his mother also seem to be willing to delay gratification. They are emphasizing schoolwork and an academic future rather than recreational activities or going out to play. They are lower income, but in many ways they are middle class. Ms. Baroque lacks the education, income, and the occupation typically associated with the middle class, but a number of the characteristics of the household—and of Pierre—appear to be those of the middle class. As Malone (1985) and Comer (1993) indicate, achievement is positively correlated with a number of the characteristics of the "mainstream," or the middle class. I am not referring to the middle income (education, income, occupation), but to what Malone calls "family values": aspirations, self-esteem, locus of control, parental attitudes and values. In a number of ways the Baroques are middle class, and I would expect the children to perform like many middle-class students. Pierre is not performing as I might have expected given what was observed. On the other hand, his performance has varied: it was at one point slightly above average but, as I have indicated, has gone down. Let us turn our attention to the next average student.

ANGOLIQUE WEAVER

Angolique's grades are somewhat higher than the grades of Pierre for the academic year 1999–2000 and were about the same the year before. She is in the eighth grade and attends the same middle school as do four other students in our study. For the 1998–1999 academic year Angolique received two B's, one B−, one B+, one C+, and one C for the winter grading period. All of the comments from her teachers were positive: She had a positive attitude, was trying harder, was making progress in each particular course, participated in class activities, and worked well with her peers. During the 1999–2000 academic year she had two B's, one B−, two C's, and one D during the winter term. She also had an A in chorus. The comments suggested that she was trying harder but could use more effort. Her grades for the winter were a bit higher than those for the fall term. Clearly, Angolique is a solid student. Angolique lives with her mother, father, and five others in a West Side neighborhood of Evanston. There are four children in the house, and the household income is considered "lower income." Ms. Weaver is thirty years old, and Angolique is thirteen, suggesting that Ms. Weaver, like Ms. Baroque, was a teenage mother. Ms. Weaver and her husband both work: she as a customer service representative and he in life insurance. Ms. Weaver completed one year of college but gave us no information regarding her husband's education. She grew up in Evanston and has lived in the current house for two years. Angolique's education is very important to her; when asked why, she replied that she didn't want her to work at McDonald's: "I don't want her to be a statistic, I want her to go somewhere in life." Like several of the families studied by Clark (1983), Ms. Weaver links education to success in life, a better job for her daughter. When asked whether she encouraged Angolique in terms of her education, she responded, "I sure do" by letting her know that "extra work means extra" and by helping her to study. She visits the school three or four times a year to "keep in touch with the teachers" and feels "confident and concerned" when she visits. This suggests high or positive self-esteem on the part of the mother, and I would not then be surprised to learn that Angolique too has positive self-esteem, an important variable in school achievement. Instead of waiting for school conferences, Ms. Weaver would rather drop into school unannounced. This also indicates confidence, especially since many poor people are intimidated by formal institutions. Think about it. Teachers are professionals. They talk like professionals, using terms often understood only by other teachers and well-educated people. They dress like professionals, they act like professionals. This is fine, but what is the impact on poor people, who might not understand some of the words and will often not be able to dress professionally? If Ms. Weaver is, as she indicates, willing to drop into her daughter's school when she wants to, then she would indeed appear to be quite confident.

According to Ms. Weaver, nothing stands in Angolique's way of obtaining a good education, and no other child tries to stop her from doing well in school. As is the case for Ms. Baroque and Pierre, Ms. Weaver places the responsibility for doing well on Angolique. As I have noted before, I believe that this involves discipline, self-esteem, and internal or self-control, each of which are very important in the educational process (Comer 1993; Furstenberg et al. 1999; Malone 1985). If students are to sit still for hours while a teacher teaches, even though they might prefer to work on the computer or play on the playground, discipline is necessary. If students are to attempt to do well in class, they generally think enough of themselves to accept the responsibility for their own performance. The lives of many poor students get in the way of these characteristics, but clearly that is not the case for all of them.

Unlike Ms. Baroque, Ms. Weaver indicates that race affects her, that "discrimination and race are a part of [her] life." Yet she does not believe that race is a factor in Angolique's education. When asked how she tried to raise Angolique, she responded that she tries "to instill self-discipline, respect, and self-esteem into her." This sounds very much like what we might expect of a "mainstream" or middle-class family. Still, the issue of race has not gone away, and this in a community that prides itself on its tolerance and diversity. One wonders what impact this might have on Angolique and her schooling.

Angolique indicates that she most likes gym, math, and chorus in school. She likes basketball and to be free "from having to think," and gym provides both. She likes math because she "likes numbers," and she likes to sing. She also mentioned two of her favorite teachers by name. She doesn't particularly like writing or major projects because they take up too much time. When asked how well she was doing in school, she answered, "well" and "pretty good." Given that she is receiving B and C grades, she seems to have a fairly clear idea about her academic prowess.

Angolique thinks that education is very important because she "needs an education to get through life and through the world" and because her parents teach that education is very important. This shows that the Weavers not only believe in the value of education, they also impress that belief on Angolique. It appears that Angolique accepts the parents' valuation of education and tries to translate that belief into achievement. This would also seem to suggest the importance of family to Angolique. She pays attention to their teachings, and this allows them the opportunity to seriously influence her development and her life.

As is the case with Pierre, Angolique indicates that she has never experienced peer pressure to do badly in school. I might have expected some pressure given that she does fairly well academically, but either there is no such pressure or she does not see it. I would suspect that it is the former, and this weakens my expectation (and Comer's [1993] as well) that a number of the poor who do well, especially minorities, will face such pressure because so many others are underachievers and are expected to be so. On the other hand, we have not yet begun to analyze the cases of the high achievers. It may be that it is the students at that level who experience the pressure. I raise the issue because if that pressure is in fact present, then we not only have a seldom-discussed explanation for the academic weakness of many poor minority students, but we also have a need for a somewhat different policy direction.

Angolique spends about two and one-half hours every evening on her homework, and like Pierre, she would like an advanced degree, a master's, but she does not yet know in what field. I am again somewhat surprised to find a young, poor, black student interested in an advanced degree already. When we think about poor black urban students, we do not appear to be thinking about students such as these. Both Pierre and Angolique seem more highly motivated and knowledgeable than most of the high achievers studied by Clark (1983). Although one of the students studied by Clark wanted a master's degree, the others were quite a bit less ambitious. I will return to this important issue later. It may well be that we are not comparing the same kinds of students. While I classify Pierre and Angolique as average, there is a good chance that several of those whom Clark terms "high achievers" would not be called such in my classification. We may thus be comparing what I consider academically average students with those whom I would consider to be actually somewhat below average, using Clark's definition. This is important because it raises the question of our expectations of poor black students. Do we expect the same of them that we expect of others, or do we expect less? We will address this issue in more depth in chapter 6. As I mentioned above, Angolique values education because she believes that it will help her to get through life and through the world. There are two points here. First, like a number of Clark's high achievers, Angolique appears to value education not for education's sake, but because she believes that it will help her later in life. Second, this is a thirteen-year-old eighth grader thinking seriously about her future and her world. This would suggest delayed gratification, a middle-class characteristic. Angolique is not only capable of conceiving of her future position in the world, she is apparently willing to work in school to achieve it.

When asked what was most important to her in her life, Angolique responded, "Education and waking up every morning." She went on to list "parents, grandparents, and sisters." So Angolique, like Pierre, thinks that family is one of the most important things in her life. This is another finding of Clark (1983). This puts the parents, and perhaps other family members, in a position to have a significant impact on the beliefs and activities of the child. It also raises the possibility of overcontrol or, as Furstenberg and his colleagues (1999) write, a lack of "support for autonomy" (76). Baumrind (1967); Furstenberg et al.; and Clark (1983) find that autonomy of the child is positively correlated with academic achievement and seems characteristic of the middle class. Clark and Furstenberg and his colleagues find in their research that poor minority parents tended to exercise a fair amount of control over their children. Indeed, Clark refers to it as "'authoritative guidance'" and raises "the danger of over control" (131). In many poor minority neighborhoods, apparently including the West Side, there are good reasons for parents to keep a close watch on their children: violence, drug abuse, gangs, and the like. If the watch becomes too close, the children may not develop the autonomy they need. If it is not close enough, the child may well face problems. I will return to this issue throughout this work.

For now, allow me to point out that Angolique wishes that her parents "wouldn't be so hard on me." She thinks that her parents fail to allow her the autonomy she desires. I would guess that most teenagers think the same thing. The critical questions are the amount of control and the type of control. Psychological control has a negative impact on academic performance, while behavioral control may be positive (Barber, Olson, and Shagle 1994). I saw virtually no indication of psychological control exerted by Ms. Baroque over Pierre. In fact, there was a great deal of the kind of give-and-take and parent–child interaction that both Clark (1983) and the Furstenberg team (1999) found to be an important predictor of academic success among the middle class.

Angolique says that her parents help her with her homework every day, and she believes that this is "too much" help. Again we see an indication of a kind of parental involvement that goes beyond PTA meetings and parent–teacher conferences. Such parents are giving the students concrete evidence of their belief in the importance of education. If poor parents with so much on their agendas find the time and energy to help with the homework consistently, then the children must realize how important education is to the parents. This increases the probability that the children will take education quite seriously, especially in light of the importance of the family to the children.

Neither Angolique nor Pierre reads a newspaper very often. When Pierre does, he reads only the comics. Angolique reads a paper once a week to see what is at the movies and "who died." It is difficult to imagine how these youngsters can keep up with what is happening in their world without reading a paper with some regularity. I did not see that Pierre was able to watch television often, and the news is not likely to be what he watches.

If she could be anyone in the world, Angolique would choose the black model Tyra Banks. because she "likes fashion and Tyra is a model." Angolique's choice does not seem to have been made on the basis of Banks's race; race is not something about which she thinks often. She did mention that there were apparently some segregated classes in the beginning of the school year, which were integrated once a group realized the problem. But in any event, there is nothing to suggest that Angolique perceives that race shapes her life.

The Observations

During the first visit to the Weaver home, the observer and Angolique mentioned to one another that they were hungry, and the observer suggested that they go to the store to buy something to eat. Angolique, however, insisted that she had to wait for her mother to return home. This is a sign that discipline prevails in this house. Angolique could not simply do what she wanted when her mother was not at home. She had to do what was expected of her. This also suggests that the mother exerts a fairly high level of behavioral control over Angolique. Such discipline is needed—indeed, required—for school achievement. It is also a characteristic of the middle class. The control or limitation of autonomy, as I have indicated, can have a negative impact on achievement. Still, as Furstenberg et al. (1999) write: "Given the neighborhoods in which many of the families in this study live and the age of the children, we expect a continuing need for high levels of extra-familial behavioral control"(115). We are beginning to see signs of this control, but the neighborhood would suggest the need for much of this control, and both Pierre and Angolique do fairly well in school despite what some might consider too much control.

As I pointed out above, Angolique does not read the newspapers often. She does, however, enjoy reading Langston Hughes and writing poetry in her spare time. This does not sound like someone alienated from academic pursuits. Indeed, when Ms. Weaver arrived home, Angolique turned to schoolwork right away, and Ms. Weaver helped her with her math homework at the same time that she talked to Angolique's four-year-old sister about wetting her pants. As was the case for the Baroques, the mother helped with homework while busy doing other things. This serves to impress on the student the importance of education. If education is important enough that the parent both works with the student on homework and does various household chores, then education must seem important to the parent, and eventually, to the child as well. While Angolique and Ms. Weaver worked on the homework, Mr. Weaver arrived home. He did not involve himself in the homework at all, but he did remind Angolique on several occasions that she should be doing it.

In the Baroque house only the mother is present, and she must do everything. In the Weaver house both parents are present, but only the mother helps with the homework. The father mentions schoolwork often, but it is the mother who actually is involved in school-related activity—and most of the home-related activity as well. Clark (1983) found much the same pattern in the two-parent families he observed: Much of the activity involving the children, including school-related activity, centered around the mothers. This would seem to place a great deal of pressure on the mothers.

Despite the fact that there are seven people in the house, the Weaver house is quiet in the evening. The same is the case for the Baroque household. The evening activity centers around school and learning, not television, radio, or recordings. During the second visit to the home, Ms. Weaver was initially sitting at the dinner table working with the four-year-old daughter, Erika, on her alphabet. Ms. Baroque helped her five-year-old with his schoolwork as well. In these cases the children would seem to learn the value of education at an early age. Instead of watching television, they are not only learning but learning how to structure their lives around learning and school, learning that school and learning come first. They are more likely to go to school prepared to learn given the value of education to the parents, the importance of family to children, and the fact that they seem to grow up in an atmosphere that reinforces the importance of education. This means that they are likely to do better in school than those for whom education is not important, those who do not learn how to study and how to learn.

Erika is learning how to read with the help of Ms. Weaver and Angolique. After Erika reads a word, Angolique repeats it to her. This is significant in two ways: It would seem to further reinforce for Erika the value of education given that even her sister seems to believe that it is important enough to help, and it serves as an example of a leadership role played by Angolique. Pierre, too, helped his brother with academic work, assisting with simple math assignments. Another time Pierre made fun of his brother, Junior, because Junior had no homework. Junior responded that he did in fact have homework and showed it to Pierre. Here is a household in which it appears to be an honor to have homework—and to do it.

Winch (1962) and Clark (1983) point out that as children become integrated into the different activities of the household, parents are in a good position to prepare them for academic and social activity. In fact, Clark finds that those who play roles in which others rely on them for assistance—helping younger siblings with their homework, for example—are the higher achievers.

While Erika and Ms. Weaver practiced her letters, Angolique asked about dinner. Ms. Weaver responded with a question about Angolique's other homework: "Angolique, let me see your social studies." "I don't have it with me." While this seemed to upset Ms. Weaver, she calmly told Angolique not to leave her books at school and returned to helping Erika with her letters. Angolique is learning to be calm even when she might be upset, a good lesson for school. While Ms. Weaver prepared dinner, she scolded Erika for playing while she should have been working on her words. Again, the children see that schoolwork is more important than play, and that it is sufficiently important to their mother that she focuses on the academic work even while she does other important household work. Furthermore, it would appear that both Pierre and Angolique, through their leadership roles, are being prepared for academic and social activity.

On another visit during a school day, the observer and Angolique did in fact decide to go to the grocery store before Ms. Weaver arrived home. However, Angolique left her mother a note telling her where she was and that she would be right back. This suggests the importance of discipline yet again and perhaps raises the specter of overcontrol.

When the observer, Angolique, and Erika returned from the store, Angolique turned on the stereo. This was unusual given that typically homework comes first and rarely is there much noise in the house during the weekday evenings. When the parents returned home a few minutes later, Mr.

Weaver said, "Turn this off," referring to the stereo, as he walked through the door. Angolique immediately turned the music off and began her homework. There was no discussion, no back talk. Mr. Weaver went into his bedroom and began to watch television.

Ms. Weaver began to help a cousin with his homework and to look over Angolique's shoulder while she worked. Clearly, on weekday evenings during the school year, academic work dominates the Weaver household, and Ms. Weaver not only pushes all students in the house to do their schoolwork, she helps them as much as she can. In the case of the cousin, she helped him to figure out words through word association and by giving him context clues. The house is orderly, quiet, and focused on academics.

There was another instance of the parents being somewhat upset with Angolique when she failed to bring home an expected document signed by a teacher. There were, however, no raised voices, no harsh words. Again, Angolique is being taught to respond thoughtfully and calmly even when emotion is present. Moreover, the parents respond warmly to Angolique even when they are not pleased with what she has or has not done. I also believe that the almost constant involvement of Ms. Weaver with the children's academic work and growth demonstrates her concern not only for school but also for them. They seem to know that they are loved and cared for. Why else would the parents pay so much attention to their work and their activities?

These are two of the three family variables that Furstenberg et al. 1999 finds a positive impact on educational success. That is, the Weaver household demonstrates parental warmth and discipline effectiveness. There are no signs of hostility or lack of concern, and Angolique seems to know what is expected of her consistently. The third variable, autonomy promotion, is, as I have written, problematic given the neighborhood with its dangers and problems. I will return to this issue.

Bempechat (1998) indicates that several variables are correlated with achievement: Students are oriented toward learning, education is set as a top priority, students are taught to work hard, high expectations are maintained, self-esteem is encouraged, and home–school relationships are maintained. The relationship between the home and school was not clear in the Weaver's case, but all Bempechat's other variables are certainly present in the Weaver household. Entwisle and her colleagues (1997) suggest that parents' help with homework, monitoring of activities, rule making and enforcement, and discipline are all important for school success. Both the Weaver and the Baroque families seem to meet most of the Bempechat and Entwisle "rules" for school success, and indeed the students in both families are successful academically. They are not the poor black urban students that the nation seems so concerned about, though they are poor, urban, and black.

During another visit to the Weaver household, the observer noted that the house was calm and quiet: "everyone was content in their own world." Ms. Weaver attempted to play a word game with Alice, the eleven-month-old. Angolique and the observer discussed school grades, and Ms. Weaver and the observer discussed a current event that had been receiving a great deal of public attention. An hour after the observer arrived (at 6:15 in the evening), Mr. Weaver came home to pick Ms. Weaver up to attend a bowling meeting. This left the house without parents, and the children, including Angolique, took advantage of the opportunity to play with each other. While no schoolwork was done before the observer left at 8:15, it is interesting to note that learning and thoughtful interaction took place much of the evening and that the house was quiet and orderly while the parents were gone.

On another visit to the Weaver house, the observer found Angolique home alone, doing homework, indicating that her parents need not be present for Angolique to do what she has been taught is correct. When her father arrived, Angolique began to tell him about school that day and that she had been asked at Family Focus to work with the younger children because it was thought she would be a good influence with them. This again reflects the leadership qualities that Angolique seems to show when she works with her younger siblings. They defer to her, and she leads, guides, and watches out for them. She finds time while doing homework to play with them.

When Ms. Weaver arrived home, Mr. Weaver hugged and kissed her and Alice together in the middle of the floor. The other family members could all see this example of familial warmth and love. Angolique then interrupted her homework to argue with the observer that homework was a waste of time. She suggested that students should be able to do the work in school and that if one knows the work, one knows it, and homework is then not necessary. Still, she did homework almost every evening, which suggests discipline. On this evening her mother found errors in one of her finished school papers. Angolique had requested permission to go to the grocery store, but Ms. Weaver made it clear that when Angolique returned she was to correct the errors. There was no argument. Angolique did as she was asked when she returned.

During this observation, as on another occasion we had observed, Mr. Weaver went to the Laundromat to do the family laundry. While I find this somewhat unusual for a non-middle-income black man, it would seem to show to the children the importance of working together and the value of family. Clark (1983) points out on several occasions how the men in his study were quite rigid in playing the masculine roles and that household activity was seen as a feminine role. This was not the case in the Weaver family. Indeed, Mr. Weaver demonstrated love and warmth, as well as strictness, consistently. Ms. Weaver and Mr. Weaver constantly impressed on Angolique and her younger siblings the importance of education and of discipline. Ms. Weaver and Angolique talked a great deal about schoolwork and about other things on Angolique's mind.

When Angolique informed her mother that she wanted a certain pair of gym shoes, her mother asked the cost and then shifted the conversation to shoes that the family could afford. When Angolique was asked to help out at Family Focus, she discussed it with her father, albeit briefly. The point is that Angolique feels free to interact with her parents, and this kind of interaction helps to prepare children for school and for the outside world. It gives them a confidence and positive self-esteem that are quite valuable.

As a part of a final set of observations of the Weaver family, the observer wrote:

> My family maintained a certain amount of normalcy. As I expected from my first visit, the Weaver family operated as a family [unit]. Important things like cooking and eating dinner together, talking as opposed to yelling, and playfulness between the parents and children were some of the things that I witnessed on almost every visit. There was always some form of communication between the older children and the younger children. Disagreements between the children were settled by whichever adult was present: they never yelled or made either child seem more or less important than the other.

The observer went on to write: "It [the observation experience] illustrated that lower-income families can very well be middle class." In fact, both the Weaver family and the Baroques appeared to be middle class in many ways important to educational achievement. They both stressed discipline in consistent ways. The student being studied in each family showed positive self-esteem and internal control. The educational aspirations of the students were high, and the value of education to the parent(s) was very high. Each home was quiet and orderly, and the parents demonstrated a warmth and concern for all of the children. In each case the student being studied interacted with younger siblings as both a leader and an educational helper. This helps the self-esteem and leadership abilities of the students and helps to keep the families close.

A number of these characteristics are very much like some of those found by Clark (1983) in the homes of high achievers. He also found "frequent parent child dialogue, strong parental encouragement in academic pursuits, clear and consistent limits set for the young, [and] warm and nurturing interactions" (111). Indeed, as we will see later in this book, I found even more similarities between the Clark families and those I studied in addition to similarities with the families studied by Furstenberg and his colleagues (1999); Bempechat (1998); and Entwisle and her colleagues (1997). In other words, there would appear to be more and more data painting a similar picture regarding the impact of the family on the academic achievements of poor children and the specific variables involved in that impact.

Before I move on to the next "average" student, I would like to make two points regarding the Weaver family. First, Angolique is involved with the school chorus. So, as with Pierre, extracurricular activities play a role in her school life. We will investigate this aspect of school in the lives of the other students to determine whether it affects academic performance. Furstenberg et al. (1999) argue that such involvement has a positive impact, and Malone's work (1985) would suggest the same if analyzed properly. The second point is that it is a bit early to determine the significance, if any, of having two parents present. It is clear that Ms. Weaver handles most of the parent–child activity. Mr. Weaver does perform at least one of the household chores, the laundry, and is involved in discipline and demonstrating love to the children. Thus he would seem to have a positive impact on the family and the children. While I will return to the issue of differences between two-parent families and single-parent families as the book progresses, such is not the focus of this work. I bear in mind, however, the findings of Entwisle, Alexander, and Olson (1997) that the children of single-parent families appear to fare worse in school than the children of two-parent families.

TRACEY LOVE

Tracey Love is eleven years old and lives with her father, mother, an older brother, and one other adult. She is in the sixth grade and in the winter grading period received one B+, one B, one B−, three C+'s, and one C−. (Tracey's grades had been slightly lower during the fall grading period.) Two teachers indicated that she has inconsistent work habits, one that she needs greater effort, and one that she cooperates well.

The lower-income Loves have lived on the West Side of Evanston for eight years, having migrated from the Bahamas. Ms. Love, forty-two, was not a teenage mother. She works full-time as a nurse at a public hospital in Chicago. It is not clear that the father was working during this research. Ms. Love has a bachelor's degree, and her husband completed the eleventh grade. Ms. Love indicated that Tracey's education is "very important" to her because education will help Tracey with her self-awareness and enable her to have a more secure future. Again, education is seen as a means to an end, with the end being a better financial future. She indicates that she definitely encourages Tracey to do well in school and that she does so by supporting her schoolwork and by encouraging her with respect to homework and her educational goals. This does not really sound like the image of the poor minority mother paying little attention to the education of her child.

Ms. Love says that she visits Tracey's school "frequently" and that she feels "confident and at ease" when she does so. I had postulated that many poor minority parents would feel uncomfortable visiting school given that schools are middle-class institutions with a style of speaking, dressing, and behaving that might intimidate some parents and therefore limit their visits to school and their involvement in school activities. Thus far I have not found this to be the case. Each parent responding to the questionnaire, Ms. Baroque, Ms. Weaver, and Ms. Love, indicated that she visits the child's school often and feels comfortable doing so. I would argue that this is largely because each mother is essentially middle class in terms of values, beliefs, and attitudes, so that the atmosphere of a school is congenial to them.

When asked what if anything stands in Tracey's way of receiving a good education, Ms. Love, like Ms. Weaver and Ms. Baroque, answered that nothing stands in her way. So Ms. Love, like the others, expects her daughter to control her own future. She, too, would seem confident and internally controlled, and I would expect that Tracey would be much the same, given that she would be influenced by her mother and not allowed many excuses. Unlike the other two mothers, however, Ms. Love says that Tracey does in fact experience peer pressure and bullying to do badly in school, though she does not seem to expect this pressure to get in Tracey's way.

Comer (1993) and I are not the only ones concerned with peer pressure on those doing decently in school. Steinberg (1998) writes: "Not only is there little room in most schools for the academically oriented, but there also is substantial peer pressure on students to underachieve" (332). Again, I submit that this pressure may well be more intense on the poor minority student who achieves because the belief is that few do so, and therefore there is little incentive for most to buck this trend. Those who do defy the expectation are often seen as "white" or as outcasts, and they therefore face pressure to fit in. Apparently, Ms. Love believes that Tracey faces such pressure. It will be interesting to see whether the higher achievers seem to face this pressure. If a student doing well or average does so, what about the student doing very well?

Like Ms. Weaver, Ms. Love feels that race and/or discrimination plays a role in her life, but she does not let it affect her. She moves beyond it, and "continues to stay focused." So none of the three respondents thus far would seem to use race as an excuse for failure. They either do not acknowledge race or discrimination as an issue in their lives, or they "move beyond" it. These women clearly believe that they, not their race, control their lives. Given the role of race and of discrimination in our society, this is interesting and powerful. Evanston has been involved for some time now in an emotional debate about why the black students perform so much worse than the white students academically and what should be done to change this situation. So race is an open and important topic in Evanston, particularly when school achievement is at issue. Still, the three mothers studied thus far indicate that it is either not an issue in their lives or that they do not allow it to affect them, and they believe that it will not hold their children back educationally.

While Ms. Love stresses the importance of education to Tracey, she noted that education was not emphasized by her own single-parent mother. Her mother stressed religion, and Ms. Love says that religion and the church are very important in her life. According to Furstenberg et al. (1999), religion may be used to provide structure and support for children in families in which students do well. The church helps the parents to positively influence peer associations and exposes the children to positive values that may very well help academically. The discipline, structure, control, and rewards for positive behavior found in most religious organizations should positively affect education. This, of course, assumes that the child is also involved in the religious organization. As we will see, Tracey definitely is so involved.

In fact, Ms. Love, when explaining how she attempts to raise Tracey, said that she stresses "values, being true to yourself, doing the best you possibly can"—excelling in your life. She also stressed growing up in church and education. Ms. Love has involved Tracey in her religious organization, and in discussing her parenting she continually came back to the importance of Tracey's education and accomplishment. The values of discipline, accomplishment, and self-control—along with the importance of education—are thus being stressed at home and probably at church as well. These are some of the more important values possessed by most children who go to school prepared to learn. As Comer (1993) suggests, many poor and/or minority children do not seem to adhere to these values, which are expected in schools, and therefore many do badly in school. As we are beginning to see in this research, however, a number of families and children do in fact seem to have these values and characteristics. They hold them in the face of many obstacles: living in neighborhoods stricken by poverty and high crime rates, surrounded by others who may not possess these same values. I have the impression that what they do is not easy.

What Tracey most likes about her school are the various extracurricular activities in which she in engaged, including theater, choir, basketball, and volleyball. She is also a member of her church choir, takes piano lessons, and is involved in dance and drama outside of school. Obviously, she is quite a busy young lady. These activities would seem to help her to develop discipline, leadership skills, and self-esteem. Discipline is required in order to perform all of these different activities on schedule, and young people who are engaged in such a variety of positive activities must realize that they are at the head of the group and that they are admired by others for their accomplishments.

When asked what she least liked about school, Tracey replied "math and math homework." She believes that she is doing well in school (as opposed to very well, fair, not so well, or poorly). Given her most recent grades, her self-assessment seems reasonably accurate, though I think that she is doing fair. Tracey indicates that education is "very important" to her, the highest level of importance that could be selected. When asked why, she replied, "Because I want to be smart, get a good education while in college, and one day have a family." At eleven years of age Tracey already thinks of college. In fact, like both of the other students, Tracey would like to go to graduate school and expects to do so. So she, like the others, has very high educational expectations.

Unlike the others, though, Tracey said that she had in fact faced pressure from her peers to do badly in school. This supports what her mother told us independently of her. She indicated that one of her peers had tried to pressure her to not attend school because the peer had failed to study and therefore did not want Tracey to show her up by doing well. While this was only one event, and it happened last academic year, she clearly thought enough of it to tell us about it, and her mother is bothered by the pressure as well. Pierre actually mentioned one event as well, but did not seem to take it as seriously as Tracey does.

Relationships with peers may well be crucial in poor minority students' efforts to do well. While the parents may nudge, support, cajole, lead, and push their children into positive activities and pro-education positions, the importance of peer-group influence, especially for the younger students, cannot be ignored. These parents must prepare their children to learn despite the obstacles wrought by race and lack of income, and they must also be particularly aware of the role of others in their neighborhoods. In Tracey's case, her mother seems to use the church to help reinforce and support her teaching and parenting strategies, which emphasize education, discipline, self-control, and achievement. In the cases of the Baroques and the Weavers, the parent(s) seem to exert quite a bit of control as a way of limiting the impact of others who might be negative. Whether this is too much control or the right amount, given the outside conditions, is an important and difficult issue, and it is an issue that I address frequently throughout this work.

According to Tracey, she devotes two and one-half hours every evening to her homework. Most of this time must be spent at Family Focus, since the observer did not see her working on schoolwork during the five visits with her and her family. Tracey goes from school to Family Focus most school days if she is not involved in one of her many after-school activities. Like the other two students observed and discussed thus far, Tracey sees no obstacles in her way to the education that she wants and expects. Like the others, she expresses confidence and internal control, which are characteristic both of students who perform well in school and of middle-class individuals. Tracey reads the newspaper once a week and responds that the church is the most important thing in her life. So she is not much different from the other two average students when it comes to reading the paper, but she is different in terms of the most important thing in her life. The other two, it might be recalled, listed their family as most important. Given the positive values and behavior stressed by most churches, the Love family is in a position to rely on the church to help provide guidance and to support their efforts to help Tracey develop positively and to see education as important. The extended family can help as well if the child believes that the family is important enough.

In either case I am referring to an institution that has enough status with the child to support the positive efforts of the parent(s). The parent is not alone in guiding the child and stressing the behavior that is important to educational success.

Unlike the other two average students, Tracey believes that race and racial discrimination are important "sometimes" because they come up a lot in conversation and "in different teachings." Like her mother, then, Tracey is sensitive to race. Neither of the other two children studied seems as sensitive. I wonder whether the child is in fact influenced by the parent. That is, perhaps Ms. Love pays more attention to race than do the other parents, and Tracey does so as a result. Tracey does not seem to think, however, that race (or anything else, for that matter) will impede her where her education is concerned. She, too, believes that she controls her own destiny, and her race, while it may be important, will not adversely affect her. So, while society seems to think that race is important and may adversely affect the efforts toward success of black students, particularly the poor, the three average students observed in this work do not seem to think so.

Tracey indicates that she receives "a lot of help" from her parents with her schoolwork and that this is about the right amount for her. When asked which one thing about her family life she would change if she could, she responded, "My brother and my dad." As I suggested above, it is not clear that

Mr. Love was working at the time of this research. In fact, he appeared to be out of the house, perhaps out of the country, for a long period of this time. Tracey might have been commenting indirectly on the father's position in the family life. Near the end of the research, Mr. Love was at home for much of the day on several different days, again raising the question of his work status. If he is not working, Ms. Love is under greater financial pressure, and many children would question his role in light of this pressure. There was not much evidence of her brother's presence while the observer was with Tracey, so I cannot say much about him or her reaction.

It is very interesting and educational, however, to note that when asked which one person in the world she would be had she the choice, she responded that she would be herself "because I like myself and I am unique." It would be very difficult to offer more concrete evidence of self-esteem, one of the more important characteristics needed for good school performance and one of the most-mentioned characteristics of the middle class. Tracey clearly believes in herself, thinks that her education is important for her success in life and to make her smart, and does not see any real obstacles in her way. With the exception of the belief that education can make her smart, she is very much like the other average students so far. Actually, I believe that Tracey thinks that she will learn more, the more education she obtains and that she substitutes "making [her] smart" for learning more. I do not think that she sees education leading to intelligence.

Like Pierre and Angolique, Tracey told us that she felt or had in the past felt close to a specific teacher—in her case, a first-grade teacher. She felt this way because the teacher was always open with the class and with herself. In Pierre's case it was with a social worker he had in the fourth and fifth grades, but he failed to explain why. In Angolique's case it was with an eighth-grade social studies teacher she had only briefly, but with whom she continues to have contact. She told us that the teacher is understanding, that she listens well, and that she can relate to the students. I think this information is important, given that there is a great deal of debate across the country about what teachers need to do differently with poor and minority students if they are to learn more and better. If we can determine what impresses the students who perform reasonably well, then perhaps we can begin to determine some of the things on which we must focus in school in order to impress and help the others. Of course, the others may well be very different and not impressed by much in school. We will have to wait until we analyze the data from the nonachievers before we can see this.

The Observations

The first time the observer visited Tracey's house, she was not at home, and her mother had some difficulty locating her. It was not, however, a case of a wandering child going where she pleased. Ms. Love checked the Evanston Media Center to determine whether Tracey was there, engaged in an extracurricular activity. Given that it was a Saturday, Tracey had many things that she could be doing. After a time Ms. Love located Tracey at the local YWCA. Tracey was practicing a song and dance routine with the themes of God and hell along with fifteen other young people. The performance was to be presented to the public in two weeks, so there was some pressure to perfect it soon. This type of extracurricular activity requires discipline and teaches young people how to get along with one another, both characteristics required for doing well in school. It may also help to teach leadership, given that some young people must be out in front and lead the others. In this case, of course, religion also plays a role, so the young people are reminded about right and wrong, good and bad, and admonished to do right and good.

Indeed, when the youngsters were performing solo, one young man's performance centered around having been a gang member and thinking that this was attractive, even though everyone who cared about him told him to stop. He didn't listen, however, and now he is in hell, wishing that he had listened earlier. This is strong support for rejecting negative influences and accepting the positive. This type of support is helpful to parents who are attempting to stress discipline, self-control, interpersonal skills, and achievement. When the drama rehearsal was over, Tracey had a piano lesson. As I have indicated, this is a busy young lady, and as I have written earlier, and as Furstenberg et al. (1999) have indicated, these activities will often have a positive impact on school performance.

When the observer made the next visit to Tracey's home, she was busy washing the dishes, while her mother was doing paperwork at the kitchen table. I believe that watching her mother doing this type of work shows Tracey the value of discipline and the importance of work. Watching parents with "homework" lets children know that it is important. Other than the sound of the dishes, the house was silent. This quiet appears to be a characteristic of the homes in which students do at least reasonably well in school. While Ms. Love did "homework," there was no evidence of Tracey doing hers or of Ms. Love's involvement in the work, which we observed often in the other two homes. According to Entwisle and her colleagues (1997), helping with homework, monitoring of activities, having rules, and discipline are important for school success. Bronfrenbrenner (1991) also stresses parental supervision, involvement, aspirations, and expectations for school success. While Ms. Love's answers to the questions on the questionnaire suggest her school involvement, high aspirations for Tracey, and expectations, the observer did not see her involved in Tracey's schoolwork.

When Ms. Love completed the paperwork she went upstairs, and Tracey washed dishes and talked to the observer about her drama performance and Family Focus. Later, Ms. Love returned and was somewhat upset that Tracey had not completed her task. Tracey has chores, which include washing the dishes and taking out the trash. These obligations help to teach discipline and to impart a sense of responsibility, both of which are important in school performance. What's more, she was performing extra chores around the house at this time in order to earn money to pay for a church choir trip to Tennessee. So this young lady learns the value of hard work at the same time she learns the sense of responsibility that accompanies household obligations.

A bit later Tracey's aunt, who lives upstairs with a son who is also a subject of this research, came into Tracey's home and began to discuss with Ms. Love the importance of parental involvement in school activities. Tracey's aunt indicated that she thought that some parents lacked the necessary education to be of much help with their children, and Ms. Love agreed. Both of these women are clear on the value of education and the importance of the involvement of the parents in the educational process. It is likely that Tracey's educational values are reinforced by listening to this type of conversation. Tracey's cousin, Peter, came in and began to tell his mother about his day. They held hands throughout the conversation. The interaction between parent and child, which is important for the child's educational success, and the indications of family warmth, which also has a positive impact, seem to be in evidence here. I will examine these variables more when I get to Peter's family.

Tracey took great pride in describing Nassau to the observer and in showing the observer a map she had made for a school assignment. Pride in one's work is obviously helpful in school performance, and both of the other two students observed thus far have demonstrated pride in some aspect of their activities: Pierre's cake, Angolique's Family Focus opportunity. This kind of pride would also suggest self-esteem; the children feel positive enough to allow themselves to feel proud of what they do. In Tracey's case, she is a self-confident and very well-organized young lady. She must be the latter in order to perform all of her many activities. Indeed, when the observer visited Tracey a week or so later, she was at Family Focus practicing for a fashion show. While some of the young people in the show practiced seriously, others did not. Those who played around were told by staff members to repeat their routine until they performed it correctly. Tracey is exposed to discipline at almost every turn.

She is also involved in quite a bit of interaction with her mother, but it is clear who the leader is in these interactions. Ms. Love makes her authority known, whether it is in playfully telling Tracey that a dish she has washed is not clean and needs to be soaked again or in letting her know that she is to be at a certain place at a certain time.

I was struck by the fact that the observer never saw Tracey doing homework and thus, of course, did not see Ms. Love helping with any homework. In both of the other two average student families, the student worked on schoolwork nearly every school day, and a parent helped all of the time. This reinforces the parents' message about the importance of education, demonstrates to the student the value of supervision, and allows parent–child interaction, all of which are related to higher school achievement. It may be, however, that the church substitutes for the parent in a sense. It reinforces discipline and self-control and, along with Tracey's myriad of other activities, it promotes self-esteem and helps to protect her from negative influences. This requires a great deal more analysis and data collection but is an intriguing possibility with interesting policy implications.

Tracey's house was always quiet and orderly, and her father was occasionally in the home but never involved in the family activities. This is somewhat different from the case of Angolique's father, who laughed and joked not only with family members but with the observer as well. Still, it is a bit too early to determine the implications of the single-parent family for school performance in this research. I have seen two two-parent families, but in one the father appears to play a very minor role, and it is not clear that this helps the student at all.

In the cases of Pierre and Angolique, both seem to delay gratification (little television watching, little socializing with friends, little playing of young people's games) in order to focus on schoolwork—during the week, at least. In both cases school seems to come first and young peoples' activities come after. In Tracey's case the church, church activities, and other extracurricular activities come first. Given that she seems gratified by these activities, she doesn't really have to delay gratification in order to do what she must.

I raise this issue of delayed gratification because it is important in school performance and because for many poor minority students it may be difficult to do. School requires young people to perform schoolwork, to sit still, and to listen when many would rather be doing something more pleasant, such as playing basketball or video games. Students give up the more pleasant activities not only because they have been disciplined to do so, but also because they have been convinced that if they do so and do a good job at the schoolwork, a big and even more pleasant payoff awaits them in the future. What if a student sees no attractive future, no prestigious, well-paying job, no security, no exciting life? Well, that is precisely the case for many poor minority students growing up in neighborhoods with few, if any, role models living these lives, showing them that the sacrifice called school is worth the effort.

The parents of these students have a very difficult time convincing them that the sacrifice has a reward later in life if they cannot point to many examples to which the children can really relate. Pointing to drug dealers and gang members, or even to store cashiers and nurse's aides, will not do the job. The lack of good examples, good role models, places more pressure on the parents to convince the students that there is an attractive future to wait and to plan for.

But while the task is difficult, it is obviously not impossible. Many manage to do it. Pierre, Angolique, and Tracey all seem convinced that their future is worth the wait and the sacrifice. This delayed gratification is, of course, another characteristic that we generally associate with the middle class. More and more, these average but solid students and their families appear to be lower income—but middle class.

SUMMARY

Life is a great deal easier when a parent can point to himself or herself or a neighbor—who is, say, a physician, attorney, professor, or entrepreneur living in a nice house, driving a nice car, taking an exciting vacation—and tell the child how good schoolwork can lead to all of this. When these successful people are not in the house or in the neighborhood, the challenge is far greater for the parent(s) and the child. Still, the Loves, the Weavers, and the Baroques appear to meet the challenge of delayed gratification and others. Let us take a brief look at what they do and how they do it.

"The interpersonal communication patterns in these homes tended to be marked by frequent parent–child dialogue, strong parental encouragement in academic pursuits, clear and consistent limits set for the young, warm and nurturing interactions, and consistent monitoring of how they used their time." While I could quite easily have conjured up this quote to describe much about my findings concerning the family lives of the three average families, the quote is not mine but Clark's (1983, 111), and he used it to describe the lives of the families of his high achievers. Our findings are obviously similar in terms of students doing at least reasonably well in school.

The homes of all three of the families with average students show no signs of affluence; they are all small and rather sparsely furnished. They are also all relatively quiet, particularly on school days, and orderly at all times. People and things seem to have their place and remain in those places for the most part. In each of the families it is the mother who guides, monitors, sets the rules, and supports the child, even in the two families in which there are two parents. The mother decides the schedule for the student, including the appropriate bedtime in two of the three families. The mother decides on the appropriate use of the student's time, and in at least one case, Angolique's, the student wishes that her parents wouldn't be so "hard" on her.

It is true that some might think that the parents in all three cases are somewhat rigid and stern or, as Clark (1983) might refer to it, overcontrolling. The parents are authoritative to some extent, but their communication with the students is loving, caring, and very often playful. I think that the parents are protecting their children from what they believe to be negative influences in their neighborhoods—and potentially in their lives. At no time were any of the parents abusive, either verbally or physically, even when the child was slow in responding to the parent.

The mother generally decided on the appropriate behavior for the child, and in two of the three families that behavior centered around school and schoolwork. In the third case, the behavior focused on the church and church-related activities, but included a number of other extracurricular activities. In the Baroque and Weaver families, where schoolwork was the central activity for the student, it was also key for the parent, because she worked with the student on that schoolwork almost every day. It was not simply a case of the parent asking the student how his or her day went and moving on to their own activities. The parent went over the homework with the student, offering help, guidance, and encouragement (perhaps too much to suit one student).

Education is a very high priority for both the parents and the students. This is evidenced by the parents' emphasis on schoolwork, by the students' very high educational aspirations, and by the amount of time devoted to schoolwork and school-related activities. All three students are involved in a number of extracurricular activities, activities that help to build leadership abilities, encourage discipline and self-control, and help with school achievement. Their parents support their involvement in these activities. While these activities are important in each of the households, education seems to be the centerpiece. Most of the students' activities are focused on school, and the parents are constantly talking about school and its importance, though this is less the case for Tracey than for the others. In her case her church-related activities would seem to offer stability, discipline, and structure, though she too believes that education is central to her life.

If there is anything in the lives of the students as important as school, it is their family. Their families are critical to them. Not only do they say this in interviews (except for Tracey, who emphasizes the church), they show this in the respect they have for their parents and the love and concern they show for their younger siblings. In fact, in the cases of Pierre and Angolique, they spend a fair amount of time working on the education of the younger siblings, both showing them love and helping them to learn the importance of education at an early age. This importance of the family allows the parents' concern for education to take on even more importance to the student, for if it is so important to those who are so important to them, its value is even greater. While Tracey emphasizes her church and religion, she shows in her actions and in her speech a great deal of respect and affection for her mother.

All three of the students are self-confident and internally controlled, and they each believe that they control their own destinies, as do their mothers. They each believe that nothing stands in their way of success in life, and that that success comes only through education. Although they are black people living in a society in which blacks do not do nearly as well as whites, they do not believe that race will hold them back. In fact, none of them seems to focus much on race. So if they fail it is not because blacks do badly or because whites contribute to this. In their view it will be because of their own deficiencies, and they do not seem to believe that they have many of these. Hard work seems to be the key for them, and they are willing to put in that work for the benefits that they believe come not just from a good education, but from a lot of education. In two of the three cases students indicate that other students tried to convince them to perform badly in school. Pierre did not seem to pay much attention to the effort or to take it seriously. Tracey, however, did take it seriously but did not allow the attempt to affect her performance. I would not be surprised to see more of these efforts as we examine the lives of the high achievers.

The children in all three households have responsibilities ranging from dish washing to helping with the younger children. These activities help to develop both discipline and a sense of responsibility, both of which are very important for school achievement. After schoolwork, extracurricular (including church) activities, family/household responsibilities, the students can do some of the things that they find attractive, but it is often bedtime by then. The parents of these three students are socializing them to think positively about themselves, to take control of their own lives, to be disciplined and responsible, to believe that education is the key to their futures, and to delay gratification: in other words, to be middle class and to go to school prepared to learn. Indeed, even the toddlers in the families are being pointed in this direction. It should be no surprise then that they do in fact appear to be learning satisfactorily in school, or at least performing satisfactorily.

This socialization is not easy given the difficulties of the lives of poor families and given the temptations and the hardships the students face. The parents must handle the stress and strain of financial difficulties while providing an orderly and apparently secure life for the children. They must encourage discipline when a number of people in their neighborhoods may seem to have frequent difficulty with control. They must constantly emphasize the value of education when it is not always obvious to the student.

They manage all of this through consistency, constancy, and rigidity. They set the rules and these rules do not change. They monitor the students constantly, and we never saw any sign that the parents allowed their own problems or concerns to interfere with the child's development. Family, familial support, and love are constants. The children are allowed to plan much of their lives, but the plans must be consistent with the rules and priorities of the family. Thus the students have relatively little discretion, except for the choice of extracurricular activities, particularly on school days. The students are surrounded by familial warmth and support. They know that they are loved and cared for. They also know that they are expected to do well. These parents did not take the students to all of their many activities (though Tracey's mother did on occasion) and stay and watch. The students handled much of this on their own. The parents do, however, visit the schools on a fairly regular basis and seem to expect the schools to perform well. They all indicate that they feel confident when they visit the school and seem to expect that the school staff will be responsive.

I also found all three students to respond positively to authority, whether that authority came from a parent, a choir leader, or a Family Focus staff member. There was no arguing between any adult and the student, no talking back. Disagreements were rare and minor. This makes it more likely that the students will respect and honor the authority of their teachers and their administrators, making success in school more realistic.

FAMILY AND THE
HIGH ACHIEVER

STEPHANIE ADAMS

Stephanie Adams is a thirteen-year-old seventh grader who, like the students we have studied so far, also lives on the West Side of Evanston. She attends the same middle school attended by a number of the students studied for this work, and the Adams family is, by the Family Focus standards, lower income. There are six family members in the Adams family: the mother, father, and four children. While their income is above the poverty line, it is not exactly comfortable, and at just over $34,000, it is below the Family Focus poverty line for a family of six. So while I would not consider the family destitute, I would consider them lower- to lower-middle income, and the neighborhood in which they live is a poor one. Her school grades leave no doubt about where Stephanie should be classified. During the first quarter she received two A's, one B+, two B's, and one B−. She also received an A in chorus. During the second quarter she received two B+ grades, one B, two B− grades, and one C. She again received an A in chorus. Clearly, Stephanie is a high achiever and well above average in terms of grades. Only one comment made about Stephanie by her teachers was negative, that she "requires greater effort" during the second quarter in social studies. Her grade in this class had fallen from an A to a B, and the teacher apparently wanted her to work harder to maintain the higher grade. She "participates in class activities," "has excellent work habits," and "has a positive attitude." All in all, she seems to be an outstanding black lower-income student.

The Adams family comes from Africa and has lived in Evanston for seven years. Ms. Adams is forty-one and was not a teenage mother. There are four children in the house, and both Mr. and Ms. Adams are college graduates and employed. Ms. Adams is a social worker, and Mr. Adams is self-employed. Here we have a two-parent family in which both parents are college graduates. This does not seem like the "typical" lower-income family. Still, their income and neighborhood place them in much the same situation in which we find many of our families. Money is a problem, and they must find ways to properly educate their children without it and the advantages it brings if they are really interested in the education of their children (which most poor families appear to be) and if they are willing to do anything about their interest.

Ms. Adams is certainly interested in the education of Stephanie. She indicates that her education is "really important" because "no one is complete without education." In this case, the value of education appears to go beyond a good job and a decent future, the aspects of education that seem to be of critical importance to the other three families studied thus far. In the case of Ms. Adams, Stephanie's education is important in her development as a person. This sounds to me very much like not only a middle-class notion but a middle-income notion as well, in which money or the job is not the primary concern. This is not, however, a middle-income family.

Ms. Adams suggests that she encourages Stephanie to do well in school partly by helping her with her homework and partly by "providing every possible support she needs." She visits Stephanie's school, the same one attended by Angolique, three or four times a year and always feels good and confident when she does. She feels this way because the children are doing well in school, so she does not think that she has any real problems with the educational process. She is not intimidated or frightened by the school atmosphere or personnel. Professionals and professionalism do not bother Ms. Adams.

Ms. Adams does not think that much bothers Stephanie, either, when it comes to her education. Indeed, like each of the parents of the average students, she thinks that nothing stands in Stephanie's way of getting a good education. So race does not hinder her, poverty does not hinder her, poor teachers do not hinder her, other students do not hinder her. Stephanie's educational future is up to Stephanie. She controls her future, and she therefore is very likely to pay attention to her teachers and to her education, inasmuch as she is expected to be responsible for her own education. While Ms. Adams does not believe that race or discrimination plays a role in her life, she does think that her "foreign nationality" has significance. Still, she does not seem likely to allow that difference to interfere with the achievement of either herself or Stephanie.

In fact, she does not seem likely to allow much at all to stand in her or Stephanie's way. Ms. Adams tells us that she was raised in a very disciplined home, and she emphasized "discipline." During her upbringing she was taught that "rules are rules, and privileges can be taken away." She is "very proud" of her strict and disciplined upbringing, and she says that she tries to raise Stephanie the same way. So, as is the case in the other homes so far, discipline is critical, though it may well be even more so in the Adams home. While this may be due to the difference in nationality, I am not in a position to know this. I do believe, however, that the possibility should be examined that those from many African nations, the West Indies, and Caribbean nations are somewhat more strict and disciplined than native-born blacks. If this is true, given the importance of discipline for school performance, we should look into this relationship.

In any event, Stephanie is growing up in a home in which discipline, education, and self-control are emphasized. It does indeed sound as though she may well be sent to school prepared to learn. Her mother does not think that anyone at Stephanie's school stands in her way of receiving a good education. Neither do any of the families of the average students. This makes me wonder about all of the discussion regarding the need to improve or change so many teachers. If the parents of average and high-achieving poor black students have no problems with the schools attended by their children, then where are the problems? Perhaps we will see them as I proceed with the analysis, but we have not seen them thus far. It does not appear that it is the schools that need to be changed, at least not in the view of the parents of those doing well.

Ms. Adams does not read the newspaper much at all, and says that she has little time to read any books. She does not appear then to spend time reading to her children, an activity that is quite good for the education of the young. She relies on "my God, first" when she has a problem and then on her husband. It appears that she has no other immediate family members in the area on whom she can rely, unlike the other parents. It should be remembered, however, that Ms. Love also relies on the Lord when she has a problem. So two of the four mothers studied thus far have close connections to a religious belief and a religious organization. As I have already indicated, this tie to the church is, according to Furstenberg et al. (1999), a positive factor in educational success, and clearly, Stephanie Adams is such a success.

When asked what she most liked about her school, Stephanie replied that she liked the teachers and the opportunity to be with her friends. I suspect that a great many teachers would love to hear students indicate that they liked them. This also suggests Stephanie's attraction to school and education, given that she did not list extracurricular activities or other school-related variables although, as we will see, she is active in athletics. She indicated that she does not like it when teachers yell. Stephanie thinks that she is doing very well in school and that her education is very important to her. When asked why, she replied, "It impacts my future." So, like the students who are doing fairly well in school, Stephanie links education with her future. This is unlike her mother, who appears to stress the role of education in the development of the person as opposed to the relationship between education and one's financial future. Still, all of the students studied thus far are focused on their future and believe that education is important for that future.

As is the case with Tracey Love, Stephanie has experienced attempts by others to sabotage her performance. In her case, as in Tracey's, friends tried to convince her "ditch" or miss class. She did not, however, accommodate them, and she believes that they tried this because "some kids don't care about their education." As I have indicated before, this bears watching. Students performing well in school who might lack the courage or support to stand up to attempts to influence them to do less well might have problems that require the attention of school personnel.

Stephanie spends one and one-half to two hours per day on her homework and plans to go to law school. So, like each of the average students, she plans to obtain an advanced degree. I cannot overemphasize the importance (and the surprise) of this finding. These are eleven- and twelve-year-old poor black students interested in education—and in a college education at that. They each want to go beyond college to an advanced degree. Students such as these must pay considerable attention to education given their lofty goals. This makes educational effort and success more likely. Like each of the other students, Stephanie sees nothing standing in the way of her meeting her goals. She is, then, not only future-oriented, she also believes that she controls her own future, her own destiny—that is, she appears to be internally controlled. She, too, seems to be a middle-class student in a lower-income setting, though in Stephanie's case her parents have the education of those we typically think of as middle-class individuals. They lack the income, however.

Stephanie reads the newspaper every Thursday, but she does so for a class. It appears that none of the students studied so far pays much attention to the newspaper, a source of quite a bit of information. She and Tracey read it a bit more than the other two, but it is not read as much as I anticipated by the students doing average to well in school.

When asked to tell us what is most important to her in her life, Stephanie responded, "My family, my health, and my friends, and my education. Without my family, I would be nothing." Her priorities are much like those of the average students, except for Tracey, who places God highest on her list of the most important things in her life. The family is a key for the others. This allows the family great influence in the lives of these youngsters, and given that education is critical to the parents, education is central in the lives of the children. These are students whom we should expect to do well, all other things being equal. But neither are really equal. These are poor black students living in an essentially poor neighborhood, students whom we might anticipate doing badly in school. They are not. Their race and their lower-income status do not appear to hinder them. I believe that this is because it seems more and more likely that they are middle class in many ways important to educational success.

Stephanie thinks about race or racial discrimination "sometimes" because she is afraid that "one day I might be affected by this." So race is on her mind but does not seem to influence her everyday thoughts or actions. She and the others do not seem to allow race to get in the way of their success, nor do they use it as an excuse for not doing well. In fact, they allow themselves no excuse other than themselves. It is not teachers, or principals, or overcrowding, or the lack of money. They accept the responsibility for their educational performance—indeed, for their performance in life. This, of course, means that they are likely to go to school prepared to learn, especially when this sense of responsibility is coupled with high educational aspirations and discipline.

Stephanie indicates that she receives "a lot" of help with her schoolwork from her parents and that this is enough for her. Like Tracey, she would choose more freedom if she could change one thing about her life, though she believes the lack of freedom "is probably for a reason, and I will probably understand it one day." Clearly, discipline is strong in the Adams household and, like many young people subjected to such discipline, Stephanie wants less. However, she does not argue with her parents on the issue. This suggests that she does not challenge adult authority, a good sign for positive school performance. After all, if adults are not respected or deferred to when appropriate, how can students do well in school? This looking up to or deference would seem to start at home and be reinforced at home by the parents.

In fact, when asked who else in the world she would be were she given the opportunity, Stephanie says, "I really look up to my parents." She says, though, "I don't want to be anybody else but myself, though Judge Judy is cool." This is another indication of the self-confidence possessed by a student doing well. Stephanie's self-esteem is clearly quite high. She likes who she is and admires her parents. Again, this allows them great influence over her, and her mother has made it clear that she stresses the importance of education to Stephanie. Stephanie has made it clear that she has received the message.

The Observations

Religion appears to be important to Stephanie, just as it is to Tracey. In Stephanie's case the religion is Muslim. The observer first met Stephanie at an Islamic worship center where she and some fifty other young people study Arabic and the Qur'an. The younger students were working on computers learning the Arabic alphabet. The older students were in a different room reciting the Qur'an, but Stephanie was helping the younger children with the computers. She is already showing signs of leadership and the ability to work with and guide younger children, both qualities that have a positive impact on school achievement. In her work with the younger students, Stephanie seemed to be quite stern and firm.

The teachers working with the students were even more firm, yelling at the students or hitting them on the shoulder with coat hangers when the children strayed too far off task. Clearly, discipline is taken very seriously in this setting, and Stephanie is exposed to this discipline. Judging from her attitude and tone with the younger students, Stephanie is herself very disciplined.

Stephanie and her siblings enjoy close, warm relationships, and she "mothers" Fermi, her youngest brother, quite a bit. She has an older brother in high school and two younger brothers, one in preschool and the other in grade school. All the children comply with the demands of Ms. Adams fairly quickly, and according to the observer, Ms. Adams "definitely rules her children with an iron fist and sternly scolds them when needed." So the discipline is not limited to the Islamic center. Their home is a small, very tidy and orderly three-bedroom house, and the Adamses have a cousin in his early twenties living with them. There are, then, seven people living in this small house which, while nicely furnished and very clean, is not the home of a family with money to spare.

One of the reasons that the house is so orderly and tidy is that Ms. Adams demands that the older children, including Stephanie, perform various household chores to keep the house that way. When Ms. Adams arrives home from work, everyone is happy to see her and expresses the feeling to her. In turn, she wants to know how the day went for everyone. In Stephanie's case the discussion centers around her school day, including talk of her soccer practice. So, like all of the average students, Stephanie also is involved in extracurricular activities, which help to develop leadership and social skills and to strengthen self-esteem, all valuable not only for educational success but for success later in life as well (Carnegie Corporation 1992). Ms. Adams, then, not only says that Stephanie's education is important but demonstrates that importance to Stephanie by putting the discussion of her school day at the top of the list of priorities in the evening. It is one thing to say that education is important. It is quite another to show it to a child, and showing it is what matters if the child is to take education seriously.

All the children in the Adams household except Fermi have his or her own bank account. They are being taught order, planning, and discipline at early ages, for this is what saving appears to teach. They are aware of and thinking about a future, and they are planning for that future. The amount of money in the accounts is not really important. What is important is that the children are learning the relationship between what they do now and their lives down the road. In a sense, education is a savings account. Children sacrifice today for something bigger and better later in life. If, however, the students do not learn to sacrifice or to visualize their future, the educational process is much more difficult. That is not an issue in the Adams household.

There is a great deal of laughing and warm kidding between Ms. Adams and Stephanie. They clearly care a great deal about one another. While Ms. Adams is warm and loving, she is also a strict disciplinarian. At one point she said to the brother in grade school, "Did you do your homework?" "Yes," he replied. "Did you pray?" "No." "Now!" was her response. He slowly trooped upstairs to comply. So in this household, both education and religion are important, and their importance is emphasized by Ms. Adams almost daily. Discipline is also very frequently emphasized, but the children do not appear to be angered or put upon by the discipline.

During this second observation, which took place at the Adams home, it was clear that one of the children had made dinner, another sign of responsibility, and when Ms. Adams asked, "Who is doing the dishes?" Stephanie quickly responded, "Me." The children are expected to do chores. Before the dishes are done, however, Stephanie must do her homework. Everyone gathers in the kitchen, and Stephanie works on her homework at the kitchen table. After a period of silent work, she asks Ms. Adams to help with a math problem and her mother complies, though even working together they cannot manage to get the correct answer. The important point is that Ms. Adams tries to help with the schoolwork. She also encourages her children and helps them to develop positive self-esteem. When the boy in grade school bragged to Ms. Adams, "Look, I am using TV time on educational stuff," referring to his watching of the nature channel on television, she laughed and responded to him, "I have such a smart boy." He is being encouraged at an early age to take education seriously, and he is being complimented—indeed, praised—for doing so.

With everyone in the kitchen and the television on, it was somewhat difficult for Stephanie to concentrate on her homework, and it was now almost 9:00. Stephanie then began to tell her mother what her grades were to that point in the academic quarter. She indicated that she was doing A and B work in every class except reading, in which she had a D at the moment. Ms.

Adams immediately told her that a D was unacceptable. Stephanie responded that the grade would rise to a B— when the current assignment was handed in. Grades seem to be taken seriously in this house. Stephanie went on to tell her mother how well she was doing in soccer, so well, in fact, that she starts every game on a junior varsity team at her school. She also participates in track.

Just before 10:00 Stephanie complained that she was making slow progress with her math homework, but her mother informed her that the work was her responsibility, and if she must take until midnight to complete the work, she had no one except herself to blame. Another lesson in responsibility and self-control, two of the important characteristics for educational success, indeed, for success in life. The younger boys had been put to bed, though not without some complaining. As the observer left at 9:50, Mr. Adams arrived home and was greeted by Stephanie with a hug. It seems that 10:00 is the designated bedtime for the younger boys, and the older children can go to bed once they have completed their chores and their schoolwork. There are, then, rules and responsibilities, discipline and order. There are no loud voices or loud noises, and everything seems to have a place and to be in that place. Everyone knows what they are to do, and they do it. If they don't, Ms. Adams makes it clear that that is unacceptable.

When the observer made the second visit to the Adams house, neither parent was at home yet. After completing the questionnaire with the observer, Stephanie began work on her Spanish homework. Soon Kolen, the older brother, came downstairs and began to argue with her about who was to prepare dinner for Fermi, the youngest brother. The older siblings obviously have responsibilities and seem to take them seriously. The arguing continued for a time, until Kolen began to prepare the dinner. There was no shouting or anger shown, just the typical sibling teasing and baiting. Throughout the debate Stephanie continued work on her Spanish homework. A bit later, at about 9:00, Ms. Adams arrived home and was warmly greeted by all four children. She asked Babe, the middle boy, "Have you done your jobs?" He replied, "Yes." She asked Stephanie, "So what have you been doing tonight?" Stephanie told her who made what for dinner, and Fermi bragged, "Mommy, I ate all my shells and cheese." So as soon as she gets home Ms. Adams wants to know whether the children have completed their responsibilities and what their days have been like.

She is not only concerned with their activities, she also wants to be certain that they do the chores they are assigned. She is showing concern for them but also stressing discipline. A little later Ms. Adams discovered a Qur'an on the kitchen table and asked accusingly, "Whose is this?" Kolen replied that it was not his; his was in her car. This made her more angry, and she informed him that he was not living up to his religious studies potential. "You must study this [the Qur'an] like your schoolbooks." He promised to study more. She then turned to Babe and rather loudly told him, "If you don't get out of your class [at the mosque] by December 15, no presents and no birthday party. You know me, I am not kidding. Aren't you ashamed of yourself? You've been in the same class for two years." Again, Ms. Adams stresses education, religion, and discipline. She also points out that there are rewards for doing what one is supposed to do and none for failure to do so. These are lessons that have a positive impact on the education of students.

Ms. Adams wanted to know whether everyone had prayed. They indicated that they had. She wanted to know who was sweeping the floor that evening. Stephanie said that she was, but she continued her Spanish homework. She did so until about 10:30, when she prepared for bed. Ms. Adams was watching the news on the television.

Ms. Adams is clearly quite stern. Indeed, she seems to be close to what Clark (1983) refers to as "authoritative," and it may well be that the children to some degree lack the autonomy that Furstenberg et al. (1999) link with academic success. On the other hand, the older children are involved to some degree in decision making. Kolen decided that he would make dinner. Stephanie decided that she would sweep the floor, and Ms. Adams did explain to Kolen and Babe why they needed to do better in their religious studies. This parental management style, strict but rational and explanatory, appears to be successful, according to Baumrind (1971), in terms of student achievement. While Furstenberg and his colleagues argue for autonomy, they also point out: "Having a say in decisions that affect them directly, such as choice of clothing, family vacations, or summer employment, provides the adolescent with a chance to practice cognitive skills, which can facilitate academic gains at school" (115). I saw no real evidence that Stephanie does not have such a say.

Furthermore, given the neighborhood in which the Adams family lives, it may well be that strictness and control are necessary to keep the children out of trouble or harm's way. I might also remind the reader that the Adams family, like the Love family, is from abroad. It could be that African and Caribbean families are culturally rather strict and limiting. As I have indicated earlier, more work needs to be done on this issue, and I lack the data to do more than suggest the topic. In any event, all of the parents studied thus far seem strict and demanding. This does not appear to have negative consequences for the academic work of the children studied, particularly not for Stephanie, and her mother may be the strongest disciplinarian of them all.

During the next visit to the Adams house, Stephanie was not doing her homework, she was using the computer while her brothers were watching television. It is important to note that the family has a computer and that the older children, at least, use it regularly. This certainly gives them some advantage in this computer-oriented society. The boys watched television and Stephanie stayed on the computer in a chat room for two hours, until Ms. Adams arrived home from work and a visit to a sick friend. Everyone, including the cousin living with them, was excited to see her, and both Kolen and Fermi proceeded to tell her about their day. Stephanie and Fermi hugged her. This kind of familial affection is shown almost every day, despite the strictness of Ms. Adams. The children seem to understand it, and if they don't, as Stephanie explained in the questionnaire, she expects that there are good reasons for it that she will understand some day.

Fermi, the preschooler, showed off his evening's drawings and started to dance to celebrate his mother's arrival. Ms. Adams responded, "I have the smartest boy in the world." Again, she works on the self-esteem of the children. In an effort to test the "smartest boy in the world," Stephanie and Babe playfully asked him math questions. He answered every question, though he had absolutely no way of knowing the correct answers. Everyone laughed, but the lessons were important. The older children were working with the younger, the importance of knowledge was emphasized, and self-esteem was encouraged.

As the family began to disperse, Ms. Adams asked each child whether he or she had prayed. Each one had done so. It is clear that religion is central to the lives of the members of the Adams family, just as it seems to be for the Love family, though the Loves are Pentecostal and the Adams family Muslim. While the religions are very different, the parents use their faith in similar ways to influence the development of Tracey and Stephanie. The religions both stress discipline, knowledge, self-control, and doing both good and right. This helps the parents as they emphasize the same things, and these qualities help the academic performance of students. In both of these cases the children are finding that the messages received at home are being supported by the religious institutions, thus strengthening the parental message.

As this evening wore on, Ms. Adams, Stephanie, and Babe discussed various extended family members. Both of the children were excited by the conversation. After a time Babe went to bed, and Ms. Adams and Stephanie discussed Stephanie's day, including the cancellation of a field trip. Stephanie read the cancellation letter out loud to her mother. She then told her about her latest soccer highlights and the rest of the school news. They talked with warmth, respect, and interest. During the discussion, Ms. Adams yelled upstairs to Babe to go to bed: "Babe, go to bed. I tell you to go to bed, I mean it." She does not accept much commotion or disagreement, and she is quite consistent about this. She asked Stephanie about her homework, but there was none for the day. She did not urge Stephanie to study. If there were no homework assignments, there was no schoolwork to be done. Stephanie and her mother talked warmly and excitedly until 10:45.

The Adams house is generally quiet until Ms. Adams arrives home. The children are busy with their own interests until their mother enters. Then they are talking to her and to each other constantly. They describe their day to her and laugh and joke with her and with each other until bedtime. There is warmth, caring, joy, and interaction whenever she is present. During our next visit the observer arrived at 7:45, and Ms. Adams arrived at 8:15. Each of the four children described their day in detail, and she admonished Babe, the middle boy: "Babe, clean the bathroom. If it isn't clean, I'll use your head to clean the inside of the toilet." Needless to say, Babe complied. A short time later a family friend arrived and was seated at the kitchen table. It turned out to be Kolen's sixteenth birthday. His mother, unimpressed, said, "Kolen, just because it's your birthday doesn't mean you don't have to take the garbage out."

After some discussion the family decided to order pizza for dinner. Ms. Adams disagreed, but the children convinced her that Kolen's birthday warranted the special dinner. The children are able to discuss things with their mother even though she is a strict disciplinarian. They know their roles and responsibilities and obviously respect her authority, but there is a great deal of interaction and give and take. As Kolen left to have his hair cut, his mother informed him that he should have had his hair cut earlier in order to look nice for his birthday.

Stephanie then proceeded to describe her day to Ms. Adams in greater detail. Ms. Adams asked frequent questions about what she was being told, including about Stephanie's latest grades (for the third time) and her volleyball tryout. Ms. Adams asked Babe about his homework and then whether he had prayed. She then told him to sweep the floor, warning that he would be in trouble if she had to continue to remind him. There appears to be something of a routine here: schoolwork, prayers, and chores, though not always in that order. Every evening Ms. Adams wants to know whether Stephanie and the others have completed their homework, completed their prayers, and done their household chores. So every evening discipline is emphasized, responsibility and self-control are stressed, and religion is underlined. Ms. Adams clearly uses her parental position to prepare her children for the academic world in which discipline, self-control, and responsibility are very important for success, and her religion provides another source of support for these values.

After Stephanie cleared the table, Ms. Adams and her guest began to eat, and Stephanie began to work on her homework. She cleared the table again after the adults finished their dinner. Once the pizza arrived at 9:15, Stephanie, Babe, Fermi, and the observer began to eat, joined a bit later by Kolen, who recounted to the others how he had managed to avoid the traditional "birthday licks" or lighthearted beating by his peers at school. When Ms. Adams joined the young people a little later, she informed Stephanie and Kolen that she wanted a clean kitchen and reminded them that their normal bedtime was 9:00. They were given an extra hour this day because of Kolen's birthday. Again, the rules are set, emphasized, and followed, though the first rule seems to be for the children to do what it takes for as long as it takes in order to perform well in school. Kolen went back to work on his paper at the computer, and Stephanie began to clean the kitchen. Schoolwork and the household obligations are clearly a part of the lives of these children.

The four children appear to be very close and supportive, and Stephanie is confident and funny. The older two watch out for the younger two and tend to treat each other as equals. They are friendly and complimentary toward each other. While they laugh and joke with one another, and the older two clearly exert authority over the younger two (so that deference to authority is ingrained early), they also help and protect one another. In fact, Ms. Adams shares many of these characteristics as well. She helps the children with their schoolwork occasionally, definitely monitors their activities, sets and enforces rules in a consistent manner, and requires discipline, all behavioral variables found by Entwisle, Alexander, and Olson (1997); Clark (1983); and Furstenberg et al. (1999) to be important for school success.

Mr. Adams arrived at 10:30, just before the observer left the house, and greeted Ms. Adams, Stephanie, Kolen, and the observer. The two older children did not talk with him excitedly the way they do with Ms. Adams, particularly when she arrives home. The children do not seem to laugh or joke with Mr. Adams as they do with their mother, and he does not ask about their day or their activities as she does. The same closeness does not appear to be there. On the other hand, he was not at home much when our observer was there; we could have missed something. Still, this is another two-parent family in which the father does not seem to be the kind of presence that the mother is. In this case, the mother is very clearly the dominant parent; she is the key where rules, obligations, discipline, and school are concerned.

During another visit to the Adams home, the two young boys, Babe and Fermi, were again watching television, along with Stephanie, who again was not doing schoolwork. It appears to be the case that she, like Tracey Love, does much of her schoolwork while at Family Focus, and she was never observed just studying. Stephanie told the observer how she had made the junior varsity basketball team at her middle school and that the soccer and volleyball seasons had recently ended. So she is involved with four different athletic teams (the fourth is track), quite busy for a student receiving A's and B's in class. Stephanie varied between watching television, discussing her athletic accomplishments, and cleaning the kitchen.

At one point Kolen, the sixteen-year-old, came downstairs and warned Babe that their mother would be angry if he did not wash his dishes. Remember, Babe is in elementary school. The Adams children learn early about their obligations—and therefore about discipline. When Ms. Adams arrived an hour or so later from the grocery store, the younger boys excitedly greeted her, Kolen took the garbage out, and Stephanie and Babe helped put the groceries away. Kolen was scolded for his failure to help with the groceries. Much of the evening was devoted to talk about Stephanie's middle school, watching television, and general children's gossip and play. While there was a great deal of talk about school, there was no schoolwork done, but Ms. Adams did a fair amount of lecturing to both Kolen and Stephanie about things of which she did not approve.

For the next visit the observer arrived at 7:20 and was greeted at the door by Stephanie. Babe was reading, Fermi was drawing (which he does all of the time when he is not watching the television), and Stephanie was preparing a hot comb for her hair. Periodically, Babe would pause with his homework to help Fermi who, when he had successfully printed the observer's name, proudly showed off his penmanship to Babe and then ran upstairs to boast to Stephanie. Academic ability seems to be important in this family, as are helping the younger family members and feeling good about what one accomplishes.

Two hours after the observer had arrived, Babe was still doing homework, Kolen was listening to hip-hop music, Stephanie was working on her hair, and Fermi was still drawing. A bit later, Kolen told Fermi that it was time for bed and began to wrestle with Babe. When the good-natured wrestling match ended a few minutes later, Kolen told Babe to complete his homework. At 9:15 Stephanie came downstairs with her hair complete and made herself a sandwich, Fermi finally went to bed, and Kolen and Stephanie began to joke with one another. Babe then asked Stephanie how to spell the word "guilty." She said that it started with "gu" and that he needed to sound out the rest. She was, as usual, helping the younger siblings with educational work, but also teaching him correctly.

Finally, at 9:30, Ms. Adams called and apologized to the observer for having to work late. After talking with their mother briefly, Kolen and Stephanie argued good-naturedly about why Stephanie gets such good grades in school. In Kolen's view, Stephanie does so well because she fears her parents, and he goes to school because he values learning. Stephanie retorts that he must go for learning's sake because he doesn't get the grades that she does. So, more joking in the warm family spirit and more talk about school and accomplishments. Kolen then went to bed. While Ms. Adams seems to want the younger children in bed by 9:00, and the older children try to enforce this bedtime, the older children, including Stephanie, seem to often stay awake past this time. Indeed, so do the younger children on many occasions, particularly if Ms. Adams arrives home late. So the time may well be 9:00, but it is far from sacred or inflexible.

Stephanie then began to practice, with the help of the observer, for her role in an upcoming school play. At the time of our study, then, she was active in four school athletic programs, a school play, a fashion show, and the preparation of a speech she was to give at Family Focus. If extracurricular activities do indeed help with school academic achievement, as they seem to, then Stephanie's school success should surprise no one.

Babe completed washing the dishes and began to playfully fight with Stephanie. Afterward they both told the observer a great deal about different young people in Evanston. Stephanie also indicated that the Adams children are considered fairly tough, not to be bothered by anyone. She once threw a chair at another girl, and she is proud of this tough image. It may well be that she avoids much peer pressure from other poor black students for doing so well because she seems to be tough and confident and would therefore fit in to some degree. This would be a good coping strategy as long as it didn't lead to trouble in school, and in Stephanie's case there is no evidence of school trouble. It is also considered "cool" and acceptable to be an athlete, and Stephanie is certainly an athlete. While she has experienced some pressure to do less well, it does not seem to be too great, nor does it bother her much. Given Stephanie's confidence and her mother's expectations and discipline, I would be surprised to find that it did.

The final visit began at 7:00 with Stephanie cooking shells and cheese, Babe and Fermi watching television, and Kolen upstairs. A short time later Kolen came downstairs to eat, and Stephanie began to use the computer. Two of Kolen's friends then came to visit. This was the first time that any other young people visited the Adams children. Indeed, visits to the other families studied were almost nonexistent as well. The students who are doing average or well do not seem to spend much time with other children either in person or on the phone. They spend time doing chores, working on schoolwork, or involved in extracurricular activities, in some cases including church-related activities. The three boys kidded one another about haircuts, and the friends left ten minutes after they arrived. At this point everyone was watching television.

At 9:00 Stephanie began to wash the dishes after giving carrots to her younger brothers to eat. Ms. Adams then arrived home and was, as usual, very warmly greeted by all the children. Kolen related that he had been given a Saturday suspension at school for play fighting with another boy. He was promptly and sternly scolded by his mother, who never raised her voice. She did, however, yell at Stephanie when she realized that the dishes had not yet been washed. "When did you get home? What have you been doing?" Stephanie replied that she had not been doing very much at all. This did not please her mother. Ms. Adams, was, however, pleased with Babe's report card, which he proudly showed her. "It's very good," she said supportively. She then told him that he must begin to read for at least thirty minutes every evening and that he must watch less television. After the mild scolding regarding the television, she said, "It's a very good report card. I am proud of it." Ms. Adams clearly wants her children to do well in school and seems aware of what they must do to accomplish this. She in this case wants less television and more reading even though the student is doing well. She maintains discipline, but she bolsters their self-esteem.

While Kolen and Fermi watched television, Ms. Adams asked if everyone had prayed. They all said they had. Fermi then showed his mother his drawings for the evening. The Adams children are all proud of their work and want their mother to be proud as well. She always takes the time to check their work and often compliments them on that work. Later, Kolen and Stephanie cleaned the kitchen, and Ms. Adams told Babe to mop the kitchen floor. She then went upstairs but called downstairs soon after to ask Kolen and Stephanie if they knew about the leader of the Senate. She then came downstairs to explain the role of the Senate leader and relate how he had been impeached for lying. She used the episode in a lecture about lying. "You might get away with it, but one day it will catch up with you. Lying is not good, it's shameful." She then said good night and good-bye and went upstairs to pray. All of the children were then, at 10:45, watching television.

While the rules and responsibilities imposed by their somewhat strict mother give the Adams children little flexibility regarding prayer, the expectation of high achievement, or the execution of one's responsibilities, certain areas are more relaxed. Bedtime, for example, is not written in granite, and the mother does play and joke a great deal with the children. There is serious discipline but a warm and caring atmosphere in the house every day. The children know their roles and take them seriously. They all defer to authority and are willing to work with each other. They are all proud of themselves and of their accomplishments. The home environment is orderly and quiet, unless Ms. Adams finds it necessary to yell at one of the children, and this does not happen very often. The television is on quite a bit, but the children are home for the most part long before either parent. This allows them some freedom that they might otherwise not have, and Ms. Adams seems interested in limiting this television time.

Stephanie does not spend much time with friends, but she is involved in many extracurricular activities and is very much involved in her religion. In many ways the family is a perfect model of the family of a high achiever. There is not as much schoolwork done in the evening as I would have expected, but there is a lot done. Stephanie is a confident, disciplined young lady who cooperates with others, helps her younger siblings, accepts her responsibilities, expects to do well, and does in fact do well. She defers to her mother's authority and teaches her younger brothers to defer to hers. She communicates and interacts well with her mother, even though her mother is strict. Learning, and not just learning that takes place in school, is highly valued. Fermi, the preschooler, is praised for his drawings and challenged in math, which he cannot possibly know. Stephanie and the others must master the Qur'an, and she helps younger students at her mosque with their lessons. Family members talk with each other when they disagree, rather than fight or yell. Their schools and their activities are central to the lives of all the children, with much of their discussion centering around their schoolwork and projects. In many ways this seems to be another middle-class family with a lower income.

MARIE THOMAS

According to Harrington and Boardman (1997), the successful blacks who grew up poor in their study thought that love and rules were the important characteristics of the successful parenting styles they experienced as children. By and large I, too, have found that parental and family love and the setting of rules by parents are characteristics of the home lives of students who do average to well in school. What about Marie Thomas and her family? Marie is a fourteen-year-old freshman at Evanston's high school and an honor roll student. She lives with a family of four, including her father, which has an income slightly above the Family Focus line for lower-income families in Evanston. She, too, lives on the West Side. In the first marking period of the 1999–2000 academic year, she received all A's and B's. In the second marking period, one A had dropped to a C, one B had dropped to a C, and one B− had dropped to a C+. For the semester, however, she had raised one of the C's to a B and another to a C+. Her grade point average is currently 3.00, and this at one of the more rigorous high schools in America. Marie is clearly a high achiever.

Ms. Thomas, forty-three, and her husband, forty-seven, have lived in Evanston all of their lives, in their current house for just over twenty years. Both parents work in the public sector, and Ms. Thomas completed high school, while Mr. Thomas completed the tenth grade. They have a twenty-five-year-old son not living with them, so it appears that Ms. Thomas was a teenage mother.

As was the case with every family studied so far, it was the mother who completed the questionnaire, and she indicated that Marie's education is very important to her. According to Ms. Thomas, Marie's education is so important because she wants to see Marie do better than she and her husband did and because the complicated future requires a good education. So, as with several other families, the importance of the student's education is tied to a desire to see the child do better than the parents, but it is also tied to the future, indicating that the parent is looking ahead and suggesting an orientation toward the future.

Ms. Thomas says that she encourages Marie in her school achievement and that she attends all of the school conferences and open houses. She also goes to school if there are any problems and appears to feel fine when she visits. According to Comer (1993), "The school is not a part of their [non-mainstream/non–middle class] social network. Their families often do not sense a right to be there and a oneness with the people and purpose of the school; and in a variety of ways the feeling is transmitted to the children" (307). I agree with this completely. However, the parents in the five families studied thus far seem to feel quite comfortable in the schools and with the schools' purposes and style. However, these families seem so far to be largely mainstream or middle-class families in terms of values, attitudes, and behavior except as that behavior is limited by income and perhaps by neighborhood. This is an important policy concern, because schools would seem to need to find ways to help poor, and particularly minority, parents become more comfortable with the school and with what the school does and how it does it. While this does not appear to be much of an issue for the middle-class poor blacks, it may well be very important for the others. On the other hand, as we will see when I turn to the policy implications of this work, it could be that family changes must be a part of this whole process.

When asked what, if anything, stands in Marie's way of getting a good education, Ms. Thomas replied, "Nothing does stand in her way." So, like all of the others with children doing at least average in school, this parent thinks that Marie's educational success is in her own hands. She expects Marie to control her own destiny, her own future. She also does not believe that any other children try to stop Marie from doing well. So she does not worry about the kind of peer pressure that I anticipated, and about which Comer (1993) and others write. So far, some experience the pressure (and apparently brush it off), while others do not experience it at all. At this point, it is not as big an issue as I would have predicted. Ms. Thomas also does not believe that there are any adults at the high school who would try to stop Marie from doing well in school. At this point, the teachers and administrators do not seem to be a concern for the parents. They place their hopes and expectations on their children, and the school does not seem to be a major concern.

Ms. Thomas does believe, however, that white children receive more attention in school than black children, and she simply wants to be treated equal to whites. So she does see some racial discrimination in the educational system but says that how much and the impact of it "depend upon the individual." Again, then, she places the responsibility on the person, not on the person's race, even though she believes that race is an issue in schools. This sense of personal responsibility is important in terms of educational success. If one's performance is the responsibility of someone or something else, then there is little pressure on one to perform well. There is always an explanation for the failure other than one's efforts.

Ms. Thomas was raised by a strict mother and had the responsibility for helping to raise her siblings. This responsibility was more important than her education in her family. She thinks, however, that the responsibility and the strict upbringing "helped . . . in the long run." I was not, then, surprised to find her say that she is "strict, but open and firm" with Marie. In her house, she is the enforcer and Mr. Thomas is "moderate," though it is important to both of them to "not lose control." So in the Thomas house there is to be control, strictness or discipline, and openness, all characteristics seen to be important parental attributes in families in which students do well in school. The Thomas parents "want to steer her [Marie] in the right direction," despite the problems in today's society.

Mr. Thomas reads the newspaper every day, while Ms. Thomas picks up her knowledge of current events from watching the news on television. She does, however, read two or three books a month. This is a family in which current events and reading would appear to be important. I think that it is good for children to know that both reading and current events are important, and the best way to learn this lesson is obviously from watching their parents. Virtually all researchers of the family emphasize reading, but I believe that children also need to have a good grasp of the world beyond their neighborhood and their own lives. This gives them a broader worldview and helps in school. Knowledge of current events can be useful here. Ms. Thomas relies on God and her husband when she has a problem. The Thomas family is thus another one in which religion seems to play a role.

When asked what she most and least likes about her school, Marie indicated that she most likes some of the teachers and students and least likes the fact that there are so many students in the school: close to 2,600. She did not indicate any real problems or concerns with the school itself or any changes that might be suggested by her concerns. To Marie, education is very important, and she thinks that she is doing very well in school. She seems to have a good sense of how well she is doing. When asked why education is so important to her, Marie responded, "you need school to get a good job." So, like several of the other decent students, Marie ties education to success later in life in general and to a job or career specifically. She, too, seems to have some focus on the future.

According to Marie, no other student has ever tried to stop her from doing well in school. She is another student who has not had a problem with this and is thus more evidence that Comer (1993) and others, including myself, may be overstating this concern. The high-achieving students may not receive as much pressure from peers to fail as we have believed. While this pressure is logical, it so far does not seem to be as widespread as I would have expected.

Marie spends about two hours a day on her homework, about the same amount of time as most of the other average or high-achieving students. She expects to go "maybe four or five more years after high school" in terms of additional education. Like the others, then, she plans to obtain at least a college degree and perhaps more. Marie sees no obstacles in the way of her educational goals or expectations. Like the others, she sees herself in control of her future. Nothing can get in her way other than herself. This is, of course, an indication of internal or self-control, a characteristic very important to educational success.

About once a week Marie reads a newspaper. Thus far, the students—the average ones and the two high achievers—do not seem to read a newspaper very often. It is unclear that they keep up with current affairs, though Ms. Thomas seems to do so and this could affect Marie. As with most of the others, her family is the most important thing in Marie's life. This means that her family is in a position to have significant influence on her and given that they value education, she is very likely to take education very seriously and to attempt to do quite well. She indicates that her parents help her "every time I need help" with her homework and that this is enough help for her. So her parents seem to be directly involved with her and her schoolwork, a characteristic that appears to have a positive impact on achievement, not just because familial interaction is positive but also because it supports the parental emphasis on education. It shows the student that the parents' push for education is not merely words. They are serious enough to devote their own time to a part of the educational process.

Race or racial discrimination is not important to Marie "because I don't care about skin color." I must admit that I am becoming more and more surprised as more students give a version of this answer. While race seems to be such a significant factor in our society, and it is mainly poor black and Hispanic students in urban areas doing badly in schools, race does not seem to concern most of the students studied so far. They appear to ignore it, and they feel fine doing so. They do not allow it to be an issue in their lives. They seem to have the power to refuse to allow it to negatively impact them. If this is the case, these are confident, assertive students, students who we might expect to do fairly well in school.

The one thing Marie would change about her family life if she could would be to have more "family time together." This is another indication of the importance of her family to her and of its possible importance in her education. If she could change herself to become any other person, Marie would become the black actress Halle Berry "because she is a wonderful actress and a strong woman." So Marie admires the strength of another woman—and another black woman at that. This is more evidence of her confidence and positive self-image, characteristics that are positively related to school achievement and to the middle class.

The Observations

The first time that the observer met with Marie and her family, the meeting took place at Family Focus, began around 6:00, and included both of Marie's parents. This is the first case of an observer meeting with both parents, and both were present for the initial interview, though Ms. Thomas was selected by the two to be the primary respondent. When the observer informed the family of the observational plans, Marie wondered aloud whether the observer would "hover" over her, correcting her homework. She was assured that the observer might talk to her about her work but would not correct it. The family seemed comfortable with this answer and prepared to leave, with the second meeting date and time to be decided. As the family left, they all held hands. The Thomas family is by all indications a close-knit family, with the father not only present but involved as well, at least to some degree. This has not really been the case so far, and if it is true here, it may help to explain the high achievement of Marie, for there are obvious benefits to there being two people to devote to her and to her goals.

For the first meeting at the Thomas house, the observer arrived just after 4:30 to find Mr. Thomas and Marie at home, both watching television but separately, Mr. Thomas watching a basketball game in the living room and Marie another show in her room. Soon after Marie began to do her algebra homework. Her mother then arrived home. After the observer greeted the mother, Mr. Thomas asked the observer to discuss his school experience, and Ms. Thomas listened intently and began to ask questions about the observer's college education. Both of the Thomases seem to be interested in the university environment. At 5:30 the family ate dinner, and Marie continued her homework while eating with the television still on, which distracted her from her work. After dinner Marie returned her attention to her homework, this time working first on art and then on her English. Just after 6:00 the observer indicated that he must leave early this time and did so.

Throughout the observation at least one television was on, but Marie continued with her homework. While neither parent was involved with her schoolwork, they both were involved with the discussion of different topics with the observer, including various events of the day. This appears to be the first of the lower-income black families in which the father seems actively involved in the family dynamics, though he has little to do directly with Marie's schoolwork.

The next observation began at 5:50, just before the agreed-upon standard time of 6:00. This time had been moved back because Marie had made the varsity basketball team and would therefore arrive home later, after practice. Here, then, we have another good student involved in extracurricular activities, activities that help to develop social and leadership skills and raise self-esteem, all of which are associated with higher school achievement. When the observer arrived, Marie was not yet home from practice, and Mr. Thomas was watching television. When Ms. Thomas left to pick Marie up, Mr. Thomas and the observer discussed war movies, with Mr. Thomas offering specific criticisms of *Saving Private Ryan,* thinking that one particular scene was "too realistic." The conversation then changed to a discussion of poor automobile drivers, with Mr. Thomas suggesting that drivers' exams should be made more difficult in order to make the roads safer. Mr. Thomas is clearly paying attention to the world around him and seems to have specific ideas about that world. His world is not just his household and his job. He has a broader view, and if this is translated to Marie, it is likely that she, too, has a broad view, which is very helpful in an educational setting.

When Marie arrived home from basketball practice, she was both excited and upset: excited because she had made the A team, upset because her friend was placed on the lower B team. Marie argued that the friend was just as good as she and therefore should be on the A team. Ms. Thomas supported Marie's position, while Mr. Thomas felt that the only important point was that Marie had made the A team. Marie disagreed, and Mr. Thomas changed his approach. He now suggested that the coach might have placed the equally good friend on the other team in order to have an equal chance of winning with either team. Marie, still not convinced, went to her room to begin her homework.

The Thomas family seems to interact quite well and quite a bit. There is a great deal of discussion and give-and-take. Marie's views are not only heard but respected, and she feels free to express those ideas. I have found this to be the case in all of the families studied so far. The students respect and defer to their parents but seem to feel confident enough to express themselves. They also learn cooperation from these discussions and from their involvement in their various extracurricular activities. Both the confidence and the cooperation are very helpful in school performance.

Marie began her algebra homework in her bedroom at about 6:30 with the television on but turned down low. At least one television appears to be on in the Thomas household whenever anyone is home, and the door to Marie's room is open at all times. She seems to have no real secrets from her family. As Marie worked on her algebra, Mr. Thomas left for the grocery store, and Ms. Thomas began to wash the dishes. During the two observations at the house, Marie had not yet been seen doing any chores, nor had the parents been observed helping her with her homework. These are differences from several of the other families. The small house, like the others, is neat, orderly, and fairly quiet. While Ms. Thomas worked on the dishes she engaged the observer again in discussion about his college experience, with specific questions about professors, classes, and campus life. College is obviously an important topic for the Thomas family.

When Mr. Thomas returned from the store, the observer returned to Marie's room, where she was now involved with her history homework. A bit later the observer and Mr. Thomas began to discuss gambling as a result of a news story that had caught Mr. Thomas's attention. The observer said that one of his friends had recently lost six hundred dollars while gambling on a riverboat casino, and Mr. Thomas was very surprised, indicating that he could not afford to lose two hundred dollars, let alone six hundred. There is not a lot of extra money in this household, but this is not at all surprising.

When this conversation ended fifteen minutes later, the observer left for the evening with Marie still doing her schoolwork. Marie's evenings appear to be fairly well structured: She goes to basketball practice after school, returns home to eat, and then spends the remainder of the evening doing homework and glancing at the television. Her life seems centered around her schoolwork. She is disciplined enough to know what she must do and to do it without any prompting. It may well be that we did not see any evidence of disciplinary action on the part of the parents because none was needed. Marie is a bit older than all of the other students studied thus far, and may be sufficiently mature that she can discipline herself for the most part.

The issue of the involvement of Mr. Thomas with the family is an interesting and important one. Clark (1983) found few significant differences between two-parent and one-parent homes, but Entwisle, Alexander, and Olson (1997) found that children in two-parent families score higher on standardized tests. They caution, however, that this issue requires greater scrutiny because single-parent families are not homogeneous. In the case of my research, I am not really dividing the families into single- and two-parent groups. To me the question is not whether there is one or two parents present, but what role is a parent playing? This would seem to be a particularly important issue for black families if Hill (1971) and Allen, Spencer, and Brookins (1985) are correct in their argument that the mother is central in the black family. It is, according to their work, the mother who plays the critical role in the shaping and molding of the child to function in his or her environment. It is not that the father plays no role, but that he plays a different role.

If this is indeed the case, then as Furstenberg et al. (1999) put it: "The generally good quality of parenting [found in bad neighborhoods] applied to households with two resident parents as well as those with a single parent," and single parenthood is not in and of itself a risk factor for poor nonwhites (217). Thus, while I have seen only one father play an active role in the family, this may not be the disaster some might believe. Although the mothers, whether single or married, may be subject to tremendous pressure (as Clark [1983] suggests) by accepting almost all the child-rearing responsibilities, that pressure has had no discernable effect on the academic performance of the students studied so far.

During the next visit to the Thomas house, the observer arrived to find Mr. Thomas in his usual place, the reclining chair in the living room watching television. Ms. Thomas and Marie had just arrived from basketball practice, and Marie was still in her room. A bit later she emerged, greeted the observer, and asked about dinner. She then fixed a plate and returned to her room to eat and watch television. A few minutes later she began work on her algebra. The routine is again consistent: basketball practice, dinner, television, and homework. While Marie worked on her algebra, her parents were in the living room reading newspapers and occasionally discussing a news item that one or the other had noticed. The family appears to pay attention to current affairs.

Throughout the evening Marie continued her homework, switching from algebra to history, saying at one point to the observer, "We just started Greece and Athens. I have to make outlines of the chapter for my class. The teacher grades us on how well we get the information down." She knows what is expected of her and has little problem responding to those expectations.

While Marie worked on her history, her parents discussed a news story involving the recent expulsion of a group of black students in Decatur, Illinois, for their involvement in a near riot at a recent football game. Mr. Thomas believed that the punishment was too harsh, "counterproductive." Ms. Thomas disagreed, arguing that the students deserved strict punishment. The discussion continued until each one of them understood the point of view of the other. The point here is that although Mr. and Ms. Thomas often disagree on issues, they always discuss those disagreements. Marie has grown up in an environment in which informed discussion is commonplace. Yelling and screaming is not the way things get done in the Thomas household. Informed discussion is the way most things are addressed in most "mainstream" or middle-class households. The Thomases negotiate rather than fight, and according to Comer (1993), students who negotiate rather than fight are viewed more positively by school staff and are therefore more likely to do well. Marie is being raised in an environment in which thought, discussion, and negotiation are the norm, and it is understandable how she is likely to be viewed positively by her teachers and school staff because she thinks and negotiates.

At about 8:00 Marie moved on to her chemistry homework without a pause after working on her history work. Every evening Marie works on her homework until bedtime, while her parents read, watch television, and discuss various activities and events. As I have indicated above, Marie's parents do not help with her work, but she could be at an academic level where her parents cannot help much. It may also be the case that she doesn't need much help. She is, after all, an honor roll student at a highly regarded high school. The parents do not ask Marie about her school day as do the parents of the average students and the other high-achieving student. It is not as though they are uninterested in Marie and her academic life, but they do not focus on this life as much as the other parents. It may be a question of Marie's age and year in school. That is, as the students get older and move into the higher grades, parents may see less need to focus on the student if the student is already showing that he or she is self-disciplined and doing well. I can check this as I study the other two high school students. Marie's parents are, however, supportive. They expect that every evening will center around her schoolwork after she completes her extracurricular activities. They both seemed happy to attend her first basketball game (which, by the way, her team lost).

The next visit began at close to the usual time of 6:00 and, as usual, Marie was in her room eating dinner with the television on and preparing to do her homework, Spanish. Her parents were quietly reading newspapers, as usual. She took a phone call, and after about three minutes she was back to her work, now a lab report for biology followed twenty minutes later by math. Commenting that her teachers increase the workload this time of the year, she nonetheless plowed through the work. She took two more phone calls during the evening but was not on the phone very long. She seems to allow nothing to interfere with her schoolwork, and her parents make certain that nothing does so.

At the start of the next visit, Ms. Thomas excitedly said, "Marie got her grades today! Go ahead, show him your grades." Reluctantly, Marie went to her room and pulled an envelope from a stack of papers on her normally very orderly desk. The envelope contained her impressive grades, all A's and B's. She then returned to her schoolwork. Mr. Thomas was in his normal position in the front of the television, this time watching the news and focusing on the World Trade Organization protests. He engaged the observer in discussion about the purposes and the methods of the protests and then switched to a discussion about how important he thought watching and reading the news was. As I have indicated above, the Thomas family manages to remain connected to the broader world through reading, watching the news, and discussion. Ms. Thomas takes advantage of several opportunities to discuss specific aspects of university life with the observer. Clearly, she wants to know as much as she can about the college experience, probably to help Marie make her decisions when the time comes. Marie spends the evening working on her schoolwork, at one point declining something to eat because "I'm studying." She takes a phone call but discusses her history assignment while on the phone. Little will distract her from her work, even though the television is on in her room most of the time.

The Thomas family interacts a fair amount and talks through their disagreements quite well. At one point there was a disagreement over whether to purchase an artificial or a live Christmas tree, with Marie and Mr. Thomas preferring the live tree and Ms. Thomas, more frugal, preferring an artificial tree because it is cleaner and less expensive over time. There was no argument, but each position was made known. At another time there was some disagreement over what to get Mr. Thomas for Christmas, with Marie disagreeing with his request. In both cases Marie was confident and secure enough to let her mother know that she disagreed, and Ms. Thomas was thoughtful, sensitive, and supportive enough to listen and take Marie's comments seriously.

At one point Marie exclaimed worriedly, referring to all her schoolwork, "I can't take this anymore!" She had a big biology test the next day, an important English test the same week, two essays due for English that week, writing for a special program, and Spanish homework. Ms. Thomas stopped what she was doing and suggested in a comforting but concerned tone that Marie should do some of the work that evening and get up earlier the next morning to get extra work time. Marie continued her complaints, but her mother counseled her to "get a grip on what [you have] to do" and to realize that she couldn't do everything. Marie felt confident enough to complain to her mother, and her mother was supportive and concerned enough to listen, pay attention, and try to guide her daughter through an obviously stressful situation. Discussion and sensitivity are the norms in the Thomas household, and Marie's schoolwork and focus on education and achievement seem to be the center of the family life.

I should also mention that not once during our ten visits with the family was there any evidence of religion playing a role in the life of the family. While Ms. Thomas mentioned relying on God when in need, there was no indication that religion plays a significant role in their lives. So the church is not responsible to any real degree as far as I can see for the discipline, cooperation, and interest in the future that was seen in the family.

The Thomas household is similar in some significant ways to the other families in which the students are doing average or well, but it is also different. Clearly, Marie is very disciplined. She spends virtually every evening after her extracurricular activity doing her schoolwork. Nothing seems to get in her way here. So, like the others, we see a great deal of discipline. On the other hand, in the other families we see a fair amount of overt disciplinary action or hear disciplinary words on the part of a parent. This is not the case in the Thomas family. The difference may be due to the fact that Marie is older than the others studied thus far. We can examine this as we study the other two high school students. The Thomas household, like the others, is structured and orderly. The same things seem to take place at roughly the same times over and over. Marie is confident and self-controlled, like the others. Also like the others, she is involved in extracurricular activities, including acting. She is confident interacting with her parents, and education is the center of her life. Unlike the others, she does not seem to have the family or household chores that help the others to be more responsible.

On the other hand, she is the only child at home and her father is somewhat involved in the functioning of the family, so there is less for her to do. There are no younger children to monitor or to help, and there is less housework. Her acting and basketball do help her to learn and to maintain a sense of responsibility, and she obviously feels responsible for her school performance. All in all, Marie is much like the others. She is disciplined, self-controlled, confident, involved, and interacts well with her parents. Her family is much like the others as well. They talk to one another in an orderly, respectful, caring, and warm manner. They expect Marie to do well in school and support her efforts. Education is highly valued, and the student is thinking about her future and the role of education in that future. The family life is structured and orderly, and the house, while the television is on almost all of the time, is quiet. This is all very much like the other houses and families—and like middle-class families. These are also the characteristics required of high-achieving students found by Clark (1983); Furstenberg et al. (1999); Comer (1993); Entwisle, Alexander, and Olson (1997); Bempechat (1998); and others. As with the other students studied, we should not be surprised by Marie's performance per se; the surprise is that the performance comes from a poor black young lady. But perhaps we should not be surprised since we are seeing this again and again.

FATIMA MARIA ROBINSON

Fatima Robinson is a thirteen-year-old eighth grader at the same middle school attended by Stephanie Adams and Angolique Weaver and from which Marie Thomas graduated. Like all of the other students thus far, she lives on the West Side. She is clearly a high achiever. In the fall quarter she received one A, one B+, three B's, and one C−. In the winter quarter she received one A, one A−, and three B's. In both quarters she received an A in chorus. Her grades in the seventh grade were about the same. The only C she received during the fall quarter was in math.

There are six members of her family, including her two parents (mother and stepfather), living with her in her house, and their family income is quite a bit below the Family Focus cutoff for her family size. Her family is clearly lower income: very low income, in fact. Ms. Robinson is thirty-two, so it appears that she was a teenage mother. I find it very interesting that a number of the mothers of these poor black students doing very well or average academically were teenage mothers, a classification that many seem to think dooms them and theirs to failure. These parents have managed to overcome this "problem" in addition to those caused by poverty and race, perhaps, as Clark (1983) suggests, through "their . . . beliefs, activities, and overall cultural style" (2). I believe that it is very valuable to learn precisely how they manage this with the students I am studying because perhaps we can use that information to help other such parents do what they need to do to send their children to school prepared to learn.

The Robinsons have lived in Evanston for five years, in their current house for a year and one-half. Ms. Robinson grew up in Chicago, as did her husband, and they have four children including Fatima. Both are employed, he as a financial coordinator and she as a dental assistant. Both of the parents completed two years of college, and to Ms. Robinson, Fatima's education is her "most important priority." As with the other parents studied thus far, the education of the student is critical to their lives. Ms. Robinson indicates that she encourages Fatima's education a great deal "with emotional support and with help with her studies." She visits Fatima's school five to seven times a year, and always feels "good" and "confident" when she does so. She, like the other parents, is not intimidated when she visits the student's school. This would suggest that she is more likely than those who might feel uncomfortable to visit the school, and therefore she is more likely to work with the school staff if Fatima has any problems. It also suggests that she has high self-esteem. She indicates that she feels confident when at the school because she knows that Fatima does well.

It is unlikely then that the low self-esteem of a parent will hinder Fatima. In fact, Ms. Robinson suggests that only money stands in Fatima's way of obtaining a good education. As with all of the others so far, Fatima's educational future and her educational success are in her hands, except that in this case Ms. Robinson points out that money could be a problem. This is a reality for lower-income parents. Still, Ms. Robinson believes that educational success is Fatima's responsibility. In fact, she says, "I raise my children to know accountability, and there is a reaction for everything that is done. School is their job, and their education is theirs to keep and is the only thing that can't be taken away." So Fatima is being raised to accept the responsibility for her performance and for her future. She is being raised to control herself and her life. Ms. Robinson indicates that other children do not attempt to stop Fatima from doing well in school. So we have another parent who does not see what I expected to find, another parent who casts doubt on Comer's (1993) peer pressure idea. While the idea is reasonable and logical, I have yet to really see it supported much with these data.

Ms. Robinson does not think that any adults at Fatima's school stand in her way of doing well. She does, however, believe that Fatima is overlooked for extracurricular activities, trips, and honors classes because of her race. She knows this because she makes it her "business to be aware of what's going on." So she believes that race plays a role for Fatima but does not think that teachers or administrators are a problem for her. On the other hand, Fatima likes her involvement in her after-school activities such as plays and dances and says that she is "not into sports or athletics." It is not then clear that race does in fact seriously limit Fatima's extracurricular activities, though there may be a problem with the honors classes and the trips. The trips probably cost money, which could be a factor. Ms. Robinson seems to expect Fatima to do well in school and doesn't think that school-related variables limit her achievement. She is very much like the other parents in this.

Ms. Robinson says that her mother was very strict, in part because she raised her children on her own, and was not very involved in her schooling. Obviously, she is raising Fatima differently and is indeed involved in her education. She reads a newspaper five days a week but "hardly ever" reads a book. So she may well be caught up with events outside of her life but, like most of the other parents, does not devote much time to other reading. When she has a problem Ms. Robinson relies on her mother and her church. Again, like the others for the most part, she leans on her family and her church. If indeed the church plays a role in the life of the Robinsons, then it is likely to help Fatima become more disciplined, more future-oriented, and have higher self-esteem, all qualities linked to higher educational performance.

When asked what she liked most about her school, Fatima answered after-school activities and her really close friends. She most dislikes her homework and gym class, but she qualifies the homework answer by indicating that although she always does her work, she believes there is too much of it. She thinks that she is doing well in school and that school is very important to her. It is interesting that she believes that she is doing only "well" as opposed to "very well," given her grades. This may suggest that she thinks she can do better. If so, then she would appear to believe that her performance is in her hands. Fatima says that school is "very important" to her because she wants "to have a good life." Like a number of the others who are doing average or well, Fatima links school and her school performance to the quality of her future life. She believes that she has a future and that her educational performance will have a great deal to do with that future.

Like her mother, she indicates that no other student has ever tried to stop her from doing well in school. She spends two to four hours per day on her homework, about the same amount of time devoted to schoolwork by the other students studied thus far. Like most of the others, she expects to go to graduate school and, like the others, she sees no obstacles in her way. So Fatima, too, believes that her future is in her own hands. She also has high educational expectations. Indeed, when asked what was most important to her in her life, she responded, "succeeding in everything." She seems to have high aspirations all the way around and expects much of herself. She says that she feels close to a teacher she had in sixth, seventh, and eighth grade because the teacher "was really understanding and took the time to help people." So she relates closely to a teacher who wanted to relate to her students.

Fatima indicates that race is important to her in that she does not want to be judged by it. Most of the other students have indicated that race is not relevant to them, and Fatima does not want it to be a factor in her life. None of them expect that race to hold them back in their attempts to do well in school or in life. In Fatima's case she appears to be confident enough in herself and in her abilities to want to be judged by those abilities and not by her race.

She indicates that Ms. Robinson helps her with her homework "whenever I need it": three or four times a week. Like most of the other parents, Ms. Robinson appears to be involved with her daughter's schoolwork. This, of course, strengthens Fatima's belief that education is very important because her mother takes the time and energy to help her with the work. It is also interesting to note that Fatima says that Ms. Robinson "makes sure that the house is quiet" so she can get her reading done. Again, one of the characteristics of the houses in which the students do well is quiet in the house. The atmosphere of the houses seems to center around the importance of the students and their schoolwork. Fatima believes that the amount of help she receives from her mother is sometimes enough and sometimes not enough, though she doesn't indicate that she wants more help.

She does, however, want "not as much arguing between my mother and my stepfather." Her biological father was never married to her mother, and they parted before her birth, only to reconcile when she was seven years old. In the beginning this was not particularly accepted by the stepfather, but he has since come to terms with it, according to Fatima. Fatima now feels close to her biological father and spends time with him. It seems, then, that she has two fathers in her life, and clearly she is very close to her mother. In fact, she indicated that if she could be anyone else in the world it would be her mother because she wanted to know what it is like to be in her shoes. She went on to add that she wanted "to make life better for her." Clearly, family is very important to Fatima, which of course allows the family great influence when it comes to shaping her values, attitudes, and beliefs. Given that education is very important to Ms. Robinson and that she expects much of Fatima, we should not be surprised to learn that Fatima has high aspirations and expects much of herself.

The Observations

The first visit to the Robinson house began at 5:00 on a weekday evening, and the observer was greeted by Mr. Robinson and his two young daughters, aged two and one-half and one and one-half. Mr. Robinson quickly began to cook dinner, commenting to the observer that there were too many children just loitering in the front of his house. Fatima's ten-year-old half brother arrived a bit later and greeted everyone, followed by Fatima a few minutes later. Her arrival was greeted with excitement by the young girls, and she responded by hugging them both. It appeared at this early stage that Mr. Robinson might play an important role in the functioning of the family and of the household, and that there was considerable familial warmth among the Robinsons.

Money is often very tight in the Robinson family, and it is difficult to make ends meet at times. Still, Fatima tells the observer that her mother would like to send her to an exclusive Catholic school in a nearby suburb. This indicates Ms. Robinson's concern for Fatima's education, particularly since they live only one block away from the local public high school, which is one of the better ones in the nation. She has taken the time and the energy to make an assessment of the value of the two schools for her daughter and to make an informed decision, even though the money may not be available.

While the observer and Fatima walked back to her house after going out for a burger, Fatima pointed out a young girl who lives nearby whose mother is a prostitute. When they arrived home, they found that Ms. Robinson had gotten home and had taken over the cooking responsibilities. Fatima told her mother that a friend had invited her to spend Friday night at her house. Her mother reminded her of a school commitment. They then discussed how she might be able to do both, just before Ms. Robinson asked how the school day went. Ms. Robinson not only has reminded Fatima of her responsibilities but also of how important school is to her by asking about the school day almost as soon as she sees Fatima. Further, the two of them seem to have a relationship that allows, if not encourages, interaction and discussion, both of which seem to be characteristics of the homes in which students do well in school.

Ms. Robinson, however, went further. She asked to see Fatima's homework and whether Fatima still wanted a math tutor. When Fatima expressed uncertainty, her mother told her that math is critical to an understanding of subjects such as economics and chemistry, obviously subjects she assumes Fatima will someday take. Mr. Robinson then joined in the discussion of the tutor, indicating that he had found someone who could help. Fatima noted that she could get a tutor at Family Focus, but Ms. Robinson thought that a personal tutor would be better. I find this discussion interesting considering that Fatima is doing C and B work in math. Apparently, this is not good enough for the family. Ms. Robinson asked Fatima to think about it and to make a decision by the end of the week. So Fatima is again given responsibility, and it is clear that she comfortably engages in interaction with her parents.

As Fatima went from the kitchen to the living room to begin her homework, Ms. Robinson asked to see the homework of the ten-year-old, who was struggling with math, and promptly began to help him. She is another parent who helps her children with their schoolwork and another who has a student doing well in school. While the two older children worked on their schoolwork, Mr. Robinson played with the younger two. In this case we do indeed see a father in a two-parent family involved in such a way that the children may benefit academically. Not only does he do some of the housework, freeing the mother to be more involved with the children, he is also involved with them himself. While this seems to support the work of Entwisle, Alexander, and Olson (1997) and some of the findings of Clark (1983), I have little data on the subject, and it is not a critical issue for my work. Still, it does suggest further study, though I am finding that students in one-parent families or in families in which the father does not seem to play a major role can do quite well, apparently thanks to the strong and persistent efforts of the mother.

The observer completed this visit at 8:10, leaving as both Fatima and her ten-year-old half brother were working on their schoolwork. In fact, Fatima did nothing that evening other than have dinner at a local eatery with the observer, discuss schoolwork and school-related activities with her parents, and do schoolwork. This appears to be another young student whose life is essentially centered around school and her achievements, one whose parents have the same priorities and make certain that the student knows that they do.

The next observation began at 5:00 as well. When the observer mentioned the local high school, Ms. Robinson informed her that if Fatima's grades drop there when she enrolls next year, she will try to send her to the Catholic school. She believes that Fatima's academic future is in her hands and expects her to do well or there will be a change. She is internally controlled and future-oriented, with high academic expectations for her daughter.

That evening Fatima indicated that her only homework was to read part of a book and informed the observer that she likes to complete her homework as soon as it is assigned. She does not like to put it off or to wait until another time. This suggests discipline on her part. While she said that she does not particularly like geography or history (she finds them boring), Fatima indicates that she studies hard whether subjects interest her or not. This is a disciplined, structured young lady. While in her bedroom with the observer, Fatima began to listen to a CD. After twenty minutes she turned it off and returned to her reading. While Fatima read silently, her two-year-old sister asked the observer to read to her, which the observer did. Fatima's parents were in their bedroom watching television news.

After a bit Fatima went into the kitchen and started to warm leftovers for dinner for her two sisters. She is responsible and has her own chores to do. In fact, she says, she and her ten-year-old brother trade off on chores. This sounds remarkably like the other families with a student doing well and more than one child of an age to perform chores. She not only has chores to do, which teaches responsibility, a key for good school performance, she also learns how to cooperate by trading off with her brother. When her mother saw that Fatima has warmed the dinner, she said, "You didn't have to do that." So she performed a task that she didn't have to do, suggesting not only responsibility but thoughtfulness as well. When the younger girls had completed their dinner, Fatima started to clean the kitchen. She and her brother trade off on cleaning the kitchen and the bathroom.

After the cleaning Fatima returned to her room and her reading, while the observer and Ms. Robinson talked in the kitchen. Ms. Robinson spoke of how frustrated she was to see students in Evanston spending so much time in the streets doing nothing when there is so much that is positive to do. She claimed that it is the parents' fault for not steering their children into these positive activities and went on to complain about the failure of minority fathers to pay enough attention to the school life and activities of their children. She pointed out that few fathers attend the family nights given by Family Focus and even fewer attend parent–teacher conferences at school. She must drag her husband to these activities, she said. This conversation suggests two things: Ms. Robinson expects solid performances from students and blames the parents for their failure; and she does not see enough familial participation on the part of minority fathers. Hill (1971) supports her observation concerning the role of the black father and argues that it is cultural. My first suggestion underlines her sense of parental responsibility and the belief that the parents should infuse the necessary discipline, sense of responsibility, and high educational expectations into their children. It also indicates that she does not seem to place blame on the school for the failure of the students. Indeed, she went on to mention virtually every extracurricular activity available to keep children positively busy and away from negative activity. The opportunities are there; the question is the family life and commitment.

Like the homes of virtually every family mentioned so far, the Robinson house is very small but very neat. Fatima sleeps in a small bedroom with her two-year-old sister, and she has a television, which she watches very little, and a stereo in a closet. The six family members share one bathroom, and the ten-year-old brother has his own bedroom. Every room is kept very neat and clean. In fact, Fatima says that she and her mother are "neat freaks." The tidiness is just another example of the order and structure that we see in the homes of the students who are doing at least reasonably well in school.

During the next visit, which took place on a Sunday afternoon, Fatima was at the local high school involved in a march to promote nonviolence and unity in the community. As the observer and Ms. Robinson walked to the school to join the march, Ms. Robinson said that Fatima is passionate about an "adopt-a-family" program in which an older child is matched with a younger child whom she tutors and to whom she donates her clothes. Fatima is not only thoughtful and concerned but involved in extracurricular activities as well, and these activities, as I have indicated, often help to develop leadership skills, cooperation abilities, and self-esteem: all important in school achievement. Ms. Robinson suggests that she believes it is the parents' responsibility to teach their children about unity and respect for others, and she is upset that many parents fail to do so. Clearly, Ms. Robinson is strong on parental responsibility. Given her belief in the primacy of education and Fatima's discipline and sense of responsibility, it is no surprise that she does so well in school.

After the march and rally Fatima and the observer returned to the Robinson home, and Fatima showed the observer her latest math test, on which she did badly. When asked how her mother had responded, Fatima replied that she'd said, "'Don't even get me started.'" Low scores don't seem to be acceptable in the Robinson household, and this again raised the issue of a tutor. Company was expected for dinner, and Fatima indicated that she had to start on her homework before the company arrived. That it was a Sunday obviously did not stop Fatima from doing her schoolwork.

In fact, very little does. She was already doing her math homework at 3:30, the time of the next visit, and expressed some apprehension about a test on the Constitution the next day. School and achievement are the center of Fatima's life. While she has friends and occasionally talks about them, she spends little time with them outside of school. Based on her interaction with girls and community people she knows at the peace march, she is quite popular. Still, she spends the bulk of her time on her school activities and her extracurricular activities. Her parents would not seem to have it any other way.

Fatima has a very complicated and extremely difficult family situation, which must place an enormous amount of stress on her and her mother. While it would certainly help the reader for me to go into detail about this situation, it would also make it more likely that others could identify the family, and this is not acceptable. I will say what I can without compromising the family's privacy. Fatima is under a great deal of stress revolving around her immediate and extended family; the complications involve her maternal grandparents, her relationship with her stepfather, and her stepfather's family. The stepfather turned out to be somewhat mean—some might say verbally abusive. We noticed that as our observations continued, Mr. Robinson did less and less of the household chores and provided less and less support to the children. It is quite possible—indeed, likely—that he appeared supportive and helpful to impress the observer and that as the observer became more and more a part of the family, he returned to his normal role, which seems to be, speaking bluntly, a problem.

The financial situation of the family is also very difficult and stressful. So Fatima must cope not only with the normal difficulties of her age but also with family problems and serious financial difficulties. Despite this she continues to do well in school. There was also no evidence of religious involvement, despite the mention of the church by Ms. Robinson. So what we expected early on, the support and involvement of the stepfather and the role of the church, did not materialize.

Ms. Robinson is herself Latino, so Fatima must also deal with the question of her identity: is she black, Latino, or both? She suggests that she is both, but this is nevertheless another issue that requires coping. While the other students discussed so far do not see race or discrimination as a serious issue, racism remains a problem in America and affects their lives directly and indirectly almost every day even though they may not yet be aware of this. They are thus coping with the problems that go along with having very little money, being black, and growing up while they work to do well in school. Their discipline, self-esteem, internal control, high educational aspirations, orientation toward the future, and sense of responsibility help them to do so. In the case of Fatima, there are also serious family problems. Still, her house is generally orderly, quiet, and structured, though the stepfather on occasion challenges this environment. It is also not clear that Fatima has the high self-esteem that the other high achievers have, and this seems to be tied to the family situation.However, she thinks highly enough of herself to expect to do well in school and in her life, and she ties the two together.

For the most part she appears much like many young middle-class girls who take school seriously and are supported in their efforts by their parents or, in the case of a number of lower-income blacks, by their mother. She is, however, poor and beset by stress-producing situations, so she has more to overcome than many. At this point, she seems to be doing so.

JOSEPH BROWN

Joseph Brown is a nine-year-old fourth grader living on the West Side close to almost every family discussed thus far. The family income is quite low, and he lives with his mother, who is single, an older brother, and his twin sister. His grades for the fall quarter of the 1999–2000 academic year indicate either "strong performance" or "acceptable performance" in almost all specified areas within the various subject areas. He could use some improvement in his communication skills, particularly with a few of his writing skills, but his math grades are outstanding. Indeed, Joseph "needs improvement" in only six of the forty-one specified areas of performance. He also shows strong performances in the nonacademic areas, including music, art, and physical education, though he does not do as well in drama. Joseph is rarely tardy or absent, and his teachers indicate that he has excellent work habits and is very cooperative. All in all, he is a very good and conscientious student who could do a bit better with some of his communication skills.

Ms. Brown, Joseph's mother, was not a teenage mother. She has two grown daughters who do not live with her, but two of her sister's children do. This places a fair amount of pressure on their small living quarters and possibly on her meager resources. Ms. Brown has lived in Evanston all of her life, in her present house for nine years, and is a single mother. She works full-time in a job she lists as "teacher," but she has only a high school diploma, so she is clearly not a professional teacher, nor does her income reflect that occupation.

She says that Joseph's education is "very important" because "It will help him better his life and know what to do." Like many of the other parents of students doing well or average in school, Ms. Brown, then, links education to improvement in her child's life. She wants him to do well in school because she believes that a good education will lead to a good life. She thus has conceptualized a future for Joseph and thinks that education is important for that future. When asked how she encourages Joseph to do well in school, she responded: "'Make sure you do your homework. Show me your homework.' Now he does it automatically." She has, then, emphasized to Joseph not only the importance of school but also the importance and value of discipline, so that now he is disciplined enough to do his schoolwork on his own. She does this by making certain that her son shows her what he is doing. This involves her in his school life well beyond simply telling him to do well. She appears to play an active role, and it is fairly clear that such a role is very important if these poor minority students are to do well in school.

Ms. Brown visits Joseph's school "about six" times a year and she feels "confident" when she does so "because they always have something good to say" about Joseph. So she visits his school a fair amount, clearly not because her son is having trouble, and she is not uncomfortable when she does so. This is not a mother who stays away because she is intimidated by the school or its staff, thereby limiting her knowledge of or involvement with her child's educational process. She does not really believe that anything stands in Joseph's way of getting a good education, though she thinks that his school is "too open," that "anybody can walk in there." This is, of course, a criticism of the school's security and says nothing about any concern that Joseph's education is being limited by any variables other than his ability and/or work ethic. His future is in his hands, in her opinion, and he is to make the most of his opportunities. Her only concern about other children trying to hamper Joseph is that some of them "might distract him in class by making him laugh." Like most of the other parents, Ms. Brown does not see others seriously trying to stop Joseph from doing well. I have, then, more evidence that the "culture of failure" that I anticipated may not really exist.

While the idea that many poor minority students face pressure from others to fail because they themselves are doing badly and can justify that failure by the failure of others makes sense and has been suggested by others, I simply do not see much support for the idea so far in this study. Nor do I find support so far for the logical idea espoused by Comer (1993) that since many poor minority parents are not mainstream or middle class and the (middle-class) school is "not a part of their social network," they fail to relate to the school and then pass this failure on to their children. I again suggest that the parents of the students who do well are in most significant respects themselves middle class but lower income and relate fairly well to the school and make certain that their children do so as well. Their children are then comfortable in and well prepared for school. It should come as no surprise that they do well in school.

Ms. Brown indicated that race and/or racial discrimination plays a role in her life. However, her example of this issue isn't clear. "One of my son's teachers told me that my efforts to call District 65 [the local elementary school district] would not help me or my son. I am going to call District 65 anyway." While race may well have been involved in this problem, it is not clear how from her remarks. Furthermore, she does not say anything to indicate that race plays any prolonged or systemic role in her life. Like the others, she does not seem to expect race to limit her, and we would then expect that she does not see race limiting her son's life or future. His education and his future are his to shape. She indicated that no adults at Joseph's school try to stop him from doing well. So race is not a problem and the school is not a problem. If Joseph fails to do well, it seems that she believes that it will be the doing of herself and Joseph. She seems very responsible and expects Joseph to be the same. She indicates that her upbringing was "very strict" and that she "got punished for wrong things." I would not be surprised to find that Joseph has a rather strict upbringing as well, though perhaps with less punishment.

In fact, when asked how she tried to raise Joseph, she replied: "He goes to church and learns about God. I am not as strict as my parents were. I will punish him if he is wrong, and then I will tell him why I punished him, and to not do whatever it is again." Like a number of the other families in the study, Ms. Brown seems religious, interacts with her son, and expects discipline. The interaction and the discipline help tremendously in school, and the religion, as I have written, helps the child learn to cooperate, work with others, and think about and expect a future, all characteristics that help in school. According to Ms. Brown, she relies on God when she has a problem. She reads a book "every day" and a newspaper three times a week. So religion does seem to be a powerful force in her life, and Joseph may well learn the value of reading from his mother. It is interesting that while a number of the parents of the students who do average to well in school place great emphasis on God and/or religion, they all appear internally controlled. They do not expect that a supreme being is responsible for the education or the future of their children. That responsibility lies with the students, as it must if the students are to do well in school. God is important, but God does not control their lives. That is up to them, and their children seem to have learned this lesson as well. Joseph can be added to this number, for he, like the others, indicates that there are no obstacles in his educational path. He is responsible for his own destiny, for his own performance. This sense of responsibility is critical if students are to do well, for if their performance is the responsibility of someone or something else, then they do not have to perform well. They can, after all, blame their failure on that someone or something else, whether that be God, another student, race, or something about the school. They then have an excuse for failure, and we should be surprised to find them doing well.

When asked what he most liked about school, Joseph replied, "I like math and gym. I like base ten numbers and extended facts. I like drama and grammar. My teacher reads us stories in drama and we have to figure out an ending. Oh, and I like the math games." Given that his strongest subject appears to be math, it should be no surprise that he likes it. He least likes "social studies. I learn stuff that I already know, so I will just be reading what I know. Music, I don't like to sing." He seems to like to reason, to think and create, skills that may serve him well in school. While he believes that his education is "very important," he believes that he is doing "well" as opposed to "very well." When asked why school is very important to him, Joseph replied, "Because they teach me things that I don't know." He seems to be inquisitive, as well, and interested in learning new things.

As does his mother, Joseph believes that other students have stood in his way of doing well in school by talking to him in class, which gets him into trouble. But he doesn't indicate any serious effort to stop him from doing well. This sounds like young children talking too much in class, not any concerted effort to limit his success. He says that this happens because "they [the other children who talk to him during class] don't want to learn. They just want to have fun all of the time." Joseph may be more serious about his education than many children of his age, his income, and his race. It is, after all, very important to him and to his mother.

Joseph says that he spends one hour a day on his homework, from 3:00 to 4:00. He was not observed once doing homework or studying during our visits to his house, but these visits all began after 4:00, and most much later, so it is possible that he had done his work before the observer arrived. Furthermore, Joseph is only nine years old, the youngest student in the study, and in the fourth grade. It is unlikely that fourth graders have a great deal of homework to do. Like all of the other students studied thus far, Joseph wants to go to college: in fact, "past college." This is a fourth grader already thinking about his post–high school education, believing that he can accomplish his goal and that it is up to him. This suggests a positive self-image, as I have written, as well as internal control and high educational aspirations. He does not appear to see any insurmountable challenges to his educational goals.

It should come as no surprise that the young fourth grader does not read the newspaper. To him his "family and friends" are the most important things in his life, his family because "they take care of me" and his friends "because they help me when I get hurt." Given the importance of his family to him, his mother can be expected to have a great deal of influence on him, and since education is very important to her, it should be no surprise that it is also very important to him. Furthermore, his family is in a position to help develop both the discipline and the sense of responsibility that are so important in his school efforts, and they appear to do so.

When asked about the impact of race on his life, Joseph responded, "What does that mean? Oh, who I am. No. I don't think about that because all of the white kids are mostly my friends, except for the ones that I don't know." It appears that Joseph is too young for race to have become an issue yet. On the other hand, it does not seem to be an issue for the other students in the study, several of whom are quite a bit older than Joseph. It may well simply not have the significance that I expected it to have. Either they do not understand it or see it yet, or they do not intend to allow it to stand in their way, if they can help it. In either event, they do not fall back on it as an excuse for academic failure.

Joseph receives "a lot" of help from his mother with his schoolwork and believes that this is enough for him. His mother is not only telling him that education is important, she is showing him. As he says: "Mostly all the time my mother is helping me if I don't go to Foster." "Foster" is another local community center visited by many young people in Joseph's neighborhood. Joseph would like to be Michael Jordan if he could become any other person, but so would a great many other nine-year-old boys, "because he is a famous basketball player." This tells us little about his self-esteem or aspirations.

The Observations

The first observation began at 7:00 P.M. on a Saturday. Joseph and his cousins were playing outside when the observer arrived. As Ms. Brown called Joseph and the observer to enter the house, she privately indicated to the observer that Joseph was the best of her children. The house was very neat and clean, though quite small. The observer and Joseph began to play dominoes which, according to Joseph, he was taught to play by Ms. Brown. In fact, while he played his mother constantly talked to him about how to play. A bit later he asked the observer to play a different game and then began to play checkers and to talk to the observer about the games he plays with his mother. Clearly, he seems to have a fair amount of interaction with his mother.

The Browns live downstairs from Ms. Brown's sister, and Joseph's twin sister spends quite a bit of time with her cousins and aunt. In fact, that evening both Joseph and his twin sister received permission from their mother to spend the night upstairs. They were both told to be back home by 7:00 in order to prepare for church the next morning. Obviously, in the case of this family, church is not just mentioned in the questionnaires as important, the family seems to be actually involved in the church, which helps Joseph develop discipline and an orientation toward the future, both of which are important to school success. The observer left a bit after 9:00 as Joseph and his twin sister went upstairs for the evening.

The next visit began at 4:00 on a Friday, and the observer again encountered Joseph playing outside. When the observer entered the house a few minutes later, Joseph began to watch *Power Rangers* on television. This day the house was not neat or orderly. The clean laundry was everywhere, bags of potato chips were in the living room, and other items were scattered about the house. This was unusual for the Brown household and for all the houses in which the students are doing average or well. By and large these houses are orderly, structured, and quiet, characteristics that make studying and concentration easier. Again, Joseph wanted to play a game with the observer but had difficulty finding the bag that contained most of the games. He did find the game Connect Four, which belongs to his mother, and he and the observer played ten games, with Joseph winning eight, before Joseph started to play with his Lego building blocks.

So far we had not observed Joseph doing any schoolwork, only playing outdoors, playing games, and watching television. Ms. Brown arrived a bit later and said nothing to Joseph about his school day or his schoolwork. This is all quite different from the activities of the other students doing well or the actions of the parents regarding schoolwork. In the other families, much of the after-school time centers on schoolwork and studying after extracurricular activities. We had seen so far no evidence of household chores, either, which help to shape discipline and responsibility. It is not really clear whether this lack of homework and chores is do mainly to the age and grade of Joseph or to differences in the family. In a few of the other households in which the student being studied had a younger sibling in school, the schoolwork of the sibling was often stressed by the parent, and the younger sibling sometimes had chores. This is not the case for Joseph and his family.

Ms. Brown did, however, show concern for Joseph's education when she told the observer that she intended to go to the District 65 administrative offices because she doesn't believe that her twelve-year-old son is learning much, and she does not trust anyone at his school. She is not content to sit back and allow whatever happens at school to simply take place. She wants to do whatever she must to try to improve the quality of her son's education. Furthermore, while Joseph seems to spend a great deal of his time playing games, he is willing to take the lead role in this process, suggesting that he is a confident young man. He also seems disciplined, future-oriented, and in possession of high educational aspirations, all characteristics of middle-class young people and of those who do well in school. During the visit when he played with the Lego building blocks, he made an impressive tower, which he placed on his dresser. During the next visit, he informed the observer in a proud tone that he still had the tower. During the same visit he and the observer played the game Connect Four, with Joseph winning five games, his twin sister winning two, and the observer winning five. He asked to play one more game before the observer left for the evening, and he won that game just as he had predicted he would. Joseph obviously feels confident about himself and is somewhat competitive, characteristics that help in school performance and that are fairly common among middle-class youth.

During the next visit, Joseph said he had a science project to do, but that he couldn't find the necessary plastic bags. Instead of going to work on the project, he immediately pulled out games to play with the observer. He informed the observer that he enjoyed learning extended facts at school and that he had beat the calculator in a game in which he had to multiply by a base of ten. He clearly enjoyed outperforming the calculator. After a time he and the observer began to play Connect Four again. He told the observer that he played this same game at school and enjoyed defeating a classmate named Tiwan, who had defeated him at the game in the third grade. Again, we see that Joseph is competitive and has high self-esteem. Ms. Brown arrived home, prepared dinner, and asked the twin sister to say grace before eating. After dinner Joseph and the observer returned to Connect Four. The observer won but was slow to realize it. Joseph did not volunteer the information, waiting until she realized it. He really wants to win, to do well. It appears that he is being raised to try hard to do well at all that he undertakes.

The next visit began at 4:00, with Joseph working on the aforementioned science project while watching television. He told the observer that the project was due in four days. This was the first time in the six observations of Joseph that he was seen involved in schoolwork. Ms. Brown had not yet said anything to him about his school performance or schoolwork. As soon as the observer arrived, Joseph pulled out the games and the table they use to play the games. Ms. Brown was sitting in the living room watching television and looking at bills. She said that she just might have to find another job because she is not making enough money to care for her family. However, she indicated that she would hate to have to do this because it would probably mean less time with her children.

Ms. Brown appears to be a thoughtful, conscientious mother struggling with her money. She is under pressure but still manages to exert discipline, to maintain a somewhat orderly and quiet home life, and to help some of her relatives. One relative with a serious drug-related problem wishes to move close to her, but she wants to avoid this to protect her children from exposure to the problem. In some ways she is the prototypical lower-income but middle-class black mother. Money is tight so she cannot allow the children to do all that she might like. The neighborhood—indeed, the family—offers temptations and pitfalls that she must steer her children around. While worrying about money and other problems, she must teach her children discipline, responsibility, high educational aspirations, internal control, and orientation toward the future. All indications are that she is successful with Joseph, though she does not appear to accomplish these goals in quite the same way as the others. Remember, however, Joseph is considerably younger than the others. He may be too young for use of the same techniques.

Not long after the observer arrived, Ms. Brown began to prepare for a Friday evening church service, and Joseph and the observer began to play dominoes. A bit later his sister arrived home from a fashion show rehearsal. The older brother was not yet home, and Ms. Brown indicated that she intended to punish him because he was expected to come directly home after school. During an earlier visit she had said the same thing to the twin sister when she was late. While she seems somewhat flexible, she is also a rather strict disciplinarian. As the observer prepared to leave at 5:30, Joseph announced that he was not going to church and intended to finish his science project. Ms. Brown instructed him to walk the observer to the door. Earlier, when Joseph's four-year-old niece had refused to speak to the observer, her mother and Ms. Brown had told her to do so and admonished her for rudeness. It appears that Ms. Brown is teaching cooperation and helpfulness. Indeed, several of Joseph's teachers comment on his report card that he is very cooperative.

During the final visit to the Brown home, the observer found Joseph's older brother in his bedroom doing his homework. His twin sister presented her science project to the observer. Joseph was sick that day. He had stayed home from school, and his mother had remained home with him. It is clear that Ms. Brown takes her parental responsibilities very seriously, and her children seem to expect that. In fact, during our observations, another family member was in need of a place to stay. Ms. Brown allowed him to stay with her family for a short time but then asked him to leave because, according to her, he drank too much, and she did not want anyone drinking near her children. So while she is very responsible where her family is concerned, she will not allow any negative influences around her children, and these include both alcohol and drugs.

The Brown home environment is not as neat or structured as some of the rest, but it is fairly orderly and quiet. Joseph expresses high educational aspirations, competitiveness, discipline, positive self-esteem, a cooperative nature, and as much responsibility as a fourth grader might express. He does not focus his activity on his schoolwork, but there may be little to do. We did not see him involved to any significant degree in extracurricular activities, like many of the other students doing well or average. We saw no evidence of any positive influence of his father, though his father was present for some of our time with the family. This, along with the clear financial difficulties faced by Ms. Brown, places severe strains on her and, as Entwisle, Alexander, and Olson (1997) point out, may well reduce her psychological resources and restrict her parenting effectiveness. Still, she expects her children to cooperate, to do well in school, to heed her directions, and to avoid trouble. She seems prepared to do what she must to help them to avoid negative circumstances, though this may hurt other family members and limit the activities of her children.

She does not discuss school with Joseph as much as the parents of the other students who are doing well, but she seems to have even more financial and family complications than many of the others. Still, when school is an issue, she is responsive and concerned, and Joseph is doing quite well in school even though most of his after-school time is devoted to playing games. She does interact with all of her children, including the grown children, and in the process the younger children, including Joseph, develop the confidence and ability to interact with others, including adults. Indeed, he never hesitated to challenge the observer to play a game and he always expected to win, though he never acted out when he lost. Joseph's mother cares very much about him and about his educational progress. She expects him to do well, and it may be that since he is doing well, she does not seem to show the same day-to-day concern as some of the other parents studied.

KAREN KENNER

Karen Kenner is a fourteen-year-old freshman at the local public high school and lives with her widowed mother, one grown brother and two sisters, one niece, and one nephew. It appears that her mother may have been a teenage mother, and several of the children have different fathers. The family income is very low, considering the number of family members living in the one house (which is located close to almost all of the others on the West Side). For the first marking period of the 1999–2000 academic year, Karen was on the school honor roll with a grade point average of 3.35. Her grades slipped somewhat during the second marking period, with one A− becoming a C+, one B a C+, one A− a B+, but one C+ became a B, and one B+ an A. The third period saw her grades slip to two C's, three C+'s, one A−, and one A, still a relatively good performance. Overall, one would have to classify Karen as a good student.

Karen's mother, Ms. Kenner, has lived all of her forty-five years in Evanston, five in her current house. She is both working full-time as a secretary/office manager and going to graduate school. As will become apparent, she is a remarkable woman: She takes care of her four children, helps with two grandchildren, works full-time, goes to school, and plans to attend law school. Karen also has five half brothers and sisters, so clearly this is a large family.

Karen's education is very important to Ms. Kenner. When asked why, she responded, "I want to see her achieve more than I did. I know that she has the potential to become someone who has made her own mark in society, to accomplish more than I did, have less struggles." Karen's education is then important not only because it will enable her to do well, better than her mother, but because through it she will make her mark in this world. Ms. Kenner expects Karen to go beyond doing well. She clearly expects a great deal of her, and Karen's education is a high priority. When she was asked how she encouraged Karen educationally, her answer was very interesting. "I tell her she has the potential to do anything she sets her mind to. There was a time when [Karen] only felt she was good at sports. So I restricted her sports and she began to focus on schoolwork. Her D's and F's became A's and B's. She has come a long way." Not only is Ms. Kenner encouraging Karen to do well in school, she has also limited her athletic activities to help her concentrate on academics. Perhaps Karen doesn't have the autonomy others think is important to success, but she lives in an environment that may well require limitations on that autonomy, and her mother clearly recognizes this and adapts to the reality. Athletics has for some time been seen by many poor blacks as a way out of the ghetto, a way to improve, an indication of status. To Ms. Kenner, it was simply an impediment to Karen's academic success, and she felt in sufficient control to place limitations on her daughter in that regard.

Given Ms. Kenner's very busy schedule, she cannot visit Karen's school often. She calls when she needs to do so, but "I also let her teachers know they can reach me at work if necessary. I also keep contact with her counselors. When I call to do phone conferences, I keep calling until I reach the teachers. I let whoever takes the message know that this is my third call and the teacher has not called back—do I need to call the chair of that department? It has happened." Ms. Kenner is a confident, persistent woman who seems to push until she gets what she needs and wants where her daughter's education is concerned. Indeed, she says, "I know that I am going to get answers to my questions or I will know where to go when I leave the school for answers." So she feels in control of herself and is knowledgeable and confident enough to have the educational system respond to both Karen's needs and her own.

When she was asked whether anything stood in Karen's way of obtaining a good education, her response was much like that of the other parents of the average and high-performing students: "Nothing but [Karen]. Sometimes her attitude can hinder her performance. As far as money, I know about scholarships." So Karen is expected to control her own educational future. Her mother has high educational aspirations for her and expects her to accept the responsibility for her performance. If the student fails to do this, then the student has relatively little chance of doing well. He or she will simply leave it to someone or something else and when failure comes, they can and do blame it on someone or thing other than themselves and therefore fail to change or to do better. Karen does not have this option, and her mother will not even allow money to limit her, even though their money is very tight. She doesn't believe that other students will hinder Karen in school because "[Karen] is a very headstrong child." Like most of the other parents, Ms. Kenner does not see peer group pressure affecting Karen's performance. She is on her own, with her mother's apparent support and guidance.

Ms. Kenner does, however, believe that a teacher did hinder Karen. "[Karen] once had a math teacher who was not good for her. He always downed the kids. He gave [Karen] F for grade all the time. When asked why she got an F, he said she deserved it. Once she was removed from his class she began to get A and B grades. The teacher was not a good match for [Karen]. I later learned from some coworkers his problem was with me. He did not like strong women. Women should not head families' situations. He had real issues." She does not believe that the school stands in her daughter's way. She pays attention to any effort at the school that she deems unfair and will clearly move to confront the situation. She is responsible, confident, and knowledgeable, very much the middle-class parent.

She believes that teachers can stop a child from doing well: "if a teacher constantly downs a kid, their self-esteem is damaged, kids need to feel good about themselves." Ms. Kenner has high self-esteem and apparently expects Karen to also. In fact, at one point she said, "[Karen] has come a long way. Her self-esteem appears to be better and she is more motivated to learn. She now knows she has the ability to do anything she wants and that's a good thing. I believe she will go on to college and I am so happy at her progress." So Karen apparently also has high self-esteem and high educational aspirations, two characteristics of successful students. She is being sent to school prepared to learn. Her mother will not accept anything other than high performance, and she seems to know this.

Ms. Kenner believes that she has had to "work harder to achieve due to my race and gender." So, while race is seen as an impediment, she overcomes it by working harder, and while Karen doesn't "really like to talk about it [because] it is uninteresting," she does not see it as a hindrance to her. So the more educated and knowledgeable mother sees race as a problem, but she will not allow it to limit her success or that of her daughter. The responsibility for the outcome of one's life lies with the individual and cannot be given over to race or gender, even though Ms. Kenner believes that each may adversely affect both of them. This is a clear example of internal control, which is very clearly tied to higher school performance. Ms. Kenner seems also to care very much for Karen, another characteristic of the families of successful students. She refuses to back down from the school when she believes Karen needs her intervention even though her schedule is difficult. This demonstrates her love and support, as do many of her comments. Like many of the others who rely on religion, she prays when a problem arises, but she also counts on herself.

Ms. Kenner says that she "was taught to believe that anything worth having is worth working hard to get. The only failure is to not try." She goes on: "I have also prided myself in being a person who if you said I could not do something I had to make you into a liar, so I did it." Again, she seems to have a great deal of confidence and determination, and she expects the same of Karen. She raises her "to be respectful of others and herself. I really don't have much reason to discipline [Karen]. She is not a child who likes to hang out in the street or party. She studies, uses the computer, and once in a while she may ask to hang out with friends. But if a problem does occur, I would punish her by taking away something she wants to do or cut her allowance. [Karen] has become much better over the past years about self-control." Ms. Kenner expects Karen to go to college, and the only issue is whether it will be local or away from home. Her grades and her interest in remaining close to home will determine which it is. She expects hard work, respect, responsibility, and self-control from Karen, and while she doesn't see much reason to discipline her, she is certainly willing to do so if needed, though the discipline is not physical. It appears quite clear that Ms. Kenner is a middle-class mother in almost every sense of the term except, and this is crucial, she lacks the income and, apparently, the occupation. She does, however, have the education, achieved after a great deal of effort and difficulty. She is precisely the type of parent who sends her daughter to school prepared to learn, and her daughter learns well.

When we asked Karen what she liked most about her school, she responded that she likes nothing about it. This is an unexpected answer from a very good student. She says that she least likes "everything." So, despite the high educational expectations and her own aspirations to go to college and to "do more if necessary," she does not seem to like school. This raises some questions about how and why she manages to do so well. While her mother seems to have the appropriate values and characteristics for a student who does well, most of the other students in our study who do well like quite a bit about their school experience. It is, after all, easy to like school when you are doing well. This is not the case for Karen, and we will have to look at this more closely.

Karen thinks that she is doing "very well" in school, so she accurately gauges her success, and she says that her education is very important to her. She believes this because "you should have an education to do your job." Like many of the others, she links education to the quality of her future life. She wants to do well in school in order to do well in a career. This is not a case of education for education's sake or for the sake of knowledge. However, when one has little money or the flexibility money brings, it is quite likely that one's attention will focus on improving one's condition, and Karen sees education as a means to that end. She, like the others, can visualize and plan to some degree for a future, and this is very important for school success. Unfortunately, many poor blacks see no positive future for themselves and they know no one close to them who has found one, thereby making it harder for them to pay attention in school, an experience designed to prepare them for a future that for so many does not exist. Many of those poor black families that do foresee and work for such a future in the midst of an environment in which it rarely exists must work very hard and hold on to values and beliefs that may well not be dominant in their communities.

Karen does not believe that any other student has tried to limit her educational success, and she studies for forty-five minutes in school and up to two hours on the weekends. So, unlike most of the other students who do well, Karen apparently does little schoolwork and this in high school, which would seem to require more. If this is true, and we will see when we turn to the observations, it should be no surprise to see that her grades, while good, have declined. She may well not pay enough attention to her schoolwork despite her aspirations, her discipline, her locus of control, and her orientation toward the future. She sees no obstacles in the way of her educational aspirations; she wants to attend college and expects to do so. She has high aspirations and the confidence she needs to make them real. Like her mother, she does not plan to allow anything other than herself to affect her educational life. She sees herself in control of her own future.

Karen reads the local newspaper once a week, concentrating on educational stories and movie reviews. When asked what is most important to her in her life, she responded, "Mom, grandmother, me, and my belongings." So she is confident, as I have written above, and tied to her mother and grandmother, like most of the other students doing well. As is the case for the others, her family is in a great position to influence her, and given her mother's confidence and expectations, it is no surprise that she is doing well so far.

Karen indicates that she gets all the help from her mother with her schoolwork that she needs and that it is not much. It may well be that Ms. Kenner is simply not available to help much given her busy schedule. We will see this when we turn to the observations. If she could change one thing about her life, Karen would spend more time with her aunts, grandmother, and cousins. Her nuclear family is important to her but so is her extended family. She would not want to be anyone else in the world if she had the option. Karen is another of the students doing well who is very confident, who has a very positive self-image, a characteristic of students who do well in school and of the middle class. We are seeing over and over that the family is important to the young students who do well in school. This puts the family in position to have great influence on the level of preparedness of the student for school and to monitor and influence the student's success. The family is critical, and we are seeing more and more precisely how the family needs to be structured, how it needs to operate, as well as the values and beliefs it needs to have if the student is to do well.

The Observations

The first observation of the Kenner household took place on a Wednesday afternoon from 4:00 until 6:00 in their two-story, neat, but very busy house. Karen spent almost all of the time in her bedroom talking to the observer. She indicated that she watches four to five hours of television a night and does homework only during commercials. As I indicated above, she was very much involved in sports in her earlier grades. She played football and basketball in fourth and fifth grades, basketball in sixth grade, and volleyball in eighth grade. She cut back on these extracurricular activities in order to concentrate on her academic work, but we really see few signs of such concentration. During this visit, her mother arrived home but not once did she mention Karen's school day or school activities. This is rather different from what transpires in the homes of most of the students who are doing well.

Karen's grandmother lives a few blocks from their home, and the family has dinner at her house once a week. Given that many immediate family members were present at some time during this visit and that the family spends time regularly with the grandmother, it appears that this very large family is a very close one. Indeed, with all of the children and grandchildren constantly moving about and talking, the house is not particularly quiet or orderly, two characteristics of most of the other families with average or high-achieving students. So we are not seeing the order or hearing the quiet of the high achievers, nor do we see the mother involving herself in the student's school activities.

During this visit Karen said that she no longer liked school because it was "boring." She also indicated that she was no longer interested in reading books from the local library and that she hates waking up in the morning. This is beginning to sound like a student whom I would not expect to do very well in school. She dislikes school, does not read many books, watches a great deal of television, and doesn't really want to wake up in the morning to attend school. While she says that she values education and wants to go into higher education, I see little evidence in her behavior or attitude to suggest this is true. On the other hand, her family is important to her, and her mother very clearly values education, including her own. It may be that Karen feels the pressure from her mother's educational pursuits and as a result tries to do well. Still, there is little about her home environment that at this point seems conducive to success except that, like most of the other students who do well, she has house chores. Karen does the dishes every Monday, Wednesday, and Friday. So she has responsibilities, and this helps to teach a sense of responsibility, which is crucial to school success.

Karen's house is not particularly large, especially given that so many family members live there. It is well worn but reasonably well kept. During our second visit, which also lasted from 4:00 until 6:00, the observer began to talk with Karen in the living/dining room on the first floor, unlike the first visit, which took place exclusively in Karen's bedroom (which she shares with a sister) on the second floor. When she was asked what were her favorite television shows, she responded *Beverly Hills 90210, Party of Five, Friends, Mad about You, The Practice, Snoops,* and *Boy Meets World.* Ms. Kenner arrives from work most evenings just before 6:00 and therefore must be aware that Karen is doing little schoolwork and is watching a great deal of television, yet she says or does little to change this. Again, this is unusual for the students we have studied who are doing well in school.

Karen lives with her two sisters, fourteen and seventeen, her nineteen-year-old brother, and the two children (two and four) of another older sister who lives nearby but cannot care for these two children. This, of course, places quite a burden on Ms. Kenner, who works and attends school. Still, she found the time to call each of Karen's teachers to ask about her progress during the first marking period. She thus calls Karen's teachers to ask about her grades but fails to ask Karen about school. This would appear to be a contradiction. Karen says that she values education, but dislikes school and devotes almost no time to schoolwork. This, too, would appear to be a contradiction. Still, Karen is doing well in school, though she is doing less well as time goes by. As the observer completed the questionnaire during this visit, another sister arrived with her two sons, as did the mother of the two youngsters living with Karen with the one-year-old girl who does live with her.

With all of the children in the house, there was a fair amount of noise and no mention at all of school. The adults and adolescents all watched television, and the young children ran about the house and played. It might actually be rather difficult for Karen to study or complete schoolwork in this environment even if she wanted to do so. It appears that Karen is doing just what she must in order to meet her mother's expectations and that she may well be intelligent enough to do this for a time. Over time, and as the educational experience becomes more difficult, it is not clear that she will be able to maintain this level of performance. We see no real signs of the kind of study habits or discipline that will be required and that we see in most of the other students.

The next observation began at 4:30 and ended at 6:30. At the beginning of the visit, the observer asked Karen how school had gone that day, and Karen responded that nothing new had occurred. She spoke about her gym class, how the teacher would not allow the class to play basketball, and how this upset many of the students. There was no mention of any other classes or of anything that she learned or of any assignment. When she was asked what university she wished to attend, Karen replied that she wished to attend a prominent California university. When she was asked why, she responded that the university looked really nice on the television program *Beverly Hills 90210.* There was no mention of the academic reputation of the school or of any reason why it might be a good fit for her interests. Karen, while apparently interested in her education and doing well, does not seem particularly well focused or motivated.

Karen told one of her older sisters, Tony, that one of her son's teachers had called to inform her that the son was not doing well in school. "So what, he never does good" was Tony's reply. She does not appear to be very concerned with the educational progress of her son. Worse still, the son was in the room listening to this reply. He may well be growing up knowing that little is expected of him educationally, and this is not what one would want if one expects high achievement.

Ms. Kenner arrived home at about 5:30. She discussed a prominent news story with the observer and asked about this study and about another family involved in the study. She told the observer several things about the mother in the other family that were not particularly positive but revealed how close many of the families in this study are and how knowledgeable they are about each other's affairs. The differences that we may see are certainly not the result of differences in neighborhoods or of income. No, these differences stem from differences in families, in familial attitudes and values, in family and home environment, and it is these variables that I strongly suspect need to be addressed in educational policy if we are to significantly improve the education of urban poor black students. I will address this issue in much more depth later in this book.

At one point Tony yelled to Marty, her twenty-two-year-old sister, that Jerry, Marty's son, had his pants down and had urinated on the sidewalk outside the house. This does not show a great deal of discipline or of supervision of the child. When Marty asked whether Ms. Kenner had any baby food for Marty's infant daughter, Ms. Kenner told her that she had no such food and that she should feed the infant whatever she could find. While Ms. Kenner ate food that she brought home with her, she told Karen that she should go to her grandmother's house if she was hungry. Marty prepared oatmeal for dinner for her two older children, and when the boy got oatmeal all over his face and clothes, both Karen and her mother yelled at Marty to "clean up after your kids." Marty did so with the same cloth that she had used earlier to wipe the floor.

While we found that quiet, order, structure, responsibility, and discipline are evident in most of the homes in which the students perform well in school, we see very little of these characteristics in the Kenner home or family. Indeed, there is a fair amount of chaos and a lack of discipline here. Still, Karen, the student, does well in school, raising questions about how she manages to do this given her family situation and home environment. Ms. Kenner, her mother, is very strongly motivated for herself to do well in school and in the world. As she drove the observer to the train station after the visit, she explained how when she was young she had been told by a guidance counselor that she was not college material. As a result she enrolled in secretarial school when she graduated from high school, and entered college only after working several years and changing her mind about her abilities. She wants very badly to prove to herself and the world that she is indeed college material.

Karen was in the car listening to this story, and I am certain that she has heard it many times before. Karen is herself interested in showing that she is college material, but it is not clear that she really knows just how to do so, beyond obtaining good grades. What will happen when and if these grades fall off? Does she have the discipline, the responsibility, the leadership abilities, the sense of cooperation that she will need and that most of the other students have? It does not appear that she does.

On the other hand, during the next visit, Karen showed the observer a recent history test on which she had received an A. She said that she had expected an F and was therefore very surprised. She did not want to tell the other students what grade she received because she didn't want them to "throw it up in her face." This does suggest that there may well be some peer pressure against high academic performance, even though Karen denied any such pressure in her interview. She is not in advanced placement classes or honors classes, so her classmates would appear to be average to below-average students, some of whom may well see little need to do well and would feel hostile toward those who do so because this might place pressure on them to do better. While we have not seen a great deal of evidence of this pressure, we have seen some. It is not outside of the realm of possibility. In fact, when she was asked why she did not take advanced placement or honors classes, Karen replied that she wanted to be seen as "regular" and not as "gay," which the students who took those classes and aimed toward Harvard, Princeton, and the like were considered. So there does seem to be the pressure to be accepted, and those who are accepted are those who do not do outstanding academic work. Such pressure would certainly limit those who succumb to it.

Karen is not involved in any extracurricular activities. Her mother wants her to join the basketball team now that her grades are good, but she indicates that she only wants to watch television. She is very different from most of the high achievers, who watch little television and are involved in a plethora of extracurricular activities, which help to build discipline, responsibility, and a cooperative nature, all of which help in school performance.

Her family situation and home environment are much more complicated than most of the others. Marty, one of the older sisters, lives with a boyfriend who has no job. After she and the boyfriend arrived at the house, her sister Tony yelled at her that she was a liar, while Karen constantly grumbled that their mother was coming home soon, with the implication that the bickering and yelling needed to stop. Tony then began to sweep up broken glass, yelling at her son that she did not need his help.

As soon as Ms. Kenner arrived at about 5:00, she started yelling that Marty had made a huge mistake. Apparently, Marty's infant daughter had fallen from a counter at a local Laundromat and hurt herself. In response, Marty had made a call that had alerted the Department of Children and Family Services, which deals with child abuse and neglect. Ms. Kenner was concerned that the call would result in the daughter being taken away from Marty and told her in no uncertain terms that she could not take care of any more of Marty's children. She also indicated that now Marty should not have to worry, since she and her boyfriend never really wanted to care for the little girl. At various times Ms. Kenner was joined in the yelling by Tony. This would not appear to be the type of home environment that is conducive to good school performances. It is loud, it is chaotic, it lacks discipline, and there are questions about responsibility and the future.

When Karen showed her mother her test grade, Ms. Kenner did not seem particularly interested. Again, this is unlike the response of the parents of most of the other students who are doing well or average. Those parents seemed to always be interested in the schoolwork of their children. Indeed, they occasionally inquired about the work more often than the students wanted them to. In the Kenner family, not once during our six visits did Ms. Kenner question Karen about her schoolwork or school-related activities.

During the next two visits, Karen and Tony and then Karen and Marty clashed over little disagreements. Karen's nieces and nephews made a great deal of noise, and there were often many baby items strewn about the house. The subject of education rarely came up during the more than ten hours that we spent with the Kenner family.

Karen Kenner does not appear to be particularly well disciplined or co-operative. While she says that education is important to her and that she intends to go beyond high school, she does very little to suggest that she takes this seriously. There was no talk about her future or indication that she is really planning or preparing for that future. Her home environment is not well structured or orderly or quiet, all characteristics of almost all of the homes in which the students are doing well in school.

Ms. Kenner's education is very important to Ms. Kenner. She works full-time, takes care of at least four of her children and two of her grandchildren, and attends graduate school part-time. She found the time to discuss her education with the observer on more than one occasion, but only once did she discuss Karen's education or that of her other children in any detail with the children or with the observer, and that discussion arose from a discussion of her own education.

Clearly, Ms. Kenner is a driven and disciplined woman, and Karen may attempt to emulate her. However, Karen spends most of her time at home watching television and arguing with one or another of her sisters. While prayer was mentioned in one of the questionnaires, there was not much evidence that religion played a significant role in the life of the Kenner family. All in all, this family is different on almost every count from the other families with students doing well in school. The answers on the questionnaires suggest a lower-income middle-class family with high self-esteem, discipline, high educational aspirations, a sense of responsibility, internal control, and an orientation toward the future. The everyday life of the family in general and Karen in particular casts serious doubt on the truthfulness of these answers. Ms. Kenner seems to have many of these characteristics, but we saw little to suggest that she works to ensure that Karen or her sisters or brother learn to share them. Still, Karen is doing well in school. I suspect that she is attempting to emulate her mother and that so far her intelligence is enough for her to do well. As the work becomes more difficult, it would be interesting to see whether she can maintain her high grades.

Karen has self-control and seems to have high educational aspirations, so she may well have been sent to school prepared to learn. When she didn't do well, her mother became involved and insisted that she devote her time to her schoolwork and not to extracurricular activities. This worked well in terms of grades but has not left her much involved with school or other activities that might have helped her to develop leadership skills or a sense of responsibility. I suspect that some changes will be necessary if she is to continue to do well.

SUMMARY

In a number of ways, four of the five families of the high achievers are very much alike, though there are important differences among some of them as well. There are also a number of similarities with the families of the average students. In three of the five families of high achievers, the activities of the students center around school and schoolwork and their extracurricular activities. This is much like the situation that prevails in the homes of the average students. When the students arrive home after school and after participation in their extracurricular activities, they focus quickly on their schoolwork, generally for the remainder of the evening. The only interruptions are household chores, dinner, and discussions with their parents, generally about school. So not only is education a very high priority, but they show its importance by focusing on it almost every evening.

The houses of three of the high achievers are quiet, well structured, and orderly, all characteristics conducive to good educational performance because they allow for the concentration on schoolwork. This is also the case in the houses of the three average achievers, leading me to conclude that quiet, order, and structure are important if students are to do well in school. Significantly, the lives of the poor are often not conducive to the maintenance of these characteristics. There are often many children of all ages in the house, and the schedules of nonprofessionals are often changeable, making order and structure difficult to maintain. Poor people must often struggle to make ends meet, and this makes predictability and order not easy to bring about. Still, the families in the cases of three of the five high achievers and all of the average achievers manage to accomplish this. They seem to understand that the characteristics are important if their children are to do well in school, and since they place an extremely high priority on this success, they do what they must. In two of the five cases, the houses lack this structure and order, yet the students do well. In one of the two cases, the student is a fourth grader and has little schoolwork to do, so the absence of these conditions may not be too problematic. In the other case, the student is a high school student who does virtually no schoolwork at home, and the absence of the characteristics may at some point prove to be a serious handicap.

Furthermore, in both of these two homes, the students either play games or watch television rather than do schoolwork, and neither student is much involved in extracurricular activities. These activities help to develop leadership skills, a sense of cooperation, positive self-esteem, and discipline, all highly correlated with higher school achievement. Still, they do well in school. Given their lack of involvement and their home environment, one wonders how long their high performances will last. In the case of Joseph Brown, the young fourth grader, the same characteristics seen in the average achievers and three of the other four high achievers, high educational aspirations, discipline, positive self-esteem, internal control, and a sense of responsibility are present. All of these characteristics are correlated with achievement. Then too, he is very competitive, and given his high educational expectations, this may very well keep him on the right track. That is, he may continue to do well because that is the way to stay ahead of the others in his classes and in his school. In the case of Karen Kenner, the high school freshman, these characteristics are not so obvious. Karen has high aspirations, but does little to achieve those aspirations and lacks the competitiveness that could inspire her to do so. She does not seem particularly responsible or motivated, and we saw little discipline on her part or pushed by her mother.

Joseph's mother is fairly strict, like three of the other high achievers and of the average students as well, though Fatima's mother does not seem to be quite as strict. She may not need to be given that Fatima does precisely what is expected of her. While this may limit the autonomy of the students, it also protects them from what must be considered a threatening environment, with relatively high crime rates, a fair amount of violence, and both gang and drug activity.

In four of the five high-achieving families, the students are supported by their families and interact quite a bit with their parents, typically their mothers, even when there is a father in the home. Much of this verbal interaction centers around school, and it is loving, caring, and often playful, the same as we saw in the homes of the average achievers. This helps to develop confidence in the students, which in turn helps them to do well in school. In the Kenner family, the interaction, what little there is, is often hostile and combative, not what we have seen to be characteristic of the average or high-achieving families.

Two of the five high achievers regularly perform household chores. This helps to develop a sense of responsibility. In the case of Joseph, the fourth grader, there is probably not much that his family could regularly expect him to do given his age. In Marie's case, she is an only child and her father is not only in the home but involved in the family activities to some limited extent. There is therefore relatively little left for Marie to do. What's more, her parents want her to focus almost exclusively on school. In Karen's case, it is not clear that anyone in the house does too much, thus Karen is not really a responsible young lady. Still, she does well in school.

By and large, then, the high achievers are much like the average students, except that the three of the former who are very much like the latter seem to focus even more on their schoolwork, and their parents, while they facilitate this focus, are not as much involved with the schoolwork, though Ms. Adams is somewhat involved. It may well be that these students are doing so well that the parents see little need to be directly involved. They show their interest, however, by discussing the work and the students' activities with them, with few exceptions. The Kenner family is an anomaly all around. The educational expectations are high, as is Karen's performance. However, the family has few of the characteristics of those in which the students are average or high performers, and Karen does not appear to have many of the traits of the other good students.

With the exceptions noted, then, we see middle-class families with little money. The students are oriented toward the future, internally controlled, have high self-esteem, are responsible, have high educational aspirations, and are disciplined. They are precisely the type of students schools want, given that schools are middle-class institutions. Neither the students nor their parents believe that anything about their schools stands in the way of their educational success, raising questions about all the fuss over the "need" to change schools. Neither, on the whole, do they believe that race will hinder them. For the most part, they do not think that other students have tried to stop them from doing well, though there is some evidence of such efforts, which must be addressed when we discuss necessary policy changes. While these attempts to stymie the educational success of the solid students are not as widespread as I expected, there do in fact seem to be such attempts, and they must be considered and somehow stopped. This is, however, easier said than done, as we will see when we turn to the policy issues.

These are students being sent to school prepared to learn. Indeed, for the most part, only success will be accepted in their homes, and their parents stress this often. If there is a big difference between these students and the average achievers it is that they generally seem to center their lives around their school activities, including the academic activities. Their parents will accept nothing less, and they create an environment in which this is not only possible but expected.

FAMILY AND THE LOW ACHIEVER

MYCELA FALWELL

Mycela is a twelve-year-old seventh grader at the same middle school attended by several others in this research. Her grades for the fall quarter were one C, one C−, two D's, and two F's. For the winter quarter, she received one C-, one D, two D−'s, and two F's. I would think that by any standard she would be considered a low academic achiever. In the sixth grade, her grades were not any better, except that she received a B+ in the fall in French. In the spring that grade was a D, and throughout that academic year she received mainly D's and F's, indicating that her grades for the seventh grade were no fluke.

Mycela lives with her grandmother, who is her legal guardian, her grandfather, and a twenty-year-old sister in the same poor West Side neighborhood in which most of the families studied in this work live. The family income is at the lowest of the lower-income levels used by Family Focus, so money is a serious problem. The grandmother, Ms. Black, grew up in the South and has lived in the same house in Evanston for some twenty years. Her husband works full-time as a machinist and completed the tenth grade, while Ms. Black completed the eleventh grade. Ms. Black thinks that Mycela's education is very important. When asked why, she responded that she would like to see Mycela do better than she did in life and that a minimal education is no longer adequate. The wish of parents or grandparents to see their children do better than they did in life and the idea that an education is needed to achieve this are very common among the poor. After all, few of them have done very well, and there is therefore a great deal of room for improvement in the next generation. This is not the case for the middle- or upper-income citizens in our country, so they will often give other reasons to justify the importance of education. For the poor, it is generally a matter of progress.

Ms. Black tries to help Mycela do well in school, like most of the other parents studied so far, and she does so by punishing her with the loss of privacy if she fails to do well. She also tries to help her remain caught up with her schoolwork. She says that she visits Mycela's school at least once a month and is upset if she is called to go, because this suggests that Mycela is in trouble. She feels "nice and good" at the standard school conference. She thinks that Mycela has many opportunities for academic help, which she apparently fails to use, and that Mycela loses some of her school assignments.

Ms. Black "can't foresee anything that is in [Mycela's] way" of getting a good education. Virtually all the other parents said the same. Like the others, then, she believes that Mycela can control her own future. The teachers are not a hindrance, the school is not an obstacle; not even the lack of money is a problem. Clearly, Ms. Black believes that Mycela should control her own life. Nor does she believe that other students attempt to stop Mycela from doing well. Given Mycela's grades, I would be surprised to learn that others try to stop her from doing well. While it is possible that others try and are successful, there is no evidence of this. Her grandmother says that her two best friends try to encourage her to do well. This is not surprising considering that one of those best friends is Stephanie Adams, one of the better and most highly motivated (and parentally controlled) students in this study. Since Stephanie does so well, I would expect her to want her friends to do well also. Unfortunately, this is not the case for Mycela, and the question is, of course, why? According to Ms. Black, Mycela's friends urge her to do better, and they occasionally study together. Their success is also a challenge to Mycela, according to Ms. Black.

When asked whether race or racial discrimination played a role in her life, she responded, "At this point not really. At sixty-three I am what I am." So we have another adult who does not see race as an obstacle in life, despite the continuance of discrimination and racism in our country. I can only conclude that these people are either relatively removed from the everyday effects of race or that they cannot see the effects. It may well be good that these individuals "refuse" to allow racism to impact their lives, at least in ways that they see.

This is quite interesting in the case of Ms. Black, who was born in the "segregated South" and experienced "segregated schooling." She did not, however, "know racism" until she came North. So segregation has not left her with a negative feeling about the role of race is this society. This would allow her to not use race as an excuse for failure, which would place more responsibility on the individual for his or her actions, a necessity for good school performance. She had a single mother and grew up in a family in which discipline was important and maintained in a "family-to-family approach." She maintains discipline with Mycela by denying her various privileges such as use of the telephone, the television, and the visits of friends. She says that she expects both maturity and self-control and that she wants Mycela to have a career and to raise a family. We have heard very few mention the raising of a family. For the most part, the parents want their children to do well enough in school so that they can go to college and become professionals. The idea of raising a family, while new for this research, is probably explained by the southern, rural background of Ms. Black. In that environment, professionalism is relatively rare, and the family is the key to economic success. Perhaps Ms. Black is simply bringing those southern, rural, poor values to Evanston.

Ms. Black "love[s] to read." She reads the newspaper six days a week but finds that she does not have as much time as she would like for other reading. It does not appear that she has passed this desire to read on to Mycela, who reads a newspaper about once a week, and then only when she is interested in specific things. Ms. Black relies on her husband when she has a problem.

Some of her answers to the questions on the questionnaire are different from some of those of the other parents/guardians. For example, she suggests that she is aware that Mycela is not performing particularly well in school. The other students are performing fairly well, and so we do not see any indication that the parents are really concerned. Furthermore, while Ms. Black says that she tries to help Mycela stay caught up in school, there is no mention of any specific help that she offers. She denies Mycela privileges if she does badly, but for the most part she relies upon Family Focus for help. She offers little herself, and this is not particularly helpful for Mycela. It may well be that Ms. Black does not really know what to do or how to do it, or it could also be that she lacks the necessary discipline, evident in most of the homes of the better students—indeed, in all but one.

Mycela herself most likes socializing with her friends at school, though she likes her math teacher. She least likes large assignments because "they are a big part of my grade." She also dislikes her science teacher. So she does not appear to like much about her school or her educational experience other than a specific teacher. She may be going to school more to socialize than to learn. If this is the case, we should not be surprised to find that she is doing badly. She thinks that she is doing "not so well" in school, so she is aware of her poor performance. Education is "very important" to Mycela "because it's my future." She does not link education to any specific goal, but at least she seems to think about her future, albeit in general terms. She appears to be future-oriented, which helps greatly in school, and she doesn't think that any other student has tried to stop her from doing well in school. She would not allow it anyway, because "I don't let nobody get in my way." Like most of the well-performing students, she believes that she can control her own future, her own progress. This sense of self-control is positive and helpful in school, but it does not seem to help Mycela. Furthermore, there is little reason for anyone to try to limit Mycela given that she is doing so badly that her success would not be a threat to others.

Mycela would like to attend college and expects to do so. However, she believes that two obstacles stand in her way: "it is so hard to pass science," and she is not doing well in Spanish. So, unlike the students who are doing well, Mycela sees obstacles to her educational future, and they are both functions of her performance in school. She seems unaware that these obstacles are for the most part hers to control, that she can and must overcome them. It is almost as though she believes that the problems are inherent in school life, not related to her effort or interest.

Mycela says that her father is the most important person or thing in her life because "he always puts up with me." A family member is thus critical to her and in a position to influence her educational performance. The observations will determine whether he plays this role. She does not think about race or discrimination very much and seems to believe that they are not very important. She gets no help from her grandmother with her schoolwork and instead asks her twenty-year-old sister or her friends. This is very interesting considering that her friends are likely to be about the same age and in the same grade. Most of the students doing well get help, sometimes more than they want, from their parents. I would expect most students to feel embarrassed to accept help with their schoolwork from friends. This would acknowledge that they are not performing up to expectations, and most young people would not want to make this admission. It is clear that Mycela is not doing well, and this is apparently accepted by her friends, at least some of whom want her to do better, but there seems to be little real adult family help.

If she could change one thing about her life, she would be older so that she could live alone or else she would like to live with her father. Clearly, Mycela is not happy with her current living arrangements, and this could negatively influence her performance. It may well be that she simply doesn't care how badly she does given that she is not comfortable or happy in her home life. Again, though, her father seems to be important. Just how is he handling this position? Mycela also does not like Evanston or her current school. She says that all of her friends are at another school that she used to attend, though this does not seem to be completely true.

Mycela, then, does not seem happy with much, and this, together with the lack or help or support with her schoolwork, could easily negatively affect her school performance. Her mother died a few years ago, and she has not been quite the same since. She has been very unhappy and somewhat confused, according to those at Family Focus. She is thus in a difficult and undesirable situation and may spend more time and energy trying in vain to find comfort and happiness than on her school performance.

If she could be one other person in the world, it would be Missy Elliot, because "she got music skills." She wants to be someone who appeals to young people. This is, of course, not unusual, but it is unlike those solid students who want to be themselves and have the confidence to say it.

The Observations

Most of the observations took place between 4:30 and 7:00. The first one began at 4:30, with the observer meeting Mycela, Stephanie Adams, and Jesse, two of Mycela's friends. The three girls and the observer moved quickly to

Mycela's bedroom because she was supposed to be cleaning her room, which was quite a mess. She did no cleaning while the observer was there, but the fact that she had the assignment does suggest some responsibilities. The girls discussed the operation of Mycela's two Walkman radios, then pizzas, and then boys. They talked about an upcoming dance at the local YMCA. This led to a discussion of the last dance there—who attended and who did not, who danced with whom, who looked nice and who did not. They moved on to a discussion about different hairstyles as Jesse fixed Mycela's hair and then began to listen to rap music on the apparently new CD player. Stephanie was now playing a video game, but soon Mycela suggested that they all play dominoes, at which Mycela won. When asked whether they watch television much, Mycela said that they watch music videos quite a bit. Neither Jesse nor Stephanie answered many questions. They seemed reluctant and allowed Mycela to do most of the talking.

Mycela then asked Jesse whether she could spend the night. Jesse demurred because she had cheerleading the next day. Apparently Jesse is involved in extracurricular activities, and we know that Stephanie is. While the girls were discussing the possibility of the three spending the night at Stephanie's house, the observer had the impression that Stephanie had few parental restrictions and little guidance. Nothing could be farther from the truth, as we have seen. Stephanie is fairly strictly guided and controlled by her mother—indeed, she has relatively little autonomy. This all sounds like young girls being young girls, and none of them would want the others to think that they were strictly controlled by their parents or grandparents. More importantly, never was school mentioned, never was any schoolwork done, never did Ms. Black ask Mycela about school that day, never were any household chores performed. This is all unlike the family situations we have seen in all but two of the families in which the students do average or very well, and in one of these situations the student is very young, and the other appears to be an anomaly. There simply was no emphasis on Mycela's education. This observation did take place on a Friday, and it is possible that this was the case because it was a weekend. Still, other observations took place on the weekdays, so the impact of the day of the week is not really clear.

The next observation took place during the week from 4:30 until 6:30 at Mycela's home. Again, Stephanie was with Mycela when the observer arrived, and this time the two of them were in Mycela's sister's room using the

Internet, tuned into a chat room with a seventeen-year-old male. After a few minutes of discussion about their age and descriptions, they moved out of the chat room. As they did so, Ms. Black came in and scolded Mycela for using the Internet too much and tying up the telephone line. She then asked Mycela whether she had completed her homework, thus expressing her concern about Mycela's schoolwork and the importance of the work to Ms. Black. Mycela said that she had completed her homework, but this was untrue, since she had previously told Stephanie that she could not finish her math because she had forgotten her textbook and planned to try to do the work during the first class period the next day.

This suggests that school may be more important to Ms. Black than to Mycela. Mycela did not seem very bothered by the fact that she had not done the math work or by the fact that she was lying to her grandmother. She is not showing much discipline or concern. Ms. Black threatens to take away Mycela's privileges if she does not receive decent grades, but the admonition doesn't appear to bother Mycela. School grades do not seem to be that important to Mycela, and the threats from her grandmother do not appear to worry her. Perhaps these threats are empty and Mycela knows this.

Ms. Black told the observer that Mycela has been living with her for a year. Before that, she and her sister had lived with both of her parents until her mother unexpectedly died. Her father fell apart and got into "bad stuff" and then failed to try to control, guide, or discipline Mycela at all. The "bad stuff" was apparently drugs, and Mycela was not being asked to do anything she did not want to do, including schoolwork. So it appears that Mycela is not particularly motivated to do well in school and that her father played no positive role in the process of guiding or motivating her, and her grandparents, while concerned, play little role themselves. They want her to perform well, but it is not clear that they quite know just how to influence this process. Mycela's older sister is attending a local public university, suggesting that education is important to the family, but for Mycela the questions are discipline and responsibility.

As the observer spoke with Ms. Black, Mycela's sister arrived home and asked Mycela and Stephanie to leave her room, which they promptly did. They went to Mycela's room, where they laughed and discussed various occurrences at school until Ms. Black came in and asked what Mycela wanted for dinner. Once that was settled, Stephanie and Mycela went back to discussing various classes and who had been asked to leave which classes. Stephanie mentioned that Mycela had been asked to leave different classes. Given that it is generally students who cause some behavioral problem in school who are asked to leave class, it appears that Mycela may well behave inappropriately in some classes in addition to performing badly: Indeed, the two often go together. While her grandmother says that she is concerned about Mycela's grades, it is not clear that she does much to actually influence these grades or to really put her concern into action. At 6:00 the observer prepared to leave, and Stephanie said that she had to leave as well because she had to check in at home, expressing the discipline that is a characteristic of her house.

Stephanie was just arriving at Mycela's home the next week when the observer got there at 4:15. This time Jesse was at the home as well, and all three girls and the observer were in Mycela's sister's room working on her computer. This time Jesse was working on her science homework, but Mycela was typing Jesse's name on the assignment. Stephanie then sat down at the computer and, after asking Jesse for her worksheet, completed the assignment for Jesse.

Stephanie is then not only doing a very good job with her own schoolwork, she is also helping her friends with theirs. Indeed, she is actually doing the work, making life relatively easy for her friends by lightening their school burdens. This may be good for friendship, but it is not particularly good for Mycela or Jesse's development of discipline or responsibility. While Stephanie was doing Jesse's science work on giant pandas, Jesse was at work on another homework assignment, and all three were discussing school grades. The observer wrote about the conversation, "It seems that [Stephanie] is the best student of the three. It appears that [Mycela] is the least concerned of the three." It will be interesting to see how long the close friendship between Stephanie and Mycela lasts. As they move on in school, as grades become more important and school more difficult, each young lady will have to devote even more time to schoolwork. It does not seem that Mycela is particularly interested in doing this, whereas Stephanie is not only interested but is given little alternative by her mother. Mycela, on the other hand, has little pressure or encouragement from her grandmother.

The three friends discussed teachers they disliked, and Mycela mentioned that she was failing two classes and not doing well in others but did not seem particularly worried or stressed about this situation. They then discussed a student they disliked and referred to her as "country ghetto," apparently meaning inarticulate, slow, and ill mannered. She and Mycela do not get along well, and Jesse and Stephanie seem to dislike her because of that. The disliked student recently moved to Evanston from the West Side of Chicago, and the young ladies think that this is a bad area to be from; it is beneath them. While they think that this girl is inarticulate, Jesse asked, "Don't she got a brother?" which is, of course, not the most articulate way to ask the question. Ms. Black, hearing the question, corrected Jesse, as she had done to Mycela several times during the observations. Stephanie has never had to be corrected, as she tends to not use slang and speaks articulately. These differences between the girls will probably push them apart as they get older and how one speaks becomes more important.

Then too, in the ghetto the manner in which Jesse and Mycela speak is fairly common, and the more articulate speaking technique is often seen as "white" or snooty. This places pressure on young people to speak in such a way that they will be accepted in their neighborhoods. This is fine for the neighborhoods but does not go well in schools, which try hard to use and to teach "proper" English. In a sense, many of those poor blacks living in the poor neighborhoods who try to do well in school must be "bilingual": speaking one way to succeed in school and another way to be accepted in the neighborhood. This pressure may well push the friends apart, given that Stephanie must speak in a manner acceptable to her mother at all times.

The three girls continued to mock the "country ghetto" girl and her brother while Ms. Black admonished them not to be so critical. The talk then turned to nicknames, and all three girls discussed their own nicknames. Stephanie went beyond her nickname to discuss her family in Africa, in the process demonstrating a great deal of knowledge of her native country. Ms. Black was impressed with Stephanie's knowledge, but Jesse and Mycela seemed uninterested in this information. They spent even more time talking about others in a derogatory manner until Ms. Black pointed out that it was getting dark and suggested that Jesse and Stephanie go home. Stephanie left almost immediately because she had to be home by dark. Jesse stayed to print out her homework (done by Stephanie).

A bit later Mycela's grandfather asked her who had been on his bed. Mycela responded that she didn't know. Her grandfather asked why the telephone book was open. Mycela answered that she was looking for Halloween costumes, and her grandfather told her to take the book off of his bed. This was the most interaction between Mycela and her grandfather we had seen thus far. Mr. Black seems to have little interaction with Mycela and Ms. Black. While what little there is seems to be pleasant and to lack tension, it is not the loving, caring, often funny interaction we have seen between many of the students and their parents. It also lacks the strictness we have often seen. Mycela seems relatively free to do what she wants, and during this observation she did no schoolwork; we had yet to see her do any.

Unlike the schedules of most of the students doing well in school, Mycela's is not centered around her schoolwork, her household responsibilities, and her extracurricular activities. It is centered around her friends and her games, and she has no one to urge or guide her in a different direction. Her house is quiet and orderly, but there is no predictable structure. She says that she is concerned about her future and realizes that education is important for that future, but does not seem interested in actually doing something to maximize the opportunity for a positive and happy future.

The next observation began at 5:15 at Family Focus, where Mycela had a choir meeting, and ended at Mycela's home at 7:30. Only three members of the choir turned out for the meeting with the choir director. While one of the three female members took notes of the dates and times of the upcoming concerts, Mycela appeared uninterested and took no notes. It is the case, however, that she is to some extent involved in an extracurricular activity, as are most of the students who do well in school. The level of her commitment to this activity is not clear. This was the first mention of it, and she did not seem very involved in the activity.

An hour and a half later the choir director said that she had to leave, and the observer drove one of the other girls and Mycela home. Ms. Black would not allow the observer to enter Mycela's bedroom because it was not clean, even though she had instructed Mycela to clean it earlier and told her that no one could enter the room until it was clean. Apparently, Mycela does not have quite the same respect for neatness and cleanliness held by most of the higher achievers, nor does she seem as concerned about the instructions of her elders as the others. Discipline and order are not as important to her.

While the observer and Mycela discussed their siblings, she referred to her sister as a "dork," meaning a person who is rather awkward, clumsy, and studious, someone very concerned with books and studying. So she speaks in a critical slang way about her sister, who is in college. This would not suggest much respect for education on her part. After she talked by phone to her father for a time, she again complained that she disliked both her science and Spanish classes but did not seem very concerned about the fact that she was failing both classes. Not much about school seems to concern her except for the social life and the attitudes of some of the other students. She seems very much uninterested in her performance and in education generally. When the observer left at 7:30, Mycela had not done any schoolwork at all.

Mycela answered the door to the observer at the next visit at 5:30. Mr. Black was watching the television news. The observer and Mycela went to Mycela's sister's room, which contains the computer. The older sister, Shayla, was busy with her Spanish homework while Mycela played a computer game. Shalya asked Mycela to stop the game so that she might use the computer for her homework, but Mycela refused, saying that she would not leave the computer until she lost the game. They argued for half an hour. Mycela then agreed to let her sister use the computer for schoolwork but instead signed on to an Internet account and checked her messages. While Shayla became increasingly frustrated, Mycela continued to use the computer for nonacademic purposes. She showed no sign that the academic work took precedence over the game or the chat room messages. Indeed, Mycela and Shayla joked about how Mycela should pay more attention to her schoolwork and how Shayla pays too much attention to hers. Shayla appears to be a serious, conscientious, hardworking individual: Not only does she attend a local low-cost public school, she also works four days a week. Education appears to be far more important to her than to her sister, and we see little sign that any adult is seriously attempting to influence or change this.

When Ms. Black arrived home, she said that she could not prepare dinner because she had to attend a meeting but that there were leftovers and she had coupons for Burger King. Both girls complained that there were no leftovers that they liked, and their grandmother said that she tried hard to keep food they preferred so there should be something. Though Shayla eventually looked for something to eat, she again complained that there was nothing there. The sisters then began a conversation about a younger girl known to both of them. Mr. Black came in, announced that he was going to Burger

King, and asked what they wanted for dinner. Shayla then returned to the computer and her homework, and Mycela complained that Shayla studies too much. Shayla replied that she must study a great deal in order to obtain good grades and that Mycela would know nothing about this since she never has good grades. Mycela protested that she was indeed getting good grades. This is interesting considering that she had recently lamented the fact that she was flunking two courses. For a while the sisters continued the discussion about the value of hard work and good grades, with Mycela taking the position that the work was not necessary and that she was doing well.

Mycela does not seem to care very much about how badly she does in school, despite what both she and her grandmother said in response to the questionnaire about the value of education. She does nothing to indicate that education is really important to her. She does no schoolwork and exhibits little discipline, self-control, or concern for her future. Her sister, on the other hand, seems very concerned with her education and spends considerable time on her schoolwork. Why her and not Mycela? It is an interesting question but beyond our ability to answer in this research. Perhaps their mother had the opportunity to exert a greater influence on Shayla before her untimely death than on Mycela, who was only ten or eleven when she died. In any event, it does not appear that Mycela is being sent to school prepared to learn, nor does she have much respect for education or its role in her life.

After Mr. Black returned with the food, the conversation shifted to whether students began the academic quarter with the grade of A in each class or with the grade of zero and then had to work up to their final grade. Mycela argued that they began with the highest grade, A, and then worked to sustain that grade. She argued, therefore, that she had all A's at that moment since it was the beginning of the quarter. It is not really clear that she believes that her grades are important, though her sister pointed out that she might be able to participate in the French class trip to Quebec next year if she received all A's, even though the fee of seven hundred dollars is very expensive.

At 7:30, as the discussion shifted to the subject of a new jump rope for Mycela, whose old one had been stolen, the observer had to leave. Mycela had again done no schoolwork. Furthermore, she had again made fun of her sister for doing so much of her own. This is very different from the students who are doing well. They seem to center their lives around their schoolwork, their chores, and their extracurricular activities. Mycela pays little attention to any of these, nor does her grandmother seem to hold her to any such obligations.

During the next visit she was again at choir practice, but when the singing began she found a position outside the view of the choir director and lip-synched the songs rather than singing. When the observer asked about this, she replied that she did not sing well and joined the choir only to go on the singing trips and to spend time with her friends. So she is not interested in the extracurricular activity and does not seem to participate in a way that helps to build her self-confidence, sense of cooperation, or leadership abilities. It is simply an opportunity to "hang out," to get out of the house. She said she wants to get out of the house because her family makes her feel that she should always be involved in something—but then she quickly changed the subject.

The final observation began at 4:20 in the living room of the Blacks' small apartment. Ms. Black explained that Mycela was at Family Focus getting help with her Spanish, at which she is not doing well. Ms. Black said that Mycela took French last year but did not do well in that language, either. She switched her to Spanish because she thought that there were so many Spanish-speaking people in Evanston that Mycela would have less trouble obtaining help with that language. The switch resulted in Mycela being behind, and she originally did not even try to do well, hoping that the school would exempt her from the requirement. When this didn't happen, she tried harder, according to her grandmother. This all underscores the finding that Mycela is not taking her education seriously and although it *is* important to Ms. Black, she does not seem to know how to encourage Mycela to aspire higher and to work to meet educational aspirations.

Ms. Black indicated that she wished that she had gone to school to study nursing, but that she has ended up a caretaker for an alcoholic couple. This has taught her the dangers of alcohol, and she works hard to teach those dangers to her family members. It appears that she sees the importance of education in much the same way that many poor blacks see it: retrospectively. They fail to do well or to do much in school, perhaps due to family obligations brought on by their poverty, and then later in life they see how much better they might have done had they pursued their education. They then admonish their younger family members not to make the same "mistake."

Admonishment is clearly not enough. There must be a home environment that emphasizes discipline and a certain set of values and attitudes, and there must be someone to encourage the youngsters to adopt and maintain the values, attitudes, and discipline. The encouragement, as we are seeing, must go beyond talking.

At about 6:00 Ms. Black left the room to prepare for a church meeting, and Mr. Black emerged from their bedroom to talk to the observer. He talked about there being too much violence on television, about how violent the young people are today, and about how he didn't want to leave his house on New Year's Eve because he was afraid of the "craziness" outside. He did not seem to be comfortable with the conversation, and it was therefore strained, but it did suggest how many older people feel a lack of connection or understanding with the youth of today. This makes it even more difficult for the elders to support or encourage the younger people.

Mycela finally arrived home at about 6:40, said that she had been working hard on her Spanish at Family Focus, and apologized to her grandfather for being late and failing to let him know where she was. There are apparently family rules concerning her schedule and whereabouts, but they are not as diligently enforced as is the case for many of the students doing well. The rules make sense given that their neighborhood is not considered particularly safe. The parents and grandparents want to be certain that the youngsters are not in threatening situations, and therefore they want considerable control over their whereabouts.

Mycela said nothing about her schoolwork or classes and nothing about extracurricular activities. Instead, she talked about two fights, one of which involved one of her friends and was broken up by a teacher quickly. The other fight was after school and started over a disagreement involving a coat. The mother of one of the girls in the fight tried to "snatch her daughter out of there," and in the process she was "swung on by the other girl." Mycela said fighting is stupid, but she watched until the mother became involved. She then felt that it was in her best interest to have nothing to do with the altercation. The observer had to leave soon after the discussion over the fights.

As I have already written, Mycela did virtually no schoolwork during our observations. Her home environment, while quiet, is not the same as that of most of the students who do well in school. She does not appear to have the discipline, self-confidence, sense of responsibility, or orientation toward the future possessed by the others, and she certainly does not show high educational aspirations. While she might have shown some discipline in leaving the fights alone, by and large she does what she wants within the broad parameters set by her grandparents and the limitations of her age. There are two adults present in the home, but the grandfather plays no real role in Mycela's upbringing, and the grandmother, while concerned, does not have a significant role, either. She has little communication with Mycela, shows little support or encouragement concerning education, and uses little discipline. Mycela seems to have few, if any, obligations, though both of her grandparents care for her and would like to see her do better than they have. Her attitudes, values, and home environment work against this, and they are doing little to change or influence these.

XENA DUNBAR

Xena is a twelve-year-old seventh grader at the same middle school attended by several of the other students in this research. During the course of our research, she and her mother and four siblings moved (with the help of the observer) very close to the same West Side neighborhood in which virtually all of the other families live. The family income is at the lowest of the Family Focus lower-income level, and Xena is doing very badly in school. For the fall quarter her grades were one C+, one C, one C−, and three F's. For the winter they were one D+, two D's, and three F's. At this point she could not do much worse in school. The question, of course, is why?

Ms. Dunbar is a single mother, as are a number of those involved with this research, and, thirty-nine now, she was a teenage mother. She grew up in Evanston. As I indicated, the family moved during the research, so the family has lived in that apartment less than two months. Ms. Dunbar has worked full-time in the same office for ten years. She has a business certificate but no degree. She says that Xena's education is very important to her because "that's the way of life now. Finish school to have a decent life." Like most of the other mothers, she seems to link education to a better position in life than she has had. Education is valued not for the sake of knowledge or for the expansion of one's horizons but for the better job to which it leads. It may well be that poor blacks have little time for knowledge or the expansion of horizons. Putting bread on the table and paying the utility bills take first priority, and more education is seen as helpful in these pursuits. Perhaps the next generation, the Stephanies and the Maries, after receiving college degrees, will have those "luxuries."

Ms. Dunbar says that she tries to help Xena with her schooling by "telling her that's the way it is. Just doing positive things." She did not specify just what these positive things are, and there was no indication that Ms. Dunbar actually does much beyond telling Xena that education is important. She visits Xena's school five or six times a year and is worried because "things seem kind of chaotic." When pressed to elaborate, she said that "things are not just going right sometimes." It was not clear whether she referred to things related to the school or to Xena or both, but unlike most of the parents of the students doing well, she is concerned and worried. The other parents would seem to have little about which to be concerned.

Xena's mother thinks that only finances stand in the way of Xena obtaining a good education. Like most of the others, then, she places the responsibility for her daughter's educational future in her daughter's hands and not in the hands of teachers or others. She expects her daughter to control her own educational future. This is, of course, positive if Xena is to do well. Ms. Dunbar does not believe that other students try to prevent Xena from doing well in school. Given how badly she is doing, there would be little for others to try to stop. Neither does she think that adults at Xena's school try to stop her from doing well. So far, only one of the parents in this research has indicated that an adult at school has limited the child's school performance. This is interesting in light of all of the policy efforts to improve the quality of teachers. These parents, the parents of the kinds of students thought to have the most trouble, do not seem to place blame on the teachers or administrators. I will discuss this issue further when I deal with the policy implications of this work, but the point is that while much of the policy community blames the teachers, the *parents* do not seem to.

Ms. Dunbar does believe that race and/or discrimination plays a role in her life. She says: "Being black is strike one. You can say your name and then your race, it's over." She says that someone at work took down a calendar she had that her boss suggested showed her "blackness." She is not allowed to wear braids anymore at work, because they highlight her blackness. "This is my country, even though I was brought here. We helped build this country too. Old railroads were built by hand, across deserts, everything. I don't treat nobody wrong." Unlike most of the other parents, Ms. Dunbar is sensitive to the role played by race in society, but she did not indicate that she expects race to limit how well her daughter can do with respect to education. So race is a problem, but it apparently is not seen as an educational hindrance for Xena.

When asked how she raised her children, including Xena, she emphasized straightforwardness and directness. There was no mention of discipline or self-control or responsibility. Ms. Dunbar apparently believes that directness with her children is critical. She said that she would rather tell them something negative than to have anyone else tell them. There was no mention of parenting style other than directness. No mention of the values she tries to instill or of the attitudes or behaviors that she thinks are important. So far there is little to suggest that this family is middle class other than the fact that Ms. Dunbar believes that Xena controls her own educational fate, except for the lack of money.

Ms. Dunbar reads the newspaper two or three times a week and reads a book every day. The book, however, is a manual that shows her how to do something correctly. It is not something that she might encourage Xena to read or to discuss with her. When she has a problem she relies on "God, because I don't have anybody. That's all I got." So, like a number of the other parents, God or religion plays an important role in her life. We will investigate the role of religion in Xena's life. Ms. Dunbar says that she relies on her father when she has financial troubles. It sounds like Ms. Dunbar is another strong, persistent black woman raising her family in a difficult situation and trying to do her best under stressful conditions. She says that she teaches Xena "to do the best you can. If you make a mistake it is not the end of the world. It won't be the end of the world because I have been to the bottom. Won't be a big thing, pick yourself up. People have less than I have. Continue to work hard to maintain what I have and get extra. Nothing wrong with faith and hope."

She clearly has a positive outlook on life and a sense of persistence. However, there was little said about education, self-control, self-esteem, responsibility, or the future. It is not really clear that she is raising Xena to value those things—which she must, if she is to do well in school. She appears to be raising her to survive difficulties, not necessarily to prepare for her future through education.

Xena most likes the other students and some classes at her school. The classes are gym, reading and language arts, art, and cooking. She most dislikes what she calls a "strict dress code." Her school does not have uniforms, but it limits certain clothes, and she wants to wear baggy clothes. When asked how well she was doing in her classes, she responded that she was doing well: a B+ in most classes. Either she really has no idea of how she is doing (unlikely given that she receives a grade report), she is not telling the truth, or she simply cannot cope with the reality. In any event, it would be difficult for her to do better if she cannot acknowledge that she is not doing well in the first place. She cannot improve if she does not think she needs to. If this is the case, she shows little sense of responsibility for her actions.

Xena says that education is very important to her because without it you "can't get a lot of jobs, or you will end up at McDonald's or at a gas station or you'll end up on the streets." It does not sound as though her aspirations are particularly high; she wants to avoid the streets and working at fast food places or gas stations. When asked whether another student had ever tried to stop her from doing well in school, she answered that yes, this had happened. It was a "girl who didn't like me because of the way I act. She doesn't like my personality. She's not a good student. I have lots of friends." This appears to be less about school performance and more about personal disagreements among young girls. It is interesting that Xena would see this as an issue of school performance when performance was not really mentioned in her explanation. Again, given Xena's grades, why would anyone want her to do worse?

Xena says about the girl: "she doesn't feel good about herself." At least Xena gives some thought to the importance of positive self-esteem, and perhaps she is positive about herself. Indeed, at one point she said, "I believe in myself." Such belief is critical to good performance. It is necessary but obviously not sufficient. According to Xena, she devotes an hour and a half every evening or weekend day to her homework. This is about the same amount of time stated by most students. She expects to go "all the way" to college. Note that a number of the better students expect to attend graduate school.

Regarding possible obstacles in her way, she points out that she did not do so well in school last year. She "didn't understand the work and didn't want to ask questions." Her mother became angry and didn't allow her to go anywhere as punishment. Now she wants to do better. Her mother is obviously concerned enough about her education to limit her activities when she does badly, or at least she did so last year. Ms. Dunbar is not simply ignoring Xena's performance. What she does to influence it we will see.

Xena's newspaper reading is limited to the comics twice a week, so she probably has little idea of what is happening in this complex world. She likes to read mysteries and fairy tales, so she has some interest in books. Her family and friends are most important to her so, like many of the other families, Xena's is in a position to greatly influence her development and her educational success. Race is not something about which she thinks much. She has "a lot of friends of other races. They act like everyone else." Unlike her mother but like virtually all of the other students, she does not see race as a problem or burden. While this is positive in our diverse society, it may well be temporary. The students may be too young to experience the negatives, and they live in Evanston, which is not only a diverse community but prides itself on its diversity and its tolerance. In any event, they do not see race as a problem.

Xena receives help with her schoolwork from her mother and a sister when she asks for that help. A number of the students who do average or very well receive help whether they ask or not. In fact, their parents are involved in their schoolwork almost every evening, thereby showing the importance of that schoolwork and also interacting with their children. Xena says that her mother is at church a great deal, which apparently limits her availability to help. If she could change one thing about her family life, it would be that her father, now living in the South, would be back with the family. In fact, her brother, John, would like to move to the South to live with the father. If she could be any one person in the world, that person would be Maya Angelou, the black poet, because she likes poetry. She thus wants to be like someone who is in a sense like herself, a black female who likes poetry. Her self-esteem may well be positive.

The Observations

The first time the observer met with the Dunbar family was at Family Focus, where Xena and her eleven-year-old brother, John, go every day after school to await the arrival of their mother. At this meeting Xena's older sisters, Lucile and Terri, were also present. They all played the board game Sorry and/or watched television until Ms. Dunbar arrived at about 5:15. Ms. Dunbar informed the observer that she attended Bible study meetings every Friday and church choir rehearsal every Monday and Wednesday, so the only good weekdays for the observations were Tuesday and Thursday. The church seems to play a significant role in the life of Ms. Dunbar, which might influence the manner in which Xena is raised by stressing discipline, sacrifice, responsibility, the future, and a strong sense of right and wrong, all of which play a positive role in school performance.

Indeed, while the observer and Ms. Dunbar spoke, Xena threw a paper wrapper out of the window and was quickly chided by her mother: "What have I told you about littering? If you do it and another person does it . . . ," implying not only that individual actions add up, but also that we are responsible for our actions. She apparently stresses discipline and responsibility. Before they all left Family Focus, Ms. Dunbar looked through a pile of donated clothes and books, asking her children to do the same and emphasizing the books to Xena. She then mentioned visiting another daughter who is away in college that weekend and noted to the observer that she was not ignoring her but that her mind was off in many different directions at that time. Ms. Dunbar appears to be a thoughtful lady, and she seems concerned with Xena's reading habits.

Ms. Dunbar has many things about which to be concerned, including the fact that one of her daughters, in high school, is pregnant. That daughter and Ms. Dunbar began a somewhat heated discussion about the price of a baby crib, with the daughter saying that she had seen a nice crib for three hundred dollars and her mother remarking that that was too expensive. "What do you want my child to sleep on, the floor?" responded the daughter. "No, I just want you to get a cheaper crib. One for a hundred dollars or less," said Ms. Dunbar, who then told a Family Focus worker that all of her children had slept with her in the same bed. Clearly, life had not been and is not now particularly easy for the Dunbars.

As they all left for Ms. Dunbar's car, Xena was holding a copy of *Little Women* and turned to the observer to say, "I love to read." At this point this love is not reflected in her reading grades. Her brother, John, also left with three different books, indicating that he intended to try to read them all. At 5:30 the observer confirmed the date and the time of the next meeting and left.

This next meeting began at Family Focus at 5:20 with the observer and Xena working on the questionnaire. A few minutes later, Ms. Dunbar arrived and after informing Lucile, one of the daughters in high school, that she was present, she again began to look through the pile of donated clothes. She then told the observer that the family was moving to the location close to the West Side to get away from a neighborhood she considers dangerous. The neighborhood has problems with gangs and kids on the streets doing drugs, according to Ms. Dunbar. Once the wayward kids cut her telephone line, which was a serious problem because her family was the only one in the building with a telephone. She then told the observer to "stick close" when they got to the apartment building. Ms. Dunbar is a thoughtful and conscientious mother struggling to make it. She apparently wants her children to do well, but it is not yet clear that she really knows how to support this. Xena is, after all, doing very badly in school, and her teenage daughter is pregnant. Still, she does have a daughter in college despite having a child, and she encourages Xena to read.

As they were all about to leave Family Focus, Ms. Dunbar informed the observer that her car was full of boxes, reflecting the imminent move, and space was therefore at a premium. The observer offered to take someone in her car, and both Xena and John asked to go with the observer. During the drive to the apartment, the observer learned about the family: Terri is seventeen, Lucile is fifteen, John is eleven, another sister is twenty and lives away from home, and another sister attends college. The observer was also told that Terri and Lucile are both on the honor roll in high school. If this is in fact the case, I am beginning to wonder about Xena's grades. Her mother stresses responsibility and reading, Xena has a sister in college full-time, and her mother clearly is attempting to place the family in a safer, better environment, showing that she is concerned about their welfare and that she is thoughtful. Still, Xena does badly in school. We see some indications that Ms. Dunbar tries to do the things needed to support a student doing well, but the student does not respond. Perhaps it is too early to draw conclusions.

The observer's first impression of the apartment was that it was messy and cluttered. It was dusty, and there was paint peeling all over. Ms. Dunbar excused the mess by pointing out that the family was in the process of moving. Cracked floors and peeling paint, however, are functions of lower income and not of moving. At one point Ms. Dunbar said to the observer, "This place is depressing." When asked where they had lived before this she replied, "In another depressing place." Fighting poverty and feeling unsafe are difficult enough. Having also to do well in school then becomes a very trying assignment. As we have seen, a number of students manage this, but it is not at all easy.

A visiting friend of Lucile had gone outside. When Ms. Dunbar realized that Lucile was not in the room, she yelled to her: "You want to go outside. Go. You know how dangerous it is. I am not going to bury a child of mine. If you get shot I'm going to cremate you cause I am not going to see a child of mine lying in a coffin. Go. You want to go. Go." Lucille put on a jacket and left. This is a mother trying hard to raise and protect her family, apparently without very much help. She then turned to John and asked to see his homework. But when he told her a few minutes later that she could look at it, she said to him, "I got my education. It's your turn." So while she indicates that she is concerned enough with John's education to want to see his homework, when she has the chance she passes with a rather snide remark. Unlike many of the parents of the students doing average or very well, she does not really work with her son on his work. During this visit Xena was not seen doing any schoolwork, nor did Ms. Dunbar ask about her school day or her schoolwork.

Most of the time during this visit was devoted to packing for the move, with the observer helping and engaging in conversational topics ranging from garage sales to the dolls collected by Ms. Dunbar to the size of the new apartment: three bedrooms. Ms. Dunbar mentioned that the quality of life in Evanston was much better in the past because "people were close." This is really a reflection of the stability of neighborhoods in the past. That stability is essentially gone from many areas, and this makes the process of education all the more difficult.

At 7:30 the observer said that she had to leave. As she stood near the door, she heard a great deal of noise from children shouting and playing in the hall. "Those parents don't care. Those parents are no good and they let their children play in the hallway," remarked Ms. Dunbar. She is a woman interested in discipline and responsibility. Still, Xena was not observed doing any schoolwork or heard discussing school, not did she have any interaction with her mother that might be considered loving or caring or supportive.

The next observation began at Xena's middle school at 2:45, the time Xena leaves school. For the most part during this observation Xena talked and played with several black friends from her school while they all walked to Family Focus. They laughed about the school pictures they had received that day, they joked about a boy, and they talked about an ice skating trip with Family Focus. There was, however, no mention of schoolwork or academics. After one student used a profane word, she was chided by Xena and told "There's a grown-up here," referring to the observer. The discussion turned briefly to a student whose house they were passing, and they then called out to that student, who peeked out of a window and then came outdoors to talk. Xena said to her, "I haven't seen you for four days." Apparently she had not been to school for four days.

The students then talked about the "cart man," a man who gathers shopping carts and talks to himself. There was a brief stop at a convenience store for candy, and then they arrived at Family Focus, where they checked in. Xena then went to the sixth-grade room rather than the seventh-grade room because she thought that room was more quiet, and she wanted to work on her math homework. She had missed math class that day due to an accident in gym that resulted in a trip to the nurse's office. She didn't have any other homework because she had had tests that day and her teachers, according to her, don't give homework when the students have testing. Xena completed the homework with the help of the observer at 4:20, at which time the observer left.

Xena appears very much like many other twelve-year-olds after school. She seems more interested in her friends and playful activity than in school, though at one point on the way to Family Focus she was concerned that she might have forgotten to bring her book for book club and was relieved to find that she had not. The next observation began at Family Focus at 4:05 with the observer waiting for Xena to finish her book club meeting. Xena showed the observer the five books she had received from the book club and explained that the students simply select the books they want from the shelves in the book room. The students in the club also maintain a journal in which they write what they learn from their readings, and Xena showed her journal to the observer. She then showed her a book of poetry written by students who attend Family Focus, including her sister Lucile. One of her poems, "Excuse Me," contained the lines: "excuse me for not wearing Tommy or

Guess"; "excuse me for being a size eleven and not a size six"; and "excuse me for not having long hair." Lucile is responding to the pressure to wear designer clothes, to be a small size, and to have long hair, all of which are unlikely when one is poor and black. Still, the pressure is there, and the young people facing that pressure must find ways to cope with it while doing well in school, growing up, and trying to maintain positive self-esteem. Many teenagers face a great deal of pressure, but it is perhaps more difficult for those who are poor and black. They often cannot afford the trendy clothes without great sacrifice, the hair of the girls is likely to be short and, given their diets, there is a good chance that many will be somewhat heavy. Lucile's work expresses her feelings and defiance about all of this.

A few minutes after beginning to write in her journal, Xena announced that her mother had arrived. Ms. Dunbar explained that the brakes on her car had failed and that she had been given a ride to Family Focus by a friend. The observer then offered to take them all back to the apartment. Ms. Dunbar called home to see if Lucile, who had the keys to the apartment, was there, but there was no answer. She decided to go home anyway, hoping that someone from the apartment complex would let them into the building. During the trip there was talk about schools but no discussion of Xena's schoolwork or school experience in particular and no interaction between Xena and her mother. They saw Lucile in front of a store near the apartment building and asked for the keys, which she finally found.

The apartment was even more chaotic on this visit, with more moving boxes piled all over. Xena asked her mother to sign a school field trip form and showed her the five books she had gotten from Family Focus. Ms. Dunbar said nothing about the books, thereby missing an opportunity not only to let Xena know that she supported her reading efforts but also to interact with her in a positive and caring manner. Xena also showed her the poetry booklet and pointed out Lucile's poems, to which Ms. Dunbar responded with a pleased smile and a question to the observer about her response to the poems. Ms. Dunbar did not, however, say anything to Xena about the poems. She seems almost to interact only when she must with Xena and then in a rather strict and uncaring manner. At one point during this visit, Xena went to get a box from her room that she said was full of toys, only to have her mother tell her that she was too old for toys. When John asked her whether she wanted to play a video game on the television, her mother said firmly, "No, turn it off." While there is certainly nothing wrong with a mother telling her children to turn off a game, this turns out to be the manner in which Ms. Dunbar typically talks to her children. It is strict and almost always businesslike, and rarely is there an opportunity for interaction. It is generally one-way.

The observer and Ms. Dunbar discussed a variety of things, including Ms. Dunbar's job, people at work, and prices for prescriptions, while Xena ate a sandwich and continued packing. She did no schoolwork, nor did she discuss any schoolwork or activities with her mother during the visit. While this visit took place just two weeks before the family was to move, Xena still went to school and still had schoolwork to do, but it does not appear to have been a high priority. The observer left at 7:10, with Ms. Dunbar and Xena watching to make certain that she got to her car safely.

The next observation began at Xena's school at 2:45. As the observer waited outside for her, she was joined by several of Xena's friends, whom she had met the last time she visited the school. As they all walked to Family Focus, there was a great deal of laughter and playing. When they arrived they all signed in, and one of the Family Focus staff members told them to start their homework, but Xena said that she had little to do and proceeded to write on the chalkboard. When pushed by the staff member regarding the schoolwork, Xena indicated that she was almost finished with the work, even though she had done almost none of it.

A bit later Xena and two others went to the book club, followed by the observer. After they had spent an hour or so reading aloud and completing worksheets concerning metaphors and similes, Ms. Dunbar arrived, and Xena left with her mother. After some discussion about which of the children would ride with whom, Terri left with the family van, and Xena, her mother, and John left with the observer for the apartment.

During the drive Ms. Dunbar talked quite a bit about how happy she was to move, to get out of the present neighborhood, in which two young people had been shot the previous week. This neighborhood, according to police data, is one of the two most dangerous in Evanston, the West Side being the other (Evanston Police Department 1999).

After they arrived Xena popped popcorn and began to watch television, while John began to work on a school worksheet. His mother asked to see the worksheet and helped him with prepositions, with which she had some troubles, but she kept trying though becoming increasingly frustrated. Soon John stopped the schoolwork and began to watch television. "Stop looking at the television," admonished Ms. Dunbar. "Your teacher has been calling me too often lately, and it is going to stop. Two wrongs do not make a right. Don't give me that. Don't tell me that you weren't doing anything, and it was all other people. Don't lie to me." John insisted that the source of the problems about which the teacher was calling was other people, though he was caught mocking his teacher. Ms. Dunbar scolded him, "You don't know how to do your homework. Look at you, you haven't done one problem by yourself. You don't know how to do it because you weren't paying attention. You were too busy making fun of her. Your teacher is a human being. Do you want people looking at you and thinking you're a little nappy-headed black boy? You need to learn proper English." "The teacher didn't explain it," said John, "she just gave the worksheet."

Ms. Dunbar is clearly concerned not only about the quality of the schoolwork done by John but also about his behavior in school, and she makes sure that John knows this. By this time she was yelling at John and he had begun to cry, still insisting that he was unfairly blamed for everything. His mother was having none of this. She wanted him to accept responsibility for his actions. She then turned to Xena and asked about the popcorn. When Xena said that she had eaten it all, her mother angrily told her that it was rude not to offer it to others. Ms. Dunbar seems to be trying to raise her children to follow a straight and narrow path, to be thoughtful, and to pay attention to school. Yet throughout all Ms. Dunbar's yelling and John's crying, Xena watched television and did no schoolwork. Neither John or Xena seems strongly motivated regarding school or schoolwork. Xena seems to think that she must attend school in order to do well in life, but doing well in school is another matter, and her mother does not seem to require this.

John then turned his attention to a television game, while Xena told her mother that basketball tryouts were beginning at school. Her mother responded that when she went to see Xena practice a few years ago, Xena had spent the entire time laughing instead of playing ball. It is not clear that she takes her extracurricular activity seriously, and given her grades it is not clear how long she will be allowed to play ball. Her mother talked about how she used to play softball in school and how good her team was. Ms. Dunbar seems to devote a great deal of time remembering her youth and upbringing.

It is almost as though she compares her youth to that of her children and wants them to have it better, though she is not clear about what she needs to do to help bring this about. She is stern and strict, but Xena does almost no schoolwork, little housework, and little outside of the house that might build a sense of responsibility, cooperativeness, leadership abilities, or self-esteem. The book club at Family Focus might help, but it seems to be a way to occupy the time until her mother arrives, and her mother pays little attention to Xena's involvement. None of this is a way to turn out a high-achieving student and is not at all similar to what we see among the average or high-achieving families.

The next observation began at Family Focus at 5:00, and at this one the observer was introduced to the two-year-old daughter of the twenty-year-old sister who is living on her own. So it appears that there will soon be four teenage mothers in the family, and as we know, teenage motherhood does not bode well for educational success. It is interesting that Ms. Dunbar seems so strict in her talking with her children, seems like such a stern disciplinarian, yet she has two daughters who were teenage mothers and another who is about to become one. The sternness and the discipline did not prevent this. This time the observer drove John, Xena, Lucile, and the older sister's child to the new apartment. While it is larger than the older apartment, it is still small, and Xena and John share a bedroom. When they arrived Xena told John to turn on the television to the Disney channel and began to talk to the observer about her favorite books, including *The Secret Garden*. Later Ms. Dunbar told the observer that she was happy about the move because it was safer in the new neighborhood. There was small talk about Halloween before Xena asked to bake a cake, only to discover that the oil and the mixing bowl had been left at the old apartment. The observer said that she would drive someone to the grandparents' house to get what they needed after Ms. Dunbar said that she did not have the money to purchase the items. The grandparents were very cordial and friendly. They also supplied the bowl, the oil, and ten dollars to Terri.

When they arrived back home, Xena and the observer started making the cake. While there was a great deal of small talk among Xena, the observer, Ms. Dunbar, and John, none of the talk concerned school or education. When the cake was finished, Xena went to watch television and her mother, John, Terri, and Lucile dressed to go back to the old apartment to pick up boxes. They all said fond good-byes to the observer and left. The observer left at 8:00. Again, Xena showed no sign of doing schoolwork, and her mother said nothing to her about it. They were happy to deal with the move, but no one paid any attention to the issue of education.

The next visit began at Family Focus as well, this time at 5:20 and ending at 7:40. The observer met John, Terri, and Xena there and after a bit of small talk drove Xena and John to the new apartment, because Ms. Dunbar had gone to Chicago. On the way John mentioned that he wished there were basketball courts near the apartment. In response to a question from the observer, he said that there were none near the old apartment, but that hadn't mattered since he was not allowed to go out anyway. His mother thought it was too dangerous. Lucile let them in, and Xena prepared a sandwich for her dinner. For the rest of the evening she watched television. At one point her sister Lucile asked why the dishes weren't washed, and Xena said that she would wash them, but Lucile responded, "If I don't do them, they won't get done." None of the children seem to do many household chores or have much responsibility. This visit the apartment was a mess, with clothes and other items spread all around. Given that the family had recently moved, perhaps this was to be expected. Perhaps we should also have expected by now that Xena would do no schoolwork that evening, either.

When the observer asked Xena how well she was doing in school, she responded that she was doing "okay" but was struggling in one class. She also said that she was planning to enter a math contest at Family Focus. Given her math grades, this is interesting. Xena is controlled and cooperative, and there are indications that she has positive self-esteem and some leadership skills. When she and her friends walk from school together, she is the one who sets the behavior standards, the one who admonishes the others for swearing in the presence of adults. She may well be the leader of her group of friends, but she is not involved in the type of activities that generally help to develop those skills. She is confident enough to tell her friends what to say and do, which may suggest that her self-esteem is not that low. These attributes do not appear to carry over into the classroom, however. But how can they when she does almost no schoolwork and does not seem to realize the importance of doing well in school? Her mother seems to want her to do well enough to get through high school and then find a "good" job. There was little mention of education beyond that. Xena pays little attention to school and her mother not a great deal more.

During the next visit, however, when Terri mentioned that a girl in her high school class was about to have a second baby, Ms. Dunbar began to explain to Terri, with Xena listening, "It's important to stay in school. Not just high school. You need to go further than high school." Terri replied that she knew this. So it seems that Ms. Dunbar is aware of the value of education, and not just middle school and high school education, but she does not seem to quite understand just how to translate that interest and awareness to Xena in such a way that it makes a difference in her performance. When Terri asked Ms. Dunbar if she could use the van, Ms. Dunbar replied "no" in a rather harsh tone. In fact, while she clearly cares for her children, she tends to speak to them without much affection and rather sternly much of the time. This does not allow for very much caring interaction. She seems to be a woman who understands that life is often very difficult for the poor and for blacks, and she doesn't have much time for niceties. This means that her children do not spend much time talking with her or relying on her for support.

Ms. Dunbar told the observer how one former coworker asked her, "Why are your people so lazy?" She went on, "Can you believe that she said that to my face?" "So I said, first of all, there are lazy people in every race." Another former coworker frequently addressed her by saying, "Hi, girl." She informed the woman that she was not a girl, that she had five children and should be treated with respect. She is aware of the difficulties that often go along with her position and wants her children to avoid that position, but does not really seem aware of what she must do to bring this about, at least not with John or Xena.

About this time Xena and John began to argue because he had poured milk back into a carton, and Xena thought this was wrong. They shouted at one another for a while, and Ms. Dunbar responded, "It's okay for them to fight. It's good for them. They think they're all tough, but you know when they get out of the house they're not." This may be a good lesson for a tough world filled with crime and discrimination but does not work very well in the middle-class world of school, where cooperation and discipline are valued. A bit later Ms. Dunbar said that she had heard enough and issued something of a threat to them if it didn't stop. They stopped the arguing and shouting quickly. She then told the observer how John had gotten into trouble with a teacher for using the word "bogus." The teacher considered it a "bad word" and didn't like John's attitude. Ms. Dunbar considered this "too strict." It may well be, but it is also what is expected, and if a student says things that bother a teacher, the teacher is likely to take offense. If the parent defends the student, the student may well continue in the behavior. This leads to trouble, and the student should be made aware of this. John was not. At 7:10, after several other stories from Ms. Dunbar that emphasized how unfair and insensitive the world can be, especially toward blacks and the poor, the observer prepared to leave.

During the next visit, which began at 5:00 at Family Focus, Xena excitedly showed her mother and the observer a booklet made of construction paper she was preparing for a class. She said that she also needed some clay for the project, for which she was constructing a diorama. While she for once seemed genuinely concerned with a school assignment, it was more an artistic work than an academic concern. Although the two are certainly related, her grades in language arts, reading, Spanish, and math suggest that she should concentrate on these subjects, but we saw no evidence that she did so over two months.

When she left Family Focus, Xena went to a nearby store to buy the clay and then returned home. John asked his mother what had happened to the television in his room and Ms. Dunbar told him that she had removed it because he watched too much television. John, now angry, replied, "Man, I'm going to live with my father." His mother answered, "If he wanted you he would have taken you by now. Did you do all your homework? Bring it here so I can see it." She again expresses her interest in John's schoolwork, but she rarely does this with John and almost never with Xena. On this occasion, however, she went over his math assignment with him though, as she had done before, she asked the observer for help. Still, working with the student shows him how important school is and that his mother takes it seriously. It goes beyond the talk that education is important.

Xena, meanwhile, was making a Mayan village out of the clay and indicated that she had chosen this assignment because it was easy. The rest of the visit was spent working on Xena's project and talking to Terri about her unborn baby.

The observer wrote in her final summary of her nine visits with the Dunbars: "I learned about her [Ms. Dunbar's] fear of living somewhere where she couldn't let her children go outside. She had to worry about guns, gangs, and drugs. I learned about struggling financially to make ends meet. Most importantly, [Ms. Dunbar] showed how she was capable of maintaining order in a chaotic life." Without question, life is an everyday struggle for the Dunbars and for most of the families we have studied for this research. Paying the rent, paying the utility bills, finding food, avoiding gangs and drugs are all high priorities—and not always easy to do. Maintaining structure and order in this environment is not a simple task. Still, order and structure seem to be characteristics of the home environment that help students to do well in school.

Ms. Dunbar struggles to maintain these characteristics, but more often than not she has a great deal of trouble. There is no real order regarding dinner or other household functions. There is little in the way of serious household responsibilities. A successful order allows predictable schoolwork times and an environment conducive to that work; responsibilities help to underline discipline and a sense of school responsibility. There is very little discussion in the Dunbar household of any aspect of school or Xena's role in it.

Ms. Dunbar, while strict, is very generous and caring. She must help her children survive in an environment that in many ways is hostile, and it seems that school is rather low on the list of priorities. The family is aware of the importance of education, but on an everyday basis there seems to be more important things, and Xena spends much more time watching television or with her friends than on her schoolwork. She has no schoolwork routine at all, and while she is a thoughtful and sensitive young lady, she does not seem particularly interested in her future or in the role of education in shaping that future. While her self-image appears to be positive, we saw little to suggest internal control, though her mother certainly tries to control her life and environment.

Overall, the family is not as middle class as a number of the others in terms of attitudes or values, though it is not as far from that position as many readers might have imagined given their circumstances. While I am not studying teenage pregnancy or its impact on education, nor am I studying Xena's sisters, I must note that three of them are or will be teenage mothers and that teenage pregnancy certainly does not improve the chances of educational success. In the case of at least two of the sisters, the pregnancy has not resulted in leaving school—indeed, one of them has gone on to college. Still, this makes their educational lives much more difficult and complicated and gives Ms. Dunbar that much more with which to cope.

We did not see any evidence that Xena is involved with the church or with other extracurricular activities in which she takes a real interest, for than matter. There was some discussion of basketball, but we did not see any real participation. So, we did not see the activities that help to build leadership skills, discipline, responsibility, self-esteem, and a sense of right and wrong. Finally, Xena and her mother do not verbally interact the same way as most of the students who do well in school. There is little playful or supportive interaction. Ms. Dunbar very clearly cares for Xena, but her interaction is typically strict and somewhat harsh, perhaps a reflection of the life they live. On the other hand, Xena addresses her mother in a very loving and caring manner and seems close to the other family members. They do not sit down to discuss Xena's concerns in a loving, sensitive way.

CAMILLE DUNN

Camille Dunn is a fifteen-year-old high school freshman who, like most of the others, lives on the West Side. (In fact, ten of the twelve families live within five or six blocks of one another, and eleven of the twelve live within walking distance of one another.) The Dunn household has two adults and three children, including Camille, and has a family income at the lowest Family Focus level. Her grades for the first marking period were mostly C's, but for the next she had three D+'s, two C's, one D, one F, and one B. In the major subject areas she received mainly C's and D's. It is safe to classify her performance as lower achieving.

Her mother, Ms. Dunn, is thirty-five and has lived in Evanston for twenty-five years, two in the current house. Her husband works for a nearby suburb in a maintenance position, and Ms. Dunn is a housewife. They both graduated from high school. Ms. Dunn indicates that Camille's education is "very important" to her because she wants to see her "be somebody"—graduate from college and make something of herself. Again, education is tied to a better life, not to self-development or to the value of knowledge. For the poor, it is about doing better than the parents, who typically lack the education. Ms.

Dunn says that she tries to encourage Camille to do well by helping her with homework and by teaching her to be unafraid to assert herself. She indicates that she does not visit Camille's school very often because she wants to "give her a break." Apparently, she wants to avoid pressuring her daughter in terms of her education. This may sound generous and concerned, but possibly it is not what is needed if Camille is to do well in school. When she visits the school Ms. Dunn says that she feels "happy, because she's having fun. That's what's important." This suggests that Ms. Dunn may well have misplaced priorities where Camille's education is concerned. It is certainly desirable for students to have fun in school; however, it is far more important for them to learn and do well.

When asked whether anything stands in Camille's way of obtaining a good education, Ms. Dunn answered money and boys. As do several of the other parents, she thinks that lack of money could be a problem but uniquely, she believes that Camille's interest in boys could be a hindrance. Obviously, money is a considerable problem for the poor, especially for college costs, but the interest in boys is a different kind of problem. Ms. Dunn believes that some of the children in her neighborhood try to stop Camille from doing well in school but that Camille is strong enough to prevent this. Camille herself doesn't really think that this happens, and given her school performance it is unclear why any other students would try to limit her school performance. Her mother is not sure how it happens, but she thinks that it does. It appears that Ms. Dunn may be imagining this to some degree.

She does not believe that any adults at Camille's school try to stop her from doing well, so it seems that the school is not the problem here. Her mother also seems to think that Camille's future is in her hands, limited only by boys and money, at least one of which she controls. Ms. Dunn believes that race and/or discrimination plays a role in her life but has no comment on how this happens. It appears that she wants to point a finger at race but is not clear on how to do so. She says that she was never concerned about much as she grew up "because I was a saint." She was popular and active and, despite having to struggle financially, she and her family made it, they survived. We see from this background information that she was poor growing up and is poor now and that she does not mention education in her description of her past.

In raising Camille, she believes discipline and respect are important; she wants Camille to be a "good person." She says that she reads the newspaper every day and reads a book every two or three weeks. If this is true, then she has some knowledge of current events, which could serve not only to enlighten her but to help Camille's own mastery of current events. Ms. Dunn relies on herself when she has a problem. She is the first respondent to fail to mention another family member or God or the church. This indicates a great deal of self-sufficiency on her part and, along with a few of the other answers, raises the question of whether she expects Camille to also be this self-sufficient and therefore not to rely on her. If so, Camille is under a great deal of pressure.

Camille herself says that she likes boys, art, and math about school. There may well be reason for her mother to worry about boys hindering Camille's performance. Ms. Dunn seems to do little to address this potential problem and has apparently done little to help Camille place this interest in perspective. Camille's grades in art and math are average, and it would seem that she might do better given her interest in these subjects. On the other hand, she is doing below average in almost everything else, so perhaps she does well in subjects she can handle and/or likes those subjects in which she can do well. She dislikes history, in which she is doing badly, and computer classes, where she does fairly well. The relationship between her preferences and her performance is therefore not altogether clear.

Camille thinks that she is doing well in school and states that school is very important to her because "I need to have an education." Not only are her notions about her success overrated, but she is unclear on the value of education to her. She wants to have an education because she needs it. Needs it for what? Like a number of the other students, however, she wants to attend both college and graduate school and sees no obstacles in her way. So she does not seem attuned to the reality of her performance and its effect on her continued education, but she does believe that she is in control of her future.

Camille reads a newspaper "every weekend," and her family and school are most important to her. This puts her family in a position to greatly influence her life, her educational life in particular. She was especially close to an eighth-grade teacher because she "could talk to her about anything." When asked whether she thought much about race or discrimination, she responded that she did, but that she did not know why. Like her mother, Camille seems confused at times about things that should not be so confusing. She says that her parents help her "anytime I need help" with her schoolwork and that is enough help for her. Camille thinks that her family life is fine, and she does not need to change anything about it. She also does not want to be any other person in the world, suggesting that she thinks fairly highly of herself. It may well be, however, that Camille is simply not thinking and wants to say very little. Her answers do not reflect a great deal of thought.

The Observations

The first visit to the Dunn household was very brief: essentially an opportunity for the observer to meet Ms. Dunn, Camille, and a sister and brother of Ms. Dunn. I mention it only because the observer noticed evidence of possible drug use by the adults, and this of course has serious implications for Camille's upbringing and education. Parents involved in drugs are unlikely to be able to offer the support, guidance, and direction children need to do well in school.

The next visit began at the Dunn house at 4:30 but quickly shifted to Family Focus when it was discovered that Camille was on her way there rather than at home. (Our observations of Camille were unusual in that they shifted in venue from Family Focus to home, unlike the sessions with the other subjects, which mainly took place in their homes.) At Family Focus Camille entered a homework room and began laughing and talking with several other students. Some of the girls were doing homework, but once Camille squeezed into a group of teenage girls at one table, they all began to laugh and joke. She did no homework during the session, which ended with a lecture by one of the counselors. The Dunn home is a small apartment showing signs of wear and water damage. There is little furniture. Rarely was dinner served while the observer was there, and never did Camille do her homework. Rather than eating at home, she often stopped at a local grocery store for treats on her way to or from Family Focus. Her mother was often not at home or left while the observer was there, leaving only Camille, her younger sister, and the observer. Other times at Family Focus some students did their homework, but Camille socialized or bought food from a vending machine. During one observation Camille's parents were both home, and her mother appeared to be preparing dinner. It was, according to the observer, the first time that she was seen performing "any type of motherly or wifely activity." A few minutes after the observer arrived and exchanged pleasantries with Mr. Dunn, Camille and her two sisters arrived. They immediately left and started toward Family Focus, though as usual, they stopped at the local grocery store to purchase treats or junk food.

As they walked the girls discussed sexual topics and boys, with Camille mentioning her boyfriend. The observer noticed what he thought were drug sentries on one of the corners on their route. When they arrived they entered a room with a number of other students, and five of the group of fifteen worked on their schoolwork. Camille was not one of the five. Soon someone began to play a music tape, and everyone paid more attention to the music than to schoolwork.

When the Dunns left some time later, the observer followed them out but said his good-byes and remained behind them so that they could not see him. The sisters joined a group of boys and girls on a nearby corner. Several members of the group passed what appeared to be a marijuana cigarette back and forth while Camille and her sisters left the group and moved toward their apartment. Several cars pulled up to the group, stayed a few minutes, and left. The observer was fairly certain that drugs and money changed hands.

The Dunn girls entered the lobby of their apartment building, but a few minutes later Camille and one of her sisters reemerged and moved toward the group on the corner. Soon someone yelled, "Scatter!" and a police car pulled up as the group dispersed. The point of all of this is not only that drugs are sold and used very close to Camille's apartment, but that she seems quite comfortable with the people selling and using the drugs.

We visited the family six times and never saw Camille doing any homework, never heard her mother or father mention school, never saw any interaction between Camille and her mother or father, and never saw any sign of familial support. The household had no structure at all, and Camille appears to be raising herself, with no adult paying much attention to her.

Camille is not involved in any extracurricular activities that might help her development and her school performance. She never discussed her future or showed any signs of responsibility. During two of the visits her mother was drinking beer. When dinner was prepared at all, it was the young girls who did it. There was very little to suggest that Camille even attends school. This is, of course, very troubling and very different from any of the other families studied. Camille shows little self-esteem or signs of internal control, though for the most part she was pleasant. She was rather quick to use vulgarities and to curse when she was not around her mother or father, which was most of the time, suggesting little self-control.

The family does not seem to have any real support system, and education was never mentioned except by the observer. It is no wonder then that Camille is doing badly in school. Virtually none of the characteristics of families with successful students or of successful students themselves are present here. The parents show nothing to indicate that they value education—or discipline, for that matter. The student has no responsibility, structure, order, or support from the home, and herself lacks most of the attitudes, values, and characteristics of a successful student. She spent a great deal of time laughing and joking and making fun of others. She seems to lack the self-control needed of a good student and does not have the parental guidance or support to help her to develop it. There is, unfortunately, little to summarize about this student or her family. In short, this is almost the antithesis of an educationally successful family.

PETER EDWARDS

Peter Edwards is a twelve-year-old sixth grader at the same elementary school attended by his cousin Tracey Love (who lives in the same building) and Pierre Baroque. He lives with his mother alone on the West Side and has a family income at the lowest of the Family Focus levels. His grades in the winter quarter were two C's, two C−'s, one D, and a B in computer technology. In the spring his grades had dropped to three F's and two D's, making him easily a lower-achieving student. The comparison with his cousin Tracey Love is interesting. She received mainly B's and C+'s, making her a solid student, while he, living in the same building and interacting with her family all of the time, was a lower-achieving student. So they are both poor, both black, both living in the same community—indeed, the same building—both going to the same school, both members of the same extended family, but they are very different when it comes to school achievement. Why?

Ms. Edwards, Peter's mother, has lived in Evanston for eight years and hails from Nassau, Bahamas. They have lived in their current house for the entire eight years, and she is thirty-eight. She works full-time in the child care business and is a single mother. She completed high school and says that Peter's education is important to her because it will help him to succeed in life. Again, education is important because of what it can do for the child's financial future, not because of what it can do for the development of the child. Ms. Edwards says that she encourages Peter in school by making sure he studies, checking up on his homework, and having him use tutors. I suspect that the tutors are from Northwestern University and work through Family Focus. She visits his school "lots"—that is eight or so times a year—and feels confident and inquisitive when she does so. She is not intimidated or frightened by the teachers; therefore, little would seem to prevent her involvement in Peter's educational process.

According to Ms. Edwards, nothing stands in Peter's way of receiving a good education, and no other students attempt to stop him from doing well. Like most of the parents, then, she believes that Peter's educational future is up to him, is in his hands, which suggests that he should control his life. Also like most of the others, she does not think that her child faces peer pressure to perform badly. Given his performance, there is little for his peers to be concerned about. She believes that one of his teachers did try to stop Peter from doing well by not trying hard enough to connect with him.

It is interesting that few of the parents point a finger at teachers, while much of the country is pushing to somehow improve teachers. These are the parents of the students most likely to have trouble with school, and few of them seem to think that teachers are a problem. While it may be that they are not in a position to properly evaluate the teachers, it is their children we are dealing with, after all, their children whose educations and futures are at stake, and it seems to me that they are the best ones to make these decisions. Without question, there are teachers who do not try very hard to reach marginal students, teachers who believe that these students can't learn and consequently do not teach them. Something must be done about these teachers. Based on what these data show and what most of these parents say, however, the larger problem would appear to lie with the families.

Ms. Edwards comes from a large family and moved to Chicago at age twenty-four. Her family was comfortable; they "saw that others had things we didn't, but we always had food in the cupboard and clothes and shoes, we weren't uncomfortable." If she felt that she needed to mention food and shoes, it suggests that things were not particularly good for her family. She tries to raise Peter in a "Christian environment, with church every Sunday." She urges Bible study and music lessons with the church. She wants Peter to be respectful and positive. This is, then, another family that says it stresses the church as a positive force in the raising of the child. As I have mentioned several times, the church can indeed have a constructive impact on the child given its emphasis on discipline, the future, cooperation, and responsibility, all characteristics that help a great deal in school. It is, of course, one thing to say things in response to a questionnaire and another to actually do them.

Peter's mother says that she reads a newspaper every day and that she reads a book every day. This would make her well prepared to discuss current events with Peter and to urge him to read about and pay attention to these events. She relies on her two sisters and on Peter as a friend when she has a problem. So, like many of the respondents, she turns to her family when problems arise, suggesting that this is another close family, which seems to be the case for many of these poor families.

Peter most likes gym about his school and least likes social studies. He thinks that most of his teachers are "okay." So he doesn't seem to like the academic subjects but has no real problem with the teachers. A dislike for the academic subjects would not bode well for high performance. He would like to transfer schools in order to be with his friends, most of whom attend a school closer to his house. His school is a magnet school quite a distance from his house, suggesting that perhaps his mother thought through the question of what would be best for him and made a conscious choice of schools. If this is the case, it implies that she is a thoughtful, conscientious mother. At this point, of course, this is speculation.

Peter believes that he is doing fair in school, "mostly C's, some D's, and some B's." He actually overrates himself but not as much as some of the other students doing badly. He says that education is important to him because "I want my mom to be proud." This is not about himself or his future but about what his mother wants. This suggests that his motivation is external, not internal, and this can make the educational process difficult because the student may not accept responsibility for his actions. He confirms his mother's belief that no other student has tried to stop him from doing well and says that he studies one to two hours a night. When asked how far he would like to go in school, he replied, "Definitely graduate high school, maybe college, if it's easy. College because my mom will make me." His aspirations would appear to be lower than those of the average and of the high-achieving students, and he clearly doesn't want to have to work too hard. He wants to do what his mother wants him to do—as long as it's easy. This does not bode well for high performances in school, which depend to a considerable degree on the motivation and initiative of the student.

Peter, like most of the others, indicated that there are no obstacles in his way to an education. He believes that he can get where he is going without facing barriers. This suggests confidence but perhaps some naïveté as well. He is, after all, only twelve years old and probably not yet aware of all of the things that could hinder him. Still, the confidence is good. He reads a newspaper twice a week and reads books for fun. When asked what is most important to him in his life, he answered, "To go to the NBA or the Olympics for track." Unlike most of the others, who answered that their families were most important to them, Peter is most interested in an athletic career. He does not seem very interested in school or education, and while his mother is clearly important to him, it is possible that his family does not have the same influence on him that we have seen with many of the others.

To Peter race is not an issue because "that's negative thinking." Like most of the other students, Peter does not want to allow race to hinder his thinking or his life. He does not allow it to get in his way. He says that he receives "lots of help" from his cousin (Tracey Love) and his aunts with his schoolwork when he asks for it, and this is enough help for him. Like almost all of the other students, he is not seeking more help from his family.

If he could change one thing about his family life, it would be that he could dribble a basketball better with his left hand. Of course, this has nothing to do with his family, but it does suggest something about his priorities. Sports may be more important than anything or anyone else—save, perhaps, his mother. If this is true, then we should not expect that Peter will place much emphasis on his education. If he could be one person in the world other than himself, Peter would be his mother "because she cares about everybody." Obviously, he cares a great deal for his mother, which places her in a position to have significant influence on him and his educational life. What she does with this influence remains to be seen.

The Observations

The first meeting with Peter was at Family Focus, beginning at 7:00 P.M. and ending at 8:00. The observer met with Peter and one of the counselors in a homework room. The conversation turned quickly to basketball and the various courts where Peter plays. Peter then began to talk about three "college girls"—Northwestern University tutors who work at Family Focus and were planning to take Peter to downtown Chicago to dinner the next day. When the counselor asked why they simply didn't eat in Evanston, he chided, "You always think of the cheap thing." He went on to add that they would be out until 3:00 in the morning. Peter is quite confident.

A bit later Ms. Edwards arrived and began to talk to the observer about the research project. She is an articulate, thoughtful, well-dressed woman, who on this occasion was carrying a copy of the book *Real Boys,* suggesting an interest in the complexities of raising sons. She was particularly interested in how our research might help Peter's education, saying at one point, "Maybe after you are done he [the author] will be able to tell me some ways to improve Peter's reading scores." She is certainly concerned about his education; she made that concern very clear to the observer. That very morning she had made an unannounced visit to his school to see a reading teacher with whom she is not satisfied. She thinks that the teacher does not try hard enough to reach Peter. Trying is one thing, having a student who cares is another.

Still, Ms. Edwards takes Peter's education seriously. "I will not allow him to attend there," she said, referring to the local middle school attended by most of the middle school students in this research. She does not believe that it is good enough for Peter, and her sister must agree, since Peter's cousin Tracey attends the same magnet school. It required repeated calls to the school superintendent to have Peter admitted. She also said that she prayed quite a bit that he would be "in the right spot." Ms. Edwards, then, behaved as many middle-class parents would: She thought through the best option for her son and then decided how to bring that option to be. While Peter is bused out of his neighborhood, she thinks that this is good for his education. At least she is thinking deeply about his education.

She mentioned that she had sent him to a "private" school in another suburb until transportation became difficult. Given her limited income, one wonders just how "private" this school could have been. Of course, Peter could have received financial assistance. According to his mother, she read to him a great deal when he was very young. It sounds like Ms. Edwards is doing or has done many of the right things to promote good school performances from Peter, yet he is doing very badly. She has thought about the best schools for him, worked to have him admitted, and read aloud to him as a young child. She says that he is not allowed to watch television during the week and that they attend church together on Friday night, Sunday morning, and many Sunday evenings. According to her, "Nothing is too good for my son." So he has the experience of the church, the love, discipline, concern, and sacrifices of his mother—and yet he does quite badly in school.

Ms. Edwards and Peter seem to talk comfortably with one another, with no tension between them. They talked at one point about what Peter would do if his dreams of a life in the National Basketball Association failed to come true. "Well, then, I'll coach a professional team." His mother pointed out that most professional coaches were themselves former pro players. "Well, then, I'll be a janitor," Peter replied. When she made it clear that her son could not be a janitor, he responded, "Well, I'll be a janitor at the United Center," which is the home of the Chicago Bulls professional team. This back-and-forth banter suggests a comfortable interaction between the two, the kind that we find often among parents and children who are doing well in school. But Peter is not one of those students.

The next visit began at 4:45. Peter was at Family Focus doing homework (unlike Camille Dunn, who never did homework at Family Focus—or at home, for that matter). He stopped when he saw the observer, and the two walked to Peter's home to retrieve his backpack, which he had left on his porch. He explained that they couldn't go into the apartment because it was being painted and there was no place to sit. They therefore returned to Family Focus. It is unlikely that there was really no place to sit in the apartment given that there was presumably someplace to sleep. It was, in fact, several visits before Peter actually allowed the observer into his apartment. He might have been embarrassed by his living arrangements.

When they returned to Family Focus, Peter resumed his homework, focusing on math and social studies. Occasionally, he talked to others at the table, mainly the girls and especially Jesse, a fourteen-year-old high school freshman. When an employee called Peter "a player"—that is, a lady's man—he responded, "I'm not a player, I'm just a gentleman." Later, at a bus stop, Peter approached a woman twice his age and asked for a hug and love. Again, here we have a confident young man—and in this case, one who does his homework when he is not flirting with the ladies. Despite his clear interest in the young ladies, he says that he has no girlfriend because his mother wants him to wait until college. We thus see more signs of the influence of his mother and the rather tight control under which she appears to have him. As I have pointed out several times before, this neighborhood may well call for restrictions on the children. Peter lives very close, after all, to the same corners on which the drug users and dealers were seen by Camille's observer.

The observer noted that Peter has trouble concentrating for an extended period of time. While doing his homework he is often fidgeting, humming, or singing. It may be that he has a attention deficit disorder, but I certainly cannot confirm that here. Suffice it to say that he wants or needs to be busy doing something even when he is doing his homework, and that this is not good for the quality of that homework.

The next visit was also at Family Focus, from 4:00 to 7:00. This was the third visit in which no time was spent at Peter's apartment with his family. It would seem that with his aunt living in the same small building, he could have gone home whether his mother was there or not, suggesting again that he was perhaps avoiding his apartment. At the start of this visit, Peter was doing math homework with the help of a tutor, but again his attention span appeared to be very short. He is always talking to others or himself and/or tapping his pencil rhythmically on the table.

This continued until 5:00, when Peter asked the tutor to play a game with him. The tutor, new to the game (Peter had to explain the rules), won both times they played, and Peter handled losing graciously. While the observer and Peter played, the tutor asked Peter what his favorite school subject was. Peter responded, "You know what I wish was a class?" "What, lunch?" "No, I wish the nurse's office was a class." "Why, do you go there a lot?" "Yeah, I play sick and go to the nurse's office. The other day she told me that if her office was a class, I'd be her best student and I'd always be the first one in there in the morning." This does not sound like a young man very interested in his education, despite what his mother says she does and what she indicates is important to her.

Peter went into the hall and talked with everyone, adult or child, who passed by. His social skills are clearly advanced. After half an hour Peter indicated that he wanted to go to his apartment to get a basketball, which he and the observer did. The observer mentioned that Peter seems to spend little time actually in his apartment, and Peter agreed, explaining that he's usually "outside" and goes home only when his mother returns from work after 7:00. This suggests that Peter spends relatively little time with his family, and the influence of his mother or his interaction with her is then in some doubt. Peter retrieved a basketball from his front porch, began to dribble, and then headed toward a basketball court, where he and several others played until dark. He then informed the observer that he had to leave because his mother would be home soon. The observer then departed.

The following week the observer met with Peter, again at Family Focus, at 4:15. Peter was again in the homework room, working without adult help on his schoolwork and flirting with Jesse. While working he sang and played with a male friend. After a few minutes he had apparently completed his homework and went outside to talk with a small group of boys and girls. The observer watched him flirt a bit more, this time with a different girl, and they then discussed his relationship with the girl before going to Peter's apartment to get his basketball shorts, which he needed for a league basketball practice at 5:30.

For the first time the observer entered Peter's apartment. The apartment is clean and uncluttered, though small, and the smell of the recent paintwork lingered. There are pictures of Ms. Edwards, Peter, and the two together all over the apartment. There are a number of magazines such as *Vibe* and *Essence* and several books, including *Growing Up Poor,* in the living room. Peter informed the observer that he sleeps on the couch "almost every night." It is unclear whether this is a function of the amount of space available or of his desire. In either case, it would make a routine or structure rather difficult to maintain given that he would have little space of his own to use.

As they were leaving the building, Ms. Love, Peter's aunt, greeted them, and they all left together, with Peter asking for change and his aunt denying him. Once outside Peter good-naturedly wrestled with Tracey in the small front yard. It is clear that Peter and his relatives get along well and care for one another, but so far there had been little said about school or education and no signs of responsibility. With a kiss from his aunt, Peter left with the observer for the gym, where he practiced basketball for about an hour.

The next visit took place on a Saturday morning at Peter's apartment. Peter's mother was away. Peter turned on the television and began to play a Nintendo game. For the next hour and a half he switched between two different games, occasionally talking to the observer about the games and about a man who had been shot recently near his apartment. Peter knew the man and commented that he had been high on drugs when he was shot. Peter asked the observer whether he thought that he, Peter, lived in a bad neighborhood. The observer responded that it was not much worse than his own neighborhood, and Peter asked, "Do you hear gunshots sometimes?" "Yeah, sometimes," the observer responded. "Me too," said Peter.

After more games and some playful conversation, Peter announced that he had to attend piano practice. The two left for a church located nearby and went to the basement, where the teacher was waiting. Peter is involved in basketball and piano lessons, so he is concerned with extracurricular activities, and they may well confer their various advantages to him. These are not apparent from his grades, however. At this piano lesson, Peter did not seem to pay much attention to his instructor's directions. This made the instructor angry, and he expressed the anger to Peter. As Peter left, the instructor gave him a piece to work on for the next lesson. "Don't waste my time, [Peter]. If you don't want to learn this, I'll just keep it. But if you want to learn this . . ." "Okay, okay, I'll do it," responded Peter.

Peter then went off to play in a basketball game but was not allowed to because "I forgot my money." It seems that the boys on the team have to pay to be a part of the team and/or league, and Peter had failed to pay his. He watched the game in street clothes from the bench, obviously let down. This was another visit during which Peter spent little time in his apartment, no time with his mother, made no mention of school, and did no household chores. When he was in his house he played games. This is all very different from the life of his cousin, Tracey, who lives downstairs and does well in school, and while his mother talks about the importance of education, I have seen little effort on her part to instill this value in Peter. He seems to do what he thinks he must in school to keep her happy, but he lacks a more personal understanding of the importance of education.

Furthermore, his mother spends little time with him, and his routine lacks the order and structure that we see in the lives of most of the students who do well. Peter is confident, demonstrates leadership abilities, and shows some signs of internal control. Indeed, most of the young people close to his age at Family Focus seem to listen and defer to him. Still, he spends so little time at home or with his mother that it would be difficult for him to do well in school. He works on his schoolwork at Family Focus but is constantly interrupted by others or by himself. Basketball seems to be more important to him, though during one visit, as he and the observer waited for an order from a fast food establishment, he mentioned that he plays the drums with his church choir and that he might make a living as a drummer. They then walked to the church, and he went in for choir practice. Later that evening his mother called the observer on the telephone to ask about Peter's whereabouts. She was unaware that he had practice that evening.

Peter seems to do mostly what he wants to do, and that does not include much schoolwork. While his mother expresses her interest in his life and his activities, there is little to suggest that she takes a very active role in his life or that her support is really there in practice. He seems to lack the order and structure that should be provided by his mother. Ms. Edwards cares about Peter's education, but perhaps does not know how to translate that care into actions that will help him to do better. Her sister, living downstairs, seems to have this knowledge and desire. The question of why Ms. Edwards does not is beyond this research, for it involves motivation and other psychological constructs as well as experience, which I cannot measure in this work. This work explores what families do and the impact of what they do on their children's education: Not *why* they do what they do.

The observer had two more sessions with Peter, one at Family Focus and one that began at his basketball game at the local middle school, moved to his church and piano lesson, and ended at the local college football game. At Family Focus Peter shifted between homework and socializing, as usual, and at the piano lesson, which his mother attended, he had his usual admonishment from the teacher for his failure to concentrate or to work hard. "This is what I mean. He does not practice, he doesn't even know the notes. It is simple. Only the right hand, not even the left, but he does not even know the simple notes. He is talented, there is no doubt, but he needs to practice so he can learn. Every week it is like this, maybe five, ten minutes we practice, the rest is messing around." This may well tell the story of Peter and suggest the failure of his mother to provide the support and environment necessary for him to do better. When the lesson was over, Peter, prodded by his mother, thanked the teacher and left the room.

On the way out they met an acquaintance who discussed with Ms. Edwards the possibility that Peter might join her Sunday School class. Ms. Edwards explained that Peter was already enrolled in a class. As the observer and Ms. Edwards walked toward her home, Ms. Edwards confided that Peter does not seem to concentrate on his schoolwork or his church work or his piano lessons for long periods. She seemed very concerned about this and how it might impact on his "being able to take care of himself," which to her would make him a success. She questioned whether she should try to push him into more responsibility if he were not ready for it.

It appears that Ms. Edwards does not expect much, perhaps not enough, from Peter, and that Peter feels he should be able to do what he likes. What he does not seem to like very much, school, he does out of fear of his mother's response. She does not seem to have done a good job of helping him to understand the value of education for his life. The discipline is there but not consistently, and when it is not Peter does what Peter likes. The absence of higher expectations, consistent discipline, and enough responsibility, coupled with no real order or structure in his home environment and little parental support for his educational life, means that not much can be expected from Peter despite his charm and leadership abilities. His future aspirations do not seem to involve much education, and he cannot seem to see how important it is. His mother does little to change this view despite her voiced opinion that education is important.

Most of the students who do well have home lives that are centered around their schoolwork. They have parents who are involved one way or another in that work and who provide the structure and support system that allow the students to focus on school, chores, and extracurricular activities. These elements are missing from the Edwards home, though it is clear that Ms. Edwards loves and cares about Peter. He may well have more freedom than he should if he is to do better in school, and he uses that freedom largely to do the things he likes. Basketball, track, flirting with girls, and playing drums are not bad or wrong, but they don't help Peter to do better in school. He spends little time at home, which should be a supportive, nurturing environment but apparently is not. Ms. Edwards does not ignore him. She attends his basketball games when she can. She went to a piano lesson when she didn't have to. She confronted a teacher on his behalf.

Be that as it may, the supportive home environment (enjoyed by his cousin living in the same building), the order and structure, the emphasis on education, the activities that encourage responsibility—these are not present. Peter has positive self-esteem—indeed, quite positive—and can be cooperative, both of which help in doing well in school. He is, however, lacking in responsibility and discipline and does not particularly value education. Wanting to be a track star or basketball player puts education in an inferior position in his life, and there is little at home to change that, despite his mother's concern. Some of the characteristics of the middle-class family are present here, and a number are not. It is also possible that Peter does indeed have a problem with his attention span. This work cannot determine this. But from what I can judge, there are other problems here in any event, including what seems to be a failure on the part of his mother to engage him in the kind of communication that helps a child feel comfortable and supported, both of which help the student to do better in school.

SUMMARY

When Xena Dunbar was asked why education is important to her, she answered that if you do not have an education, you "can't get a lot of jobs, or you will end up at McDonald's or at a gas station or you'll end up on the streets." It is important to Peter Edwards because "I want my mom to be proud." For Camille Dunn it is "because I need to have an education." None of these students express high educational aspirations or an understanding of the role of education in achieving life goals. They want an education because they must have one to avoid poverty or because it is required. They do not seem to expect much from their lives, and in response they do not put much into their educational lives.

Mycela Falwell thinks that education is important "because it's my future," not because of a specific goal. Her grandmother, like the mothers of the other low achievers, seems to value education but fails to do the things that support higher achievement. There is little consistent discipline in any of the homes of the low achievers. The parents and grandparent talk about discipline, but little was seen during the observations. To a considerable extent the students did what they liked, not what was required of them, and none of them liked schoolwork. In two of the four cases, the parent or grandparent was not much of a presence in the student's life, and in two of the cases, the students seemed to spend more time outside of the home than in it, and they were not spending the time involved in extracurricular activities that developed a sense of responsibility or discipline. In the case of the other two, while they were in the home a fair amount, they spent their time watching television or playing games and not on schoolwork.

In fact, none of the four students devoted much time to schoolwork. The only one who did any real amount of it worked away from home and spent as much time laughing and playing as working. These are students who, when asked what they most like about school, answered, "boys" or "gym" or "socializing." They do not take school or education seriously, and their parents are either uninterested in this or don't know how to alter it. They do not for the most part interact with their children in a way that fosters confidence or a sense of being supported. As a result, only one of the students really seems to have a positive self-image, and he is the only one who seems to feel in control of his life. On the other hand, he does a number of things not because they are good or right, but because he thinks that his mother wants them done.

None of these students have an orientation toward the future conducive to higher achievement in school. One wants to be a professional athlete, and the others just want to get by. Why should a student try to do well in school when getting by requires nothing more than an occasional visit to class, and becoming a professional basketball player requires even less? They have no reason to attempt to do better, and they have parents who provide neither the reasons to succeed nor the means to do so: structure and order. None of the homes of these students have much structure or much order, and there is no real role for educational work in the homes. Nor do these students have responsibilities in the home, which the better students usually do. Having household tasks to perform helps to foster the sense of responsibility that is essential to good school performance.

If a child has no experience of an obligation to do something and do it well, how can a teacher convince that student of an obligation to do schoolwork and do it well? These students have no commitment to learning and no home environment that fosters learning. There is no coming home, going to your room or the kitchen table, and opening the books. No mother asking about your school day, insisting on seeing your homework, and discussing your school day. There is no mother showing interest in your extracurricular activities and telling you to get to bed at a reasonable hour—after your schoolwork and house chores are complete.

In one case the mother seems caught up in drugs and cannot help the student, and the father is occasionally present but is not a factor in the student's life. In another the grandmother may lack the energy, knowledge, and motivation to support, guide, and discipline the child. In another the mother is trying to hold together a family that includes four children at home, one of whom is pregnant, at the same time helping with her two grandchildren. She tries to provide a structured and orderly environment for her children and to administer discipline, but both are difficult given the obstacles she faces. Her children, like several of the low achievers, look at the local social service agency as a home away from home, as a baby-sitter until the mother arrives from work, often too tired to actually mother.

While religion is said to be important to several of these families, it is not clear that it plays much of a role in the lives of the students themselves. We did not see much churchgoing or hear much discussion about the church from these students. As a result, it is unlikely that the discipline, sense of cooperation, and orientation toward the future that religious bodies often foster are nurtured in these students, at least not by the church.

It was somewhat surprising to observe these students spending so little time on schoolwork, expressing so little interest in school-related activities or in their futures, and then to observe so little effort on the part of their parents or grandparents to alter any of this. Again, the adults expressed the interest and concern, but did little to translate words into action that might help these students in school. Admittedly the obstacles are formidable, but those faced by the parents of the high achievers and of the average students are equally tough, yet they raise their children quite differently.

It should be stressed that the parents and grandparents of the low achievers do not for the most part see teachers or the schools as obstacles for their children or grandchildren. They do not indicate that any real changes are necessary in the schools despite all that we hear about how such changes will improve the education of students like those involved with this research. I suggest that the focus is wrong. Yes, changes should be made in schools. Some teachers should be more motivated. Others need to really believe that poor black students can learn. Still others need to learn how to relate better to many of these students. Some schools need better facilities and more supplies. It seems, however, that what is most needed are changes in families and homes. The adults in this study do not believe that the schools are the problems that require changes. Based on this work's findings, neither do I.

The families are very different, as are the performances of the students. While there are a few characteristics of the middle class among these families, particularly the Dunbars, by and large these are not middle-class families. These are not families high in self-esteem and educational aspirations, with a keen sense of the future, a great deal of self-control, discipline, and a sense of responsibility. These are not homes with structure, order, and quiet, all of which are conducive to sound school performances, and the performances are not there. Nor are they homes in which the parents spend much time communicating with or encouraging their children concerning school performance, both characteristics of families in which children perform well in school, according to Mordkowitz and Ginsberg (1987), Clark (1983), and Furstenberg et al. (1999).

FINDINGS AND ANALYSIS:
SO, WHAT DO WE KNOW?

The purpose of this book is to examine how and why some poor black children do well in school yet others, who live in the same community and attend the same school systems, do not. Given that urban education is a vitally important issue that seems to hold a great deal of the nation's attention, it is imperative that we find answers to this puzzle. It is not true that all poor black students do badly in school and could therefore all benefit from the same policy changes. In fact, as we will see in the next chapter, it is unlikely that any of the policy changes being tried now can be successful given that they seem to assume that all of the affected students and families are the same. This book examines the ways in which they are different.

According to Bempechat (1998), "barring serious learning difficulties or mental retardation, all young children have the basic intellectual skills and the potential to learn" (2). Yet some poor black students learn well and perform well in school, and others, though they appear similar in important ways, do not. I selected students who were equally poor, knowing that income affects school performance. Black students do less well than white students, and all of the students in this work are black. They all live close to one another, so the neighborhood should not be a factor. They attend the same two related school systems—indeed, many attend the same school—so differences in the schools should not explain why some do better than others. The biggest differences here are in the families themselves and in the characteristics of the students, which are shaped by the families.

According to Clark (1983), "Increased knowledge of the home functioning patterns in different ethnic communities will enhance the prospect of developing appropriate school policies and procedures for increasing the knowledge levels of all categories of school children, while preserving the integrity of 'the school' and 'the home' in each neighborhood" (213). This work seeks to increase our knowledge of the home/family dynamics in a poor black community to help define what policy changes should be designed to increase the learning of those who need help. I believe that we have learned a fair amount in the process.

As Entwisle, Alexander, and Olson (1997) point out, family and neighborhood resources have a significant impact on student school performances. These authors emphasize the impact on performance in the summer; most others, including me; Clark (1983); and Furstenberg et al. (1999) examine the impact overall. Clark's work is limited to the family, as is my own: Given that the families live in basically the same neighborhood, differences cannot be attributed to significant neighborhood variations. The questions, then, are: What is it about the family that best relates to how the student does in school, and what impact do these things have on the student's performance?

It is not that these poor black children are suffering from inadequate parenting. There are some questions about the rearing of a few of the children in this research, but on the whole it would appear that the children are adequately raised. Still, some of the students do very well in school and others in the same income bracket, the same school, the same neighborhood—indeed, in one case, the same building—do badly. What varies in this work are the family and the home environment. The families of the students who do average work and those of the high achievers have a great deal in common, and both are significantly different from the families of low achievers. Similarly, the students themselves are quite different, and to a significant degree the individual differences stem from the familial differences. The homes of the average and high achievers are relatively quiet, orderly, and structured. There is not a great deal of noise or commotion when the students are at home, and much of the talking at home centers around the students' school concerns, which often include extracurricular activities. In fact, involvement in extracurricular activities is common among the high achievers and the average students, but not among the low achievers: Only one of the low achievers is so involved compared to most of the others.

The order, quiet, and structure create an environment conducive to homework and to the discussions that the parents—always the mothers in our cases—very often have with the students about their schoolwork and activities. One of the higher achievers, Karen Kenner, and her family do not seem to be like most of the others. The house is noisy and disorderly. There is little discussion between the mother and Karen regarding school, and Karen does almost no schoolwork at home. The other high and average achievers come home from their activities and go straight to their schoolwork in a quiet environment or to their household chores and then to their schoolwork. The chores help them to develop a sense of responsibility and order, both of which are very useful in school. After all, if students do not feel that they are really responsible for their grades or their performance, how can we expect them to do well? The good students have home responsibilities and the obligations that go along with extracurricular activities, while the low achievers, with the one exception, have no such responsibilities, and this one student has no home responsibilities.

The parents of the average students are very much involved with the students' schoolwork. That is, they not only ask the students what they need to do that day for the next school day, they often help them on this work. The parents of the high achievers are less involved with the schoolwork of their children, though they have high expectations of them and they do ask about the work. I think that these parents are aware that their children are doing very well and that their help is probably not required. They do, however, express their interest and concern regularly. This is not the case for the parents of those not doing well. These parents (in one case grandparent) indicate their interest and concern on a questionnaire, but it was not seen much during the observations. They seem to say what they think is right but fail to do it. Karen Kenner's mother is much the same, and Karen is, for the time being, a high achiever. I say for now because her grades seem to be going down, and her home environment does not seem supportive.

The parents of the average and high achievers are very supportive of the schoolwork of their children. Indeed, for the most part, the school activities structure the home life. The involvement in extracurricular activities, common to all of the average achievers and three of the five high achievers, helps them to develop leadership abilities, discipline, self-control, and cooperation, all of which help in school achievement (Furstenberg et al. 1999). The average and high-achieving students, with two exceptions, play few games and watch little television on school nights. They spend their time on schoolwork, housework, and discussing school activity with their parents. The low-achieving students tend to devote a great deal of time to television and games and almost none to schoolwork, and their parents and grandparents do almost nothing to change this.

The high achievers and the average students have high educational aspirations expressed both in the answers to the questionnaire and in their devotion to schoolwork, except for the two who do very little schoolwork. One of these two is a fourth grader and has little schoolwork to do, so it is really only one high-achieving student with high aspirations verbally expressed who fails to demonstrate those aspirations in schoolwork, and this one lives in a somewhat chaotic household. The households of the average and high-achieving students demonstrate a great deal of discipline and control—or restrictiveness, as Furstenberg et al. (1999) put it. This may well limit the autonomy of these students, which could be problematic in terms of development. However, given the crime and other dangers of the area in which the families involved in this work live, thoughtful families have little choice. The students who are low achievers have no such discipline or control. They seem to spend a great deal of time and energy doing what they like, not what their parents want them to do.

The average and high-achieving students have positive self-images, are internally controlled, and are oriented toward the future. They seem to believe that they control their academic lives and that their performances are up to them. This is essential for good school performance. The average and high-achieving students are concerned about their futures and appear to link their academic performances and their other school activities to those futures. Their parents also express concern about their futures, but so do the parents of the low achievers. The parents of the high-achieving and average students, however, demonstrate their concern by establishing a home environment conducive to academic pursuits and by emotionally and practically supporting the students' educational work, though in several cases the support is mainly emotional, as the parents do not often actively help with schoolwork.

The parents of the high and average achievers spend considerable time with the students and are always calm and supportive. The parents of the poor achievers spend much less time with the students and are on occasion rather loud and short-tempered. The high and average achievers are expected to pursue college and in some cases post-graduate educations. Indeed, in many families very young children indicate an interest in a post-graduate degree. Clearly, they understand a fair amount about the educational process and expectations, and their family is supporting this understanding. The adults very frequently urge the students to do well in school and relate this achievement to the future. The lower achievers have lower expectations, and their parents say very little to them about school or its relationship to the future. As I have indicated, there is one high-achieving family in which this is not the case. In this family the mother is focused on her own education and future and says little to the daughter about hers. It is not clear how long this student's achievement will last.

As I have suggested above, several of the parents of the good students work with them on their schoolwork. This reinforces the parents' spoken position that school is very important and helps to establish the schoolwork process at home. As the students go along in school, this is less likely to occur. It occurs very little with the lower-achieving students, only in one family, and not consistently in that one.

In short, I define the characteristics of the average and high-achieving students as discipline, positive self-esteem, internal locus of control, high educational aspirations, orientation toward the future, and a sense of responsibility and cooperation. The characteristics of the home environments are order, discipline, quiet, and support. The parents talk with the students about their schoolwork and extracurricular activities, they make certain that the homes are sufficiently structured so that the homework is doable and predictable, and they make certain that the students do their assigned household chores, which build discipline, responsibility, and leadership. Not every family fits this pattern, but almost all do, and not all of the four low-achieving students and their families fit an opposing pattern, but all except for one does, and that one is close.

All of the students and families studied in this work express a belief that education is important, but clearly this belief is not always reflected in performance. It is not true that poor black parents have no respect for or interest in the education of their children. All of these parents and their children indicate this respect. All of these parents respond that they visit the schools of their children and feel comfortable doing so. They all seem to care, but they do not all know what to do to translate this care into better grades and more interest on the part of their children. As we will see later, then, policy should not center around somehow increasing the level of care, but translating existing concern into action for those families in which this can take place. If drugs are an issue, we have a serious problem. If a parent is seldom present, we have another problem. Concern, however, is not the main problem.

Fordham and Ogbu (1986); Neisser (1986); Suskind (1998); Bempechat (1998); Clark (1983); and Comer (1993) all raise the concern that minority students who do not do well in school exert pressure on the good students to perform badly. As Clark puts it, "We also need more research into the *negative* consequences of being a high achieving student in a community dominated by low achieving youth" (214). This society has come to expect little of poor black students in school, and those students have therefore found an excuse—indeed, two excuses, poverty and race—for their poor performances. When other poor black students do well, these two excuses become problematic; the students using the excuses believe that more might be expected of them. They might therefore pressure the students who reject or do not use the excuses. This peer pressure could result in the potentially good students doing badly in order to be accepted by the other students.

As a poor black student, I myself faced several efforts from other students to force me to limit my educational performances. Based not only on these experiences, but also on the work of other scholars mentioned above, I expected to find similar pressure in my research. Bempechat (1998), referring to the work of Fordham and Ogbu (1986), writes: "By third grade, however, [black] mothers found themselves competing unsuccessfully with their children's peers, who became increasingly influential in distracting their children from the good study habits they had installed in them. This scenario appears to play itself out as children get older" (88).

The low-achieving students in this work indicated that they faced no such pressure. On the one hand, this could be expected. After all, these students already performed badly, so their peers really didn't need to pressure them into lowering their performances. On the other hand, it is possible that peer pressure had caused the unsatisfactory performance in the first place. This is very unlikely given that their home environments and their own characteristics are explanation enough for limited school performances. That is, they have lives that work against good school performances. Further, these students are old enough to be aware of such pressure, and they indicated that they face none, with one exception: And in this case what the student, Xena Dunbar, described was more social pressure than academic pressure. A fellow student did not like "my personality" or the fact that Xena had "a lot of friends." This does not seem to be academic pressure.

Of the three average and five high-achieving students, four indicated that they had faced such pressure. In two cases the student revealed that other students tried to convince the good student to skip class "because some kids don't care about their education." In another case a student said that others talk to him during class, and if he responds he gets into trouble. Another student was asked by a peer whether he had done his homework. "When I say yes, [he's] like, 'Oh, man,' but he's not stopping me from doing well." It appears that this young man is resisting the pressure quite nicely: Indeed, all of them are. In fact, in this last case the student, Pierre Baroque, said that the boy raising the question does his homework as well; this may well be a case of competition, which can also be a form of peer pressure. In one of the cases of pressure to skip class the student, Stephanie Adams, said that it exists "because some kids don't care about their education." She clearly cares about her own education, and this is reflected not only in her grades but also in her approach to school.

So some peer pressure exists that *could* limit the performances of some students who are doing well in school but does not appear to do so. The pressure could also exist without the students being aware of it, but this is unlikely given the ages of the students. For the most part, these students have high academic expectations of themselves, high expectations from their parents, and great support from these parents that allows them to resist the pressure—in fact, almost requires them to do so. I expected more of this pressure because the solid students live in a neighborhood that has become largely poor and not very upwardly mobile. Many of the people in the area are not doing well and would not seem to expect others to do so. This could lead to quite a bit of pressure for those doing well. While there is some, there is not as much as I would have predicted.

Then, too, the two related school systems in Evanston have reputations for being quite good, and while the black population of Evanston is substantial, the majority of the students in the systems are middle-income white students. I suspect that these students face pressure from upwardly mobile parents and their peers to do well. So the majority of students in the schools feel the need to perform well, and this may create an atmosphere in which higher performance is expected. If so, the poor black students could also be exposed to this pressure while in school. This would all work against the pressure to do badly. Educators need to be aware of this pressure, however, in order to fully understand what some poor minority students must cope with every day. I will return to this issue in the next chapter when I discuss social policy in light of my findings.

Clark (1983) writes: "The interpersonal communication patterns in these homes [of high-achieving students] tended to be marked by frequent parent–child dialogue, strong parental encouragement in academic pursuits, clear and consistent limits set for the young, warm and nurturing interactions, and consistent monitoring of how they used their time." He goes on: "The interpersonal processes of the communication style used by these parents can generally be described thus: parents consistently use their legal, psychological, and physical power to define 'appropriate' behavior rather authoritatively for family members and then to allocate resources and delegate responsibilities to others in the household" (111). These findings are very close to my own with the parents of the average and high achievers. These parents expect the best of their children, define these expectations to them, hold the children to them, and create an environment in which the students have the best opportunity to meet them. Furstenberg et al. (1999) write: "Youth who are doing better than expected are most likely to have the benefits of a supportive family environment" (133). I find this environment in almost all of the cases of the average and high-achieving students. In short, the families are what most would consider middle class without the education, occupation, or income of the middle class. I will return to this when I turn to the theoretical implications of this work.

For now, let me examine the issue of single-parent versus two-parent households. Clark (1983) studied both kinds of households, thinking originally that the difference in structure might influence student performance and concluding that it did not. Furstenberg et al. (1999) find that poor two-parent households are more likely than single-parent households to have successful students. They conclude, however: "Overall, family structure makes very little difference in the competence or mental health of both African-American and white children, though a strong marriage offers significant advantages on family climate and parental support in both groups" (143). Entwisle and her colleagues (1997) write: "It is becoming increasingly clear that children growing up in single-parent families do not do as well in school as their counterparts in two-parent families. What is not so clear is why family structure affects schooling" (99). Obviously, there are differences in the findings on this topic, and I am not trying to clear up these differences.

It would seem that children in two-parent households would have a better chance of experiencing parental monitoring and supervision—and perhaps a better chance of parental support—if only because the parents could have more time available because they share domestic chores. In this work I found that two of the four low achievers live with a single parent. Another lives in a situation in which the father is not present in the home consistently. The fourth student lives with her grandmother and grandfather. In the cases where there is a male present at all, he has very little to do with the raising of the child. In fact, there is almost no communication between the males, when they are present, and the students. In five of the eight cases where the students are doing average or very well, there is a father present. I did not find that the father is much of a factor in supporting the child, discussing the student's schoolwork, monitoring the student's activities, or encouraging the child. In every case in this study the mother or grandmother answered the questions for the questionnaire and was the adult with whom we communicated and watched in every visit to the homes. In the case of Marie Thomas the father was often present and occasionally talked to the observer. Mr. Thomas is clearly interested in and concerned about Marie and her school performance. In fact, he is one of the very few fathers who visited Family Focus for events. Nonetheless, it was Ms. Thomas who spent the majority of the time with Marie.

Even with the fathers present, it is the mothers who encourage the students, the mothers who visit the schools, the mothers who discuss the schoolwork with the students, the mothers who ask about the extracurricular activities, the mothers who assign and monitor the household chores.

With the possible exceptions of the Thomas family and the Weaver family, and an occasional comment from the father in the Robinson family, the males played little observable role in the lives of the students. It may be that in the other cases the fact that a male is a wage earner allows the mother more time and energy to devote to the student. However, almost all of the women involved in this research work themselves, so they have two jobs.

The role of family structure in shaping the performance of the students is, then, not altogether clear. There is not a father consistently present in any of the families in which the students do badly. However, when there is a father present and the student does well or average, that father is not much involved with the student, with a few exceptions, and these are not great exceptions. The bottom line seems to be that the mother in these poor black households is the key, and if she does certain things to maintain the order and structure in the house and to support the self-esteem, sense of responsibility, educational aspirations, leadership, and internal control of the student, the student does well in school. If she does not do these things, the student does badly. The father may be present, but he does little, though I must emphasize the few exceptions, given that the others do so very little.

That fathers are not a significant factor when students do badly suggests that their presence might help, but then they are not much of a factor when students do well, either, suggesting that their presence does not help. The mothers are critical and under a great deal of pressure in the families in which the students do well. The responsibility is essentially all theirs. "A co-resident father is available on a daily basis to tell stories, answer questions, help with homework or monitor the child's activities, and having more than one parent helps in the communication of family rules and discipline" (Entwisle, Alexander, and Olson 1997, 115). I find that even when the father is in residence, he seldom engages in the activities mentioned in this quote, though his presence may free the mother to do more of these things. The mother is the key to the success of the student.

The issue of parental involvement is raised often in discussions about improving the education of poor minority students. According to Entwisle, Alexander, and Olson (1997), this is tied to parental expectations of the student's performance. That is, "parents who expect their children to do well in school are more likely to take steps to encourage this outcome such as attending parent–teacher meetings and providing resources at home to help their children to do well in school" (115). School staff tend to believe that if parents are involved, then they are more likely to do the things at home to encourage better performance. While self-selection may well be an issue here—that is, the parents who most want their children to do well and are most interested in ways to help this come about are the parents most likely to become involved—the point is that involvement and performance seem to go together.

I saw very little parental involvement in the school itself, though the parents of the better-performing students are involved in the schoolwork and activities of their children. They ask about the work, look at the work, help with the work, and talk about the importance of school and school activities. They say that they visit schools and that they feel comfortable doing so, but in only one instance did we see evidence of such a visit. I am not, then, convinced that getting parents to come to school will automatically help the students to do better. The parents of the better students are probably more likely to attend school functions, but in this case the schools are preaching to the converted. The parents of the students doing badly need to make serious changes in the home environment and in how they develop and support their children and what they expect of them. Going to school does not really bring this about.

The parents of the average and high-achieving students believe strongly that their children will be successful and that education is critical to their success. They also believe that this successful future is up to their children and that little other than money stands in their way. The children share these beliefs, though they do not mention money as an obstacle. They think that their futures are in their own hands, and they expect to do well. They are also prepared to wait for that future and for gratification. Remember that for the most part the low-achieving students did what satisfied them. They played a great deal; they watched a lot of television. They were out of the house a fair amount. The better students did what they were required to do.

So, then, they are pointing toward a future, believe in their ability to get there and to do well, and believe that the execution of the task is up to them. These beliefs come from their parents (generally one parent), who create an environment that supports and encourages these beliefs and their execution. As Bempechat (1998) writes: "Many [poor and minority parents] do the same kinds of things that have been documented in white middle class parents" (34). This is true for the parents of the students doing well, but not true for the parents of the others. The characteristics of the successful parents and the students, noted above, are middle-class characteristics, and given that schools are middle-class institutions, it should be no surprise that these students do well. The critical public policy question is: How do we manage to encourage and allow others in these groups to do the same? I will address this very important issue in the next and final chapter.

THEORETICAL AND PUBLIC POLICY CONCERNS: SO, WHAT DO WE DO?

As I pointed out at the beginning of this analysis, the issue of the educa tion of poor minority students has received a great deal of both public and social policy attention in the past decade or so. While much of this attention has focused on the question of changes in the schools, an increasing amount of research, including this work, has concentrated on the role of the family in the educational process. As we will see a bit later, this work at the least implies that familial changes are necessary to improve education, as opposed to changes in schools and/or the educational process itself. I do not want to suggest that there should not be changes in schools to improve the education of poor minority students, but I do think that the potential impact of most of these changes is overrated. Comer (1993) is correct. As middle-class institutions, schools work best for middle-class students, or at least for those capable of thinking and acting like middle-class students.

I believe that middle-income white students perform better in schools, not because they are inherently more intelligent than others, but because they live family lives that emphasize discipline, delayed gratification, responsibility, internal control, self-esteem, and cooperation: All characteristics that are not only helpful but essential in school performance given the structure and goals of schools. Schools are not only structured in such a way that these middle-class characteristics are necessary, they exist to prepare students for lives in the middle class. Thus, students who are leaning toward this life and are comfortable with these characteristics do best. Comer's (1993) point cannot be overemphasized: "Children from social networks with similar attitudes, values, and ways to those of the school and the most powerful school people have the best opportunity of meeting the expectations of the school" (305).

The real question, then, if educational improvement is our concern, should be: How do we shape and mold the students who are not from these networks, not from Comer's "mainstream" or from my middle class so that they can meet the expectations of the school, so that they can do well? It is not clear to me that the policy changes being discussed today are aimed at this question at all, raising the possibility that many are missing the point. Keeping students in school for a longer school day or school year does little to encourage delayed gratification or internal control or discipline or familial support. Having students wear uniforms does nothing to encourage parents to ask about homework on a consistent basis. Holding a student back a grade does nothing to create order and structure in a home. I will return to these issues later, but for now the question is: How is it that eight of the twelve families I studied can send their students to school sufficiently prepared to learn (and even the average students can do better than several of Clark's high performers), while four of their peers and neighbors cannot or do not?

In many ways these eight are middle-class families with lower-class incomes. Clark (1983) found much the same thing, as did Furstenberg et al. (1999); Bempechat (1998); and to some degree Entwisle, Alexander, and Olson (1997), all of whom studied the relationship of the family to either education or to success through education. The issue of middle-class lower-income families raises the theoretical question of how to define class. For years social class has been defined for the most part by rankings on income, education, and occupation scales (Sampson 1973). Other scales are occasionally brought into use, but for the most part these three dominate our definition of social class. In this case the poor would be considered "lower class," a term I am very uncomfortable with, because they would rank low on the income scale, the occupation scale, and probably on the education scale.

For social scientists—indeed, for most observers—while one's education, occupation, and income are important, probably more important are the values, behavior, attitudes, and beliefs that are related to and would seem to follow from these more observable and more easily measurable variables. These values, behavior, attitudes, and beliefs have often been lumped into a "culture" (Frazier 1957; Glazier 1963; and Valentine 1968). My interest is not whether the issue is indeed cultural but in the possession of the characteristics so often attributed to the middle class by those with lower incomes. Banfield (1970) described the middle class as oriented toward the future, self-confident, internally controlled, creative, and independent. The lower class was seen as low in self-esteem, apathetic, and externally controlled. Or, as Oscar Lewis (1966) wrote, characterized by "a weak ego structure, confusion of sexual identification, lack of impulse control, little ability to delay gratification and to plan for the future, resignation and fatalism, belief in male superiority, tolerance for psychological pathology . . . very little sense of history" (xlvii–xlviii). Frazier (1957); Glazier and Moynihan (1963); Lewis (1966); Mead (1986); and others have attributed these various characteristics to those with certain incomes, educations, and occupations. In other words, the characteristics follow from the incomes, educations, and occupations and, to some, in turn lead to them because the characteristics limit the upward mobility of people who possess them.

The problem with this association for me is that I do not see it. I see poor black families with many of the characteristics attributed to the middle class. Indeed, that is precisely what I have found in this research. Of the eight families with average or high-achieving students, seven of them appear to have a number of the characteristics of the middle class. The students are oriented toward the future, are internally controlled, have relatively high self-esteem, are disciplined and cooperative. Several demonstrate leadership skills as well, and their parents, at least their mothers, support and encourage these characteristics not only through what they say to the children but also through the environment they maintain in the home. These seem to be middle-class families with lower incomes. On the other hand, the families with students doing badly appear to be non–middle-class families with lower incomes. For the most part the students lack discipline, pay little attention to the future, lack self-control and, with one exception (Peter Edwards), seem to be low in self-esteem. Their parents and grandparents do little to alter this situation; indeed, for the most part they create a home environment that supports it.

Of course, it is not particularly easy for lower-income families to maintain middle-class characteristics, particularly in neighborhoods in which many of the residents do not share these characteristics and therefore do not support them. Still, many do and find their way out of poverty through schools, middle-class institutions. Indeed, of the families I studied, most do have many of the characteristics of the middle class, and I suspect that this is the case for most of the poor. Some of the poor apparently do not have many of these characteristics, making education more difficult. Or, as Comer (1993) writes: "The experience of children who grow up in social networks that are marginal to the mainstream of society is often quite different, more likely to produce social and academic failure in school" (306). I am not arguing here about whether there is a culture of poverty or about whether the poor are basically different from the nonpoor. My only point is that many of the poor are in ways important to education middle class and should not be termed lower class. They are middle-class and lower-income people, and given the opportunity their children can do just fine in school.

The question of why some people have many of these characteristics and some do not is beyond this work, though I have asked myself many times why this is the case, especially when most of the families involved with this work live in the same neighborhood. The neighborhood is not responsible for the differences. Neither is race. Neither is income. To determine the source or sources of the differences is beyond me. My original question was: Why do some poor black students do well in school and others do not? The answer seems to lie with the family and not so much with the neighborhood or the schools. The short answer is that middle-class students do well, and the poor are often middle class in terms of the things that count in schools.

If, in fact, the family makes such a significant difference, what does this suggest about policy? Indeed, almost all of the efforts to improve the education of urban poor nonwhites center on the schools, when it seems to be the case that the family is central, and I am not the only one nor the first one to make this case. The major difference between this work and most other research concerning the family and education is that I do not see family socioeconomic status as the key. Some, perhaps many, poor families have many of the important characteristics of those with much higher socioeconomic status. It is not the status, it is the noneconomic characteristics of the status, and poor families may have them as well as middle-income families. If the family is the key or primary construct where education is concerned, then why do most policy efforts to improve the schools of urban poor minority students focus on schools? Why don't these efforts center around families?

I am not suggesting that what occurs in and about schools is not important. It is—indeed, it is critical. However, it is secondary. Children sent to school prepared to learn appear to do so. The key policy issue is then: How do we manage to help parents who need the help to send their children prepared to learn? The politicians and policymakers appear to ignore this question and to focus on the schools. Former vice president Al Gore, as a presidential candidate, proposed to spend $50 billion to make preschool possible for almost all three- and four-year-olds. He wanted to spend federal dollars to help families pay for college and to pay for new school construction and modernization. He proposed to increase the number of teachers in inner-city schools by 75,000 and to reduce class size and the size of schools. He also proposed to increase teacher salaries.

During his campaign for the presidency, Texas governor George W. Bush proposed educational vouchers for students in low-performing public schools that failed to improve after three years. He also proposed standardized tests for third through eighth grades in reading and math and spending $1 billion a year for five years to establish reading problems in kindergarten and first grade. He proposed to reward states for increases in student performance, to spend $3 billion to establish or improve 2,000 charter schools, to increase the amount that parents can put into educational savings accounts, and to help recruit retired military personnel to become teachers.

Both the candidates proposed to spend more money to improve education, though Mr. Bush wanted the bulk of the money to go to states and private sources while Mr. Gore preferred to see the money go to public sources and be controlled by the federal government. None of this is surprising given their parties and their political differences. What should be surprising is that they both proposed to spend money and aim it at schools when schools, while critical, are secondary. If the schools are the primary construct in terms of how well students do, then why is it that four of the twelve students whom I studied do badly when they have about the same income as the others, live in the same neighborhood as the others, attend the same schools as the others, and are of the same race as the others? The variables that we might expect to affect their performance do not vary among them: The families themselves do vary. If the schools made the difference, the performances should be much the same, assuming roughly equal ability. They are not, however, and the only construct that varies enough to explain the differences is the family.

As Laurence Steinberg (1998) correctly put it: "A sizable part of the variability in student performance is determined by factors outside of school" (322). He goes on to write: "Education reformers have, for the most part, been guilty of a sort of myopia that has zeroed in on schools and classrooms and has paid only passing attention to the broader context in which schools and classrooms function." He is entirely correct. Both politicians interested in education and educational policymakers focus on schools as the institutions to be changed and ignore the reality that other institutions, such as the family, have a great deal to do with how students perform in schools. The bulk of the research on educational performance focuses on schools. Furthermore, it is much easier to change teachers, or to increase teacher requirements or expectations, or to build more schools, or to require more tests or higher scores than to even discuss the changing of families. This discussion must, however, take place given that the other changes do not appear to make much of a difference, at least not among the urban nonwhite poor.

In his book *Changing Urban Education* (1998), Clarence Stone asked contributors to examine a number of "solutions" to the urban education problem. The chapters on reform have such titles as "The Challenge of School Reform in Baltimore: Race, Jobs, and Politics," "Grassroots Action in East Brooklyn: A Community Organization Takes up School Reform," "Corporate Influence on Chicago School Reform," and "Education and Regime in Charlotte." While there are several other chapters, not one of them examines the educational problem much beyond the schools. There is some, though not very much, discussion of parental involvement, but for the most part the entire book focuses on schools, politics, and corporate involvement in educational change. Here is a book that centers on changes in urban education and fails almost entirely to pay attention to the family, as though the family has nothing to do with education.

In their book *The Manufactured Crisis* (1995), David Berliner and Bruce Biddle argue that there is no real problem in America's schools, that all the fuss over schools and students is just a liberal hoax. They make very few references to the family, and when they do it is within the context of improving the quality of life for poor families, not the relationship of the family to the education of the student. The fact that family socioeconomic status is a factor in predicting student performance is not new. The fact that blacks do worse than whites is not new. Clark tied the performance of poor blacks to their families back in 1983, and several authors have since focused on the family when studying educational performance and achievement. Still, the policy discussion virtually ignores the family.

We seem to think that changing buildings and teachers and funding will do the trick even though past changes in these have led us nowhere. In Chicago it was thought that the students would improve their performance if their parents were more involved. So the city developed local school councils to share in the policy making and governance of the schools. The councils were elected and included parents, so the schools were essentially decentralized. After five or six years the performances went nowhere. The power in the schools was then centralized, a turn of 180 degrees, and the performances changed not one whit. In the meantime thousands of students are learning no more and doing no better.

Based on my research it is not clear that the kind of parental involvement often discussed—that is, spending considerable time at school—is the key in any event. Parents need to be involved with their children at home: looking over and discussing the schoolwork of the student and talking to their child about his or her school day and school activities. What's more, the parents who are most likely to participate in school activities are probably the parents most likely to do the necessary things at home. That is, self-selection is probably a factor, and the parents we most need to reach are probably least likely to be reached through school elections.

While this society does occasionally discuss how families can help their children, Furstenberg et al. (1999) are correct when they write, "Americans strongly adhere to the ideal of a family system protected from government interference, in which children's fates are almost entirely in the hands of parents" (226). The family is sacrosanct in America. Yet this research suggests that some of the poor black families must be changed if their children are to do well in school. They need to become more like the families of the students who do well, and providing vouchers, or charter schools, or teachers with stronger credentials, or more tests, or longer school days, or stopping social promotions will do little to accomplish this. The students in this study who do well do not have vouchers. They do not attend charter schools. They have for the most part the same teachers, or at least teachers with the same credentials and supervision, as the others. They have the same school day and the same promotion policy. No, these students perform differently because of different family environments and different family approaches to their education and development, and it is these environments and approaches that must be changed if students are to perform better. This is not going to be easy considering the fact that Americans resist government interference with the family.

Furstenberg et al. (1999) suggest that families that do well socially and culturally are in that position because they possess economic and educational advantages. This is not altogether true, fortunately. As I have shown, a number of the families in this study have few advantages, yet their children manage to do well in school. Poor black parents can and do raise their children as though they are middle-class parents, as though they have the economic and educational advantages they lack. This is, of course, not easy, but we need to find ways to help the other families who do not do this learn how. This, of course, requires fundamental familial change. Not all families will be amenable to this change. It is not likely, for example, that the Dunn family could make such a change given what seems to be a drug problem in the family. That problem would have to be solved first.

What I am talking about here is more basic parenting knowledge, which would involve changes in the home environment, and support for changes to help the students develop greater discipline, higher self-esteem, more responsibility, and more internal control. I do not believe that the school can accomplish much of this. It is not the school's responsibility, nor do the schools know much about this. They may be able to help teach pregnant teenagers how to feed and care for their soon-to-be-born children. How can they teach mothers in their twenties and thirties how to establish and maintain order and structure in their homes? How to make certain that the house is quiet when the child is doing homework? Indeed, the importance of the homework or how to discuss it with the child systematically? How can they teach parents that children must learn to believe that their future is up to them and that they can control it, and how to teach this to the children? Yet all of this must happen if we seriously want to improve the educational future for many poor black students, and schools are not the institutions that can bring this about. They can help, but they cannot do it.

Entwisle, Alexander, and Olson (1997) may well be correct when they argue that summer programs may significantly help poor students because "living in a poor neighborhood . . . hinders achievement because it does not support cognitive growth in periods when school is closed" (163). This would support the idea that schools can indeed make a significant difference for poor students, but mainly in the summer and perhaps after school. I would never argue that schools are not critical for poor black students. They certainly are, but families are primary and need to be addressed while we look into what we should do with schools. I am not certain that more summer schools or stricter standards for grade promotion can help Peter Edwards or Mycela Falwell. More school cannot help much if they go home to the same family environment or if there is not some effort to help them become more disciplined, internally controlled, and responsible. If students do not believe that they are responsible for their education, or if they are not willing to forgo television or games for homework, then what will more education accomplish? How can summer school help if the parent indicates no concern for the student's education when the student returns home? The student must be sent to school prepared to learn if the schools are to work. This is the responsibility of the family, and I am not certain that any other institution can do it, unless there is some substitute for the family. I am convinced that many poor black families can and do accomplish this.

But what happens when middle-class lower-income families send their children to school prepared to learn and the school is unprepared to teach? These parents then behave like the middle-class parents they are and make decisions about what is best for their children. Parochial schools, vouchers, charter schools, or magnet schools come into play. This leaves fewer middle-class students in schools with a higher percentage of non–middle-class students or students from families that have not prepared them for school. This makes the school experience worse for teachers and students: Teachers will have fewer role models to point to and students fewer middle-class peers to emulate. The smaller number of middle-class students left may face more pressure from the other students. As I have indicated, I did not find as much of this pressure as I expected nor as the work of John Ogbu (1990) might suggest. Evanston is, however, a suburb that has many middle-income, middle-class white students who may well serve as the role models and provide pressure to succeed.

Race and poverty are obstacles, but many families overcome them quite nicely, and others can do the same with some help. While Bempechat (1998) and others believe that parochial schools do a better job than others in helping poor black students overcome these obstacles, I believe that these schools enroll those middle-class poor black students who will do well almost anywhere. If the parochial schools enroll those prepared to learn, those whose parents support their learning at home, then these students will perform well. The fact that they do is less an indication of how special the schools are than a manifestation of the specialness of the family.

The issue then becomes: How does society provide the help necessary to change the families who need it? How do we turn Mycela Falwell into Stephanie Adams, Mycela's family into Stephanie's family? I strongly believe that this is possible and reject the arguments of scholars such as Loury (1995) and Rosen (1959), who suggest that black families either cannot be helped to succeed or that they can be helped only very little, and then only by moving away from other poor blacks. All twelve of the students in this study live in a poor black neighborhood with poor black families, and eight of the twelve do just fine in school. Whether they will do fine in life is another issue, but they are certainly on their way. Their race, their poverty, their neighborhood has not limited them so far.

Before I turn to the question of what society needs to do to help the families that need the help, let me be clear about the role of schools. I do not mean to imply that we should not do all that we can to improve the quality of education. There are many teachers who do not try to teach poor minority students because many of the students do not try to learn. There are many schools that lack adequate space and resources. Schools can and should do a great deal more. However, we must be aware that these improvements alone are unlikely to significantly help many poor minority students, and if they do not, then we should not rant and rave that the improvements have failed and move on to the next idea. The family is clearly critical. In this research there are students living in the same neighborhood, going to the same schools, often with the same teachers, in one case living in the same building, and some do well while others do badly. The schools cannot explain this. Still, the schools should be addressed.

Schools are critical in two ways. One, the shift in the economy has in many communities meant that the factory jobs that required minimal schooling are gone. The jobs in most urban areas today require more education and greater skill. A student cannot drop out of school in the tenth grade and become a meat packer or welder and make almost as much money as his or her high school teachers. This places more emphasis on schools. Second, what does or does not go on in school of course affects the education of students. Preschool education can help to teach students how to behave in school and how to learn, but the students still need to go home to supportive environments. Small class sizes (fifteen to twenty students) can allow teachers to devote more time to each student. If, however, the student lacks the discipline or internal control, the conducive home environment, the understanding from parents (which must go beyond talk) that education is important, then the teacher is still facing a very difficult challenge.

So, while schools are critical, the family seems to be the primary construct, and we must focus on ways to change or to strengthen these families if we are truly concerned with the education and the future of poor black students. Fortunately, we have a road map provided by the families whose children are doing well. We now need a strategy. Furstenberg et al. (1999) suggest making "local institutions multi functional" (229). That is, churches, schools, and health service agencies would furnish not only religion, education, and health services, they would also provide services to help "strengthen" or positively change the family.

I am not a big supporter of having schools provide much more than education. This is a difficult enough task. However, some agency, some facility, would need to exist that carries the trust of poor blacks and can convince those families whose children are doing consistently badly to allow intervention. Workers must be able to come into the homes of poor black families for a sufficiently long time to help them change their home environment and to teach the parents what they must teach the child for academic success—and equally important, *how* to teach it.

There are several problems here, though, and the first is trust. As Furstenberg et al. (1999) and Clark (1983) correctly point out, many of the poor do not trust outsiders or most institutions. Some have legal problems that they prefer to keep to themselves, many would be embarrassed or resentful dealing with people who might consider themselves superior, and many have been treated badly and unfairly by similar institutions or people. Why would they allow others into their homes for extended periods of time to teach them what they probably believe that they already know? After all, we are not talking about how to change a baby's diaper or which formula to use. We are talking about changing the home environment, about what to teach and how to teach it to children already taught. We are talking about understanding the importance of discipline and how to provide it and teach it consistently. We are talking about fundamental changes in the family.

The first issue is therefore trust if we are to get close enough to these families to have the desired impact, and not every institution has that trust. I will address the question of which ones do soon. For now, allow me to make the important point that I have relied a great deal on the work of Clark (1983) and Furstenberg and his colleagues (1999) not just because I believe that their work, while not without problems, is quite good. More importantly, most of the work on poor black families and their children focuses on why and how they fail, ignoring all of those who don't. Clark and Furstenberg et al. focus, as do I, on why and how the students in these families succeed.

Furstenberg et al. (1999) offer basically two ideas: an increase in functional communities and "expanding educational and developmental opportunities" (231). Functional communities, according to Coleman and Hoffer (1987) as stated by Furstenberg et al., are "institutions that provide a collective purpose that reinforces parents' beliefs and values. Churches and private schools are the most common form of functional communities, but other institutions could be constructed intentionally to involve the family as a social entity" (230). In other words, they want government support for institutions that poor parents might trust that can support the parents' efforts to raise their children appropriately. These functional communities also allow like-minded parents interested in achievement to enable their children to associate with children who are like themselves. Clark makes the same suggestion. However, what about the children of parents who are not "like-minded"? That is, what do we do about four of the twelve students whose parents express support for education but do little at home to send their children to school prepared to learn? We cannot help only those who need little help.

Expanding educational and developmental opportunities does largely that. It will help those most amenable to help, those prepared to take advantage of the opportunities. These families are certainly a concern, but I am more concerned with those not interested in these opportunities. The parents of Fatima Robinson and Marie Thomas will find and take advantage of the opportunities, though they should certainly have more opportunities. Opportunities will probably not help Peter Edwards because he is not prepared for them. The opportunities matter significantly only for those ready to take advantage of them and ready to support the use of them at home. Furstenberg et al. (1999) want poor parents to acquire improved skills at managing the external world, but they also want, as I have indicated, more opportunities. I believe that it goes well beyond managerial skills and opportunity for those poor black parents at the bottom. The opportunities cannot be used if parents do not know how to successfully parent, and the managerial skills assume that parents can prepare their children for school and go beyond that to determining what school experience is best for them. But the first step is preparing them, and the issue is how to get poor black families to successfully do this to take advantage of the opportunities. As I have written, schools must present these opportunities, but they are available in Evanston and four out of twelve students are not taking advantage of them. We must help to change one-third of the families, and more educational and developmental opportunities will not, in my opinion, do it. Opportunities must be there for change to take place, but they are not enough.

Clark (1983) thinks that the parents need to establish rules for behavior for every situation, to monitor the students' use of time and space, to establish leadership opportunities, to encourage the child to be academically ambitious, to make certain that homework is regularly performed, and to respect authority figures. Sound familiar? These are all things done by the parents of all but one of the eight students in this study who do average or well in school. Most importantly, Clark wants parents to do things, including those listed, that "serve well in equipping school children with the comprehensive writing, reading, verbal, and social skills and personal qualities needed for learning classroom lessons and coping with adults and peers" (215). He wants them to do the things done by the parents of the successful students in this research. He wants children to be sent to school prepared to listen and to learn. The families of those who are not, need to change, and as I have indicated, while we talk a great deal about the family in America, we do not want to interfere with it. I do not see how we can avoid it if we truly want to improve the education of poor blacks, and this is eminently possible.

Furstenberg and his colleagues (1999) are correct when they state: "We must think about whether the cultural model that assigns almost exclusive responsibility to parents is in need of revision" (232). On the one hand, we want parents to send their children to school ready to learn—indeed, we expect it.

On the other hand, when this is not done we do not want to look to the family in any serious way. We want to attempt to pass the responsibility on to other institutions, beginning with the schools, and to try to change them to respond to the problem. Again, many of the schools serving poor black students do indeed have problems that need to be addressed, but the four families in my research that have children doing badly do not function much at all like those that have students doing well. Much as we might like to, there is no getting around it: We need to address the families.

We can do this by providing more funding and staff for the Family Focuses of the nation. Trust is critical here, and agencies that have gained the trust of poor families are very important. If we are to ask poor black families to allow us into their homes to assess their parenting skills and styles and then to allow us to suggest to them over time what changes are needed, the families must trust whoever is doing this. Teaching a mother how to discipline a child consistently is not easy and will take time. Teaching a parent how to ask the student about his or her school day every day and to look at the student's homework and to help with it is not easy, either. The parent will need to be taught what to do and say to help the student become responsible and feel in control of his or her own life. The parent will have to realize the value of quiet, order, and structure when the child returns from school and to determine ways to provide these in the home. Teaching these qualities to parents who may well have trouble paying the rent or buying groceries, who may have many mouths to feed and a lot of noise to quiet will take time and commitment both from the parents and the staff member attempting to do it.

Since eight of the twelve families involved in this research (though I have my doubts about one) seem to do the necessary things, I see little reason to think that most of the others can't, with the proper guidance and help from the proper people. All of the poor black families in this research say that education is important to them. But all do not know how to translate that sense of importance into a home environment and a family life that will allow their child to take advantage of the educational experience. Not every one of the four families will want to allow the change agents into their homes. Who wants nonfamily members in their homes three or four evenings a week for several weeks, especially when these nonfamily members are telling them what they are doing is wrong and must change? On the other hand, who wants their children to do badly in school and thereby limit their future lives, possibly heading straight for the poverty parents say they want the children to escape?

These are not easy choices, but they must be at least available. It is to be expected that some families will simply reject the help, but if two out of four agree, I would argue that two out of four is better than none, and we are currently helping none. Former president Clinton pushed for federal funding for two hundred thousand new teachers in order to reduce class sizes around the country. Reducing class size from thirty-two to thirty in a city is nice, but it will not do much to improve education. I would suggest instead that the money be used to hire two hundred thousand staff members for community agencies that have the access to and trust of the poor, people who can go into homes and begin to teach parents what they must do to send their children to school prepared to learn. In other words, I propose to hire trusted community workers who could spend considerable time in the homes of some poor parents teaching them how to parent based on what I have found in this work.

These staff members would have to be able to work with the schools in their efforts to help particular students as they are working with the parents at home. This is not an easy task, as I have stated, but what is the alternative? Most of the parents in the families that I studied do a great job of parenting, especially when we consider the obstacles that many face. We see that this is achievable and that it is happening. These parents are doing what they must in order for their children to do well in school. It is not that they send their children to different schools, live in different, more supportive neighborhoods, or have more money than others. Some have suggested that the neighborhood is key. While I believe that it can be if it has many middle-class—not necessarily middle-income—residents, I did not find this to be the case in my study.

It is not that neighborhoods do not matter. They may indeed be important, but not independently of the family. Certain values, beliefs, behavior, and attitudes become acceptable in a neighborhood, and others are denigrated by the residents. When neighborhoods were segregated by race, middle-income blacks were forced to live next to poor blacks, and factory jobs were available to support a working class, the attitudes, values, and behavior of the middle-income/middle-class blacks tended to dominate, and most others accepted them. The neighborhood atmosphere was determined largely by the middle-income population with support from the working class. The neighborhood residents could see the cars, the clothes, the living arrangements of the middle income, believe that these advantages followed from their behavior, their values, their beliefs, and then attempt to emulate them. Furthermore, the middle-income residents would insist that their way was the "right" way, the "good" way. All of this would influence families to act like middle-class families, and they found a great deal of support for their actions. Those who failed to adopt these characteristics were seen as "bad" and avoided.

As black neighborhoods changed due to desegregation and the movement and demise of local factories, the middle-income and working-class blacks moved, leaving fewer and fewer of those who supported the values, beliefs, attitudes, and behavior of the middle class. Obviously, there are many who do support these left in these communities, but changing conditions have made their family tasks much more difficult—but clearly not impossible, based on my data. We now must make holding these middle-class values possible for those who have not yet adopted them. Changing neighborhoods would help, but changing families is more realistic; we cannot force people to live where they might not want to live. We can make it attractive to do so, but not without great costs, both human and financial. Gentrification is not easy.

If teachers do not teach, students will not learn, but teachers did not make the difference in our study, either. The parents—the families—made the difference. We must begin to work to change parenting if we want to make a difference with education. Fortunately, we have examples that not only suggest that it can be done but also point us in the right direction. Am I suggesting that we pay no attention to the schools in our effort to improve the education of many poor black students? Not at all! As I have stated, we know that small classes, fifteen to twenty students, make a significant difference. This is, however, a very expensive strategy. We would have to almost triple the educational expenditures in most cities to do this, because not only would we have to cut the classes in half, we would also have to build new classrooms, many of which would not be necessary for very long given demographic trends. We also know that preschool education can help, but it, too, is expensive, and at this point very few young people are enrolled.

While both efforts may be effective, the children still go home to their families, and it is my position that these families, at least many of them, can become effective at preparing their children for school, and these prepared students can do well as long as the school does its job, whether the classes are small or not and whether the student had a preschool experience or not. I believe that this research gives us a fairly clear view of what has to be done to accomplish this. A great many people who have the trust of the poor would need to be hired, trained, and gain access to the homes of the families that agree to attempt to change. They would need to be in the homes for a fairly long period of time, and much of this time would be in the evening and on weekends when children are at home.

This form of family education—family change—will not be easy, particularly in some of the more difficult neighborhoods. But what is the alternative? Do we continue to complain and moan about how urban educational systems fail poor nonwhites? Do we continue to try solutions that would not seem to have much chance of being effective? (Remember, the parents do not see the schools as a problem.) Are we prepared to spend the money on school-related efforts that could help? In the end, the family is still there and still the key. We must begin to focus our efforts there, as difficult as this will be.

APPENDIX: INTERVIEW QUESTIONNAIRES

The questions used in each of the interview schedules were designed to gather background data on the families and students and to obtain some attitudinal and behavioral information. The observers administered the questionnaires when they were comfortable doing so and when they believed that the parent/grandparent and the student felt similarly comfortable. The interviews were quite open, and some of the questions served mainly as guides.

PARENTAL QUESTIONNAIRE

Hello, I am (*interviewer's name*) from DePaul University. We are, as you know, studying how parents or guardians in Evanston relate to their children. I would like to conduct a short interview with the person responsible for the children in this household. May I talk to that person? (*Once you have been introduced to that person*) I would like to ask you your name, though no real names will be used in the study.

Respondent's name
  (1) What is your relationship to the children in this house? (*Probes: father, grandfather, mother, aunt*)
  (2) How are you related to the head of the house? (*Probes: spouse, head, parent, child*)

(3) How long have you lived in Evanston?

(4) In what city or community did you grow up?

(5) How long have you lived in this house? (*Years or months*)

(6) How many adults (over 18 years old) including yourself live in this house with you?

(7) How many children live here?

(8) How old are you? (*Age in years at last birthday*)

(9) Is the head of the household working or doing something else at present?

    1. Working (*Go to question 10*)

    2. Unemployed, but looking for work (*Go to question 12*)

    3. Going to school (*Go to question 12*)

    4. Retired (*Go to question 13*)

    5. Housewife (*Go to question 12*)

    6. Unemployed, not looking for work—this does not include housewife (*Go to question 12*)

(10) (*If employed*) What is his/her (your) job?(*Job title, description*)

(11) (*If employed*) In what type of business does he/she (you) work? (*What does company do?*)

(12) (*If not working at present*) Has the head of the household (you) ever had a job?

Yes (*Go to question 13*)

No (*Go to question 16*)

Not applicable (*Go to question 16*)

(13) (*If not working at present*) How long ago was it that the head of the household (you) worked? (*Record in months*)

(14) (*If not working at present*) What was the head of the household's (your) last job? (*Job title, description*)

(15) (*If not working at present*) In what type of business did he/she (you) work? (*What did company do?*)

(16) Are you married or single? (*Ask only if not obvious from question 2*)

    1. Married, includes common law

    2. Single

    3. Separated or divorced

    4. Widowed

(17) (*If married*) Does your spouse live in the house with you?

(18) (*If married*) Where is your spouse from? That is, where did he/she grow up?

(19) (*If married, separated, divorced, or widowed*) How far did your spouse or ex-spouse go in school?

Grade

Degree

(20) What is the last grade that you completed in school?

Grade

Degree

(21) How important is (*child's name*) education to you? (*If not important, go to question 23*)

(22) (*If at all important*) Why is it so important?

(23) If not important, why not?

(24) Do you try to encourage (*child's name*) to do well in school?

(25) (*If yes*) How do you encourage him/her?

(26) How many times a year do you visit (*child's name*) school?

(27) How do you feel when you visit the school? (*Probes: happy, worried, afraid, confident, concerned*)

(28) Why do you feel this way?

(29) What, if anything, stands in (*child's name*) way in terms of getting a good education? (*Probes: health, teachers, lack of a future, money, family responsibility*)

(30) Do other children try to stop (*child's name*) from doing well in school? (*If no, go to question 32*)

(31) (*If yes*) How do they do that?

(32) Are there adults at school whom you think try to stop (*child's name*) from doing well in school?

(33) (*If yes*) How do they do that?

(34) Do you believe that race and/or discrimination plays a role in your life? (*If yes*) How? (*If no, go to question 35*)

(35) Tell me about your upbringing. What was it like?

(36) How do you try to raise (*child's name*)? (*Probes: What is important in raising children? What about discipline? What about self-control? What about the future?*)

(37) How many times a week do you read a newspaper?

(38) How many times a week do you read a book?

(39) Upon whom do you rely when you have a problem?

(40) Is there anything else that you wanted to say or to add?

STUDENT QUESTIONNAIRE

Hello, I am (*interviewer's name*) from DePaul University. As you probably already know, we are studying how some families in Evanston get along with their children, and how those children do in school. I would like to conduct a short interview with you about yourself, your family, and school. I would like to know your name for the record, though no real names will be used in the study, and everything that you say is confidential.

Respondent's name
Respondent's gender
    Male
    Female

(1) How old were you on your last birthday? (*Age in years*)

(2) What grade are you in in school?

(3) What school do you attend? (*Name of school*)

(4) What do you like most about the school? (*Probes: The teachers? Your teachers? The principal? A specific teacher? The after-school activities? The homework? The students?*)

(5) What do you like the least about the school?

(6) How well are you doing in school? (*Circle one*)
    1. Very well
    2. Well
    3. Pretty good/fair
    4. Not so well
    5. Poorly

(7) How important is education to you? (*Circle one*)
    1. Very important
    2. Important
    3. Kind of important

4. Not very important

5. Not at all important

(8) Why is this? That is, why is school (*use the answer from above*) to you?

(9) Has any other student ever tried to keep you from doing well in school?

    1. Yes (*Go to question 10*)

    2. No (*Go to question 12*)

(10) When and how did this happen?

(11) Why do you think that this happened (or happens)?

(12) How much time do you spend on your homework every evening or weekend day?

(13) How far would you like to go in school?

(14) How far do you expect to go in school?

(15) Are there any obstacles in your way? (*Circle one answer*)

    1. Yes (*Go to question 16*)

    2. No (*Go to question 17*)

(16) What are these obstacles?

(17) How many times a week do you read a newspaper?

(18) What is most important to you in your life?

(19) Is there one specific teacher to whom you really feel close or to whom you used to feel close?

    1. Yes (*Go to question 20*)

    2. No (*Go to question 21*)

(20) In what grade was this, and why do/did you feel close?

(21) Is race or racial discrimination something that you think much about? Why or why not?

(22) How much help do you get from your (*parent(s)/grandparent/aunt/ uncle/whatever is appropriate*) with your schoolwork? That is, how often would you say they help you?

(23) Is this enough help for you? Not enough help? Too much help?

(24) If you could change one thing about your family life, what would it be?

(25) If you could be one person in the world, who would it be? Why is that?

(26) Is there anything else that you would like to add?

BIBLIOGRAPHY

WORKS CITED

Allen, W. B., M. B. Spencer, and G. K. Brookins, eds. 1985. *Beginnings: The social and affective development of black children.* Hillsdale, N.J.: Erlbaum.

Banfield, E. 1970. *The unheavenly city.* Boston: Little, Brown.

Barber, B. K., J. E. Olson, and S. C. Shagle. 1994. Associations between parental psychological and behavioral control and youth internalized and externalized behaviors. *Child Development* 65:1120–36.

Baumrind, D. 1967. Socialization and instrumental competence in young children. In *The young child: Reviews of research,* edited by W. W. Hartup. Washington, D.C.: National Association for the Education of Young Children.

———. 1971. Current patterns of parental authority. *Developmental Psychology Monograph* 4, no. 1:1–103.

Bempechat, J. 1998. *Against the odds: How "at risk" children exceed expectations.* San Francisco: Jossey-Bass.

Berliner, D. C., and B. Biddle. 1995. *The manufactured crisis: Myths, fraud, and the attack on America's public schools.* Reading, Mass.: Perseus Books.

Blau, P., and O. D. Duncan. 1967. *The American occupational structure.* New York: Wiley.

Bronfrenbrenner, U. 1991. What do families do? *Family Affairs* 4:1–6.

Campbell, F. A., and C. T. Ramey. 1995. Cognitive and school outcomes for high risk African-American students at middle adolescence: Positive effects of early intervention. *American Educational Research Journal,* 32: 743–72.

Carnegie Corporation. 1992. *A matter of time.* New York: Emerson Hall.

Clark, R. 1983. *Family life and school achievement: Why poor black children succeed or fail.* Chicago: University of Chicago Press.

Coleman, J. S., and T. Hoffer. 1987. *Public and private high schools: The impact of communities.* New York: Basic Books.

Coleman, J. S., et al. 1966. *Equality of educational opportunity.* Washington, D.C.: U.S. Office of Education.

Comer, J. P. 1993. Inner-city education: A theoretical and intervention model. In *Sociology and the public agenda,* edited by W. J. Wilson. Newbury Park, Calif.: Sage.

Entwisle, D. R., and K. L. Alexander. 1996. Family type and children's growth in reading and math over the primary grades. *Journal of Marriage and the Family* 58:341–45.

Entwisle, D. R., K. L. Alexander, and L. S. Olson. 1997. *Children, schools, and inequality.* Boulder, Colo.: Westview Press.

Evanston (Illinois) Police Department. 1999. Police reported crime, January–December.

———. 2000. Comparison of selected crime and incident codes by beat, 1 January 1999–31 December 1999. Office of Administration, Planning Bureau.

Fordham, S., and J. Ogbu. 1986. Black students' school success: Coping with the burden of acting white. *Urban Review* 18:176–201.

Frazier, E. F. 1957. *The Negro family in the United States.* Rev. ed. New York: MacMillan.

Friedman, M. 1962. *Capitalism and freedom.* Chicago: University of Chicago Press.

Furstenberg, F. F., Jr. 1993. How families manage risk and opportunity in dangerous neighborhoods. In *Sociology and the public agenda,* edited by W. J. Wilson. Newbury Park, Calif.: Sage.

Furstenberg, F. F., Jr., et al. 1999. *Managing to make it: Urban families and adolescent success.* Chicago: University of Chicago Press.

Gilles, J. L., S. Geletta, and C. Daniels. 1994. What makes a good school? A methodological critique and reappraisal. Paper presented at the annual meeting of the Midwest Sociological Society, St. Louis, Mo., March.

Glazer, N., and D. P. Moynihan. 1963. *Beyond the melting pot.* Cambridge: M.I.T. Press.

Harrington, C. C., and S. K. Boardman. 1997. *Paths to success: Beating the odds in American society.* Cambridge: Harvard University Press.

Hill, R. B. 1971. *Strengths of black families.* New York: Emerson Hall.

Jencks, C., et al. 1972. *Inequality: A reassessment of the effect of family and schooling in America.* New York: Basic Books.

Jencks, C., and P. Peterson, eds. 1991. *The urban underclass*. Washington, D.C.: Brookings Institution.

Karweit, N. 1976. Quantity of schooling: A major educational factor? *Educational Researcher* 5, no. 2:15–17.

Kornblum, W., and J. Julian. 1998. *Social problems*. Upper Saddle River, N.J.: Prentice Hall.

Lareau, A. 1989. Family-school relationships: A view from the classroom. *Educational Policy* 3, no. 3:245–57.

Lefcourt, H. M. 1982. *Locus of control: Current trends in theory and research*. 2d ed. Hillsdale, N.J.: Erlbaum.

Lewis, O. 1966. *La vida: A Puerto Rican family in the culture of poverty*. San Juan: Random House.

Lieberman, M. 1993. *Public education: An autopsy*. Cambridge: Harvard University Press.

Lightfoot, S. 1978. *Worlds apart: Relationships between families and schools*. New York: Basic Books.

Lord, S. E., J. S. Eccles, and K. A. McCarthy. 1994. Surviving the junior high school transition: Family processes and self perceptions as protective and risk factors. *Journal of Early Adolescence* 14:162–99.

Loury, G. G. 1995. *One by one from the inside out: Essays and reviews on race and responsibility in America*. New York: Free Press.

Malone, P. J. 1985. Socioeconomic status, family culture, and academic achievement: A study of black and white pupil performance in an interracial school. Ph.D. diss., University of Wisconsin–Milwaukee.

Mead, L. 1986. *Beyond entitlement: The social obligations of citizenship*. New York: Free Press.

Mele, Alfred. 1995. Current patterns of parental authority. *Developmental Psychology Monograph* 4, no. 1:1–103.

Mordkowitz, E., and H. Ginsberg. 1987. Early academic socialization of successful Asian American college students. *Quarterly Newsletter of the Laboratory for Comparative Human Cognition* 9:85–91.

Neisser, U., ed. 1986. *The school achievement of minority children*. Hillsdale, N.J.: Erlbaum.

———. 1990. Literacy and schooling in subordinate cultures: The case of Black Americans. In *Going to school: The African American experience*, edited by K. Lamatey. Albany: State University of New York Press.

Rodman, H. 1971. *Lower class families: The culture of poverty in Negro Trinidad*. New York: Oxford University Press.

Rosen, B. 1959. Race, ethnicity, and the achievement syndrome. *American Sociological Review* 18:176–206.

Sampson, W. A. 1973. The relative importance of ascribed and achieved variables as family social status determinants. Ph.D. diss., Johns Hopkins University.

Schweinhart, L. J., et al. 1993. *Significant benefits: The High/Scope Perry preschool study through age 27.* Ypsilanti, Mich.: High/Scope Press.

Steinberg, L. 1998. Standards outside the classroom. In *Brookings papers on educational policy,* edited by D. Ravitch. Washington, D.C.: Brookings Institution.

Stone, C. 1998. *Changing urban education.* Lawrence: University Press of Kansas.

Suskind, R. 1998. *A hope in the unseen: An American odyssey from the inner-city to the Ivy League.* New York: Broadway Books.

Traub, J. 2000. Schools are not the answer. *New York Times Magazine,* 16 January.

U.S. Department of Commerce, Bureau of the Census. 1990. *1990 census of the population and housing: Summary of population and housing characteristics, Illinois.* Washington, D.C.: U.S. Department of Commerce.

Valentine, C. 1968. *Culture and poverty.* Chicago: University of Chicago Press.

Winch, R. F. 1962. *Identification and its familial determinants: Exposition of theory and results of pilot studies.* Indianapolis: Bobbs-Merrill.

Winerip, M. 1998. School choice: A new beginning for public education or the beginning of the end? *New York Times Magazine,* 14 June.

Zigler, E., and S. Styfco, eds. 1993. *Head Start and beyond: A national plan for extended childhood intervention.* New Haven, Conn.: Yale University Press.

ADDITIONAL SOURCES

Anderson, E. 1990. *Streetwise: Race, class, and change in an urban community.* Chicago: University of Chicago Press.

Borstein, M., ed. 1995. *Children and Parenting.* Vol. 1 of *Handbook of Parenting.* Mahwah, N.J.: Erlbaum.

Brooks-Gunn, J. 1995. Strategies for altering the outcomes of poor children and their families. In *Escape from poverty: What makes a difference for children?* edited by P. L. C. Landsdale and J. Brooks-Gunn. Cambridge: Cambridge University Press.

Bryk, D., V. E. Lee, and P. B. Holland. 1993. *Catholic schools and the common good.* Cambridge: Harvard University Press.

Coleman, J. S. 1961. *The adolescent society.* Westport, Conn.: Greenwood Press.

Comer, J. P. 1988. Educating poor minority children. *Scientific American* 256, no. 11:42–48.

Cook, T. D., and T. R. Curtin. 1986. The mainstream and the underclass: Why are the differences so salient and the similarities so unobtrusive? In *Social comparison, social justice, and relative deprivation: Theoretical, empirical, and policy perspectives,* edited by J. C. Masters and W. P. Smith. Hillsdale, N.J.: Erlbaum.

Crouter, A., et al. 1990. Parental monitoring and perceptions of children's school performance and conduct in dual and single earner families. *Developmental Psychology* 26, no. 4:649–57.

Drake, St. Clair, and H. Cayton. 1962. *Black metropolis: A study of Negro life in a northern city.* New York: Harper and Row.

Eccles, J. S., et al. 1991. Control versus autonomy during adolescence. *Journal of Social Issues* 47, no. 4:53–68.

Epstein, J. 1987a. Parental involvement: What research says to administrators. *Education and Urban Society* 19:119–36.

———. 1987b. Toward a theory of family–school connections: Teacher practices and parent involvement. In *Social intervention: Potential and constraints,* edited by K. Hurrelman, F. Kaufman, and F. Lasel. Hawthorne, N.Y.: Aldine de Gruyter.

Furstenberg, F. F., Jr. 1997. The influence of neighborhoods on children's development: A theoretical perspective and a research agenda. In *Neighborhood poverty: Policy implications in studying neighborhoods,* vol. 2, edited by J. Brooks-Gunn, G. Duncan, and J. L. Aber. New York: Russell Sage Foundation.

Gans, H. J. 1995. *The war against the poor: The underclass and anti-poverty policy.* New York: Basic Books.

Garmezy, N. 1993. Children in poverty: Resilence despite risk. *Psychiatry: Interpersonal and Biological Processes* 56:127–36.

Ginsberg, H. 1986. The myth of the deprived child: New thoughts on poor children. In *The school achievement of minority children: New perspectives,* edited by V. Neisser. Hillsdale, N.J.: Erlbaum.

Hannerz, U. 1969. *Soulside: Inquiries into ghetto culture and community.* New York: Columbia University Press.

Jencks, C., and S. Mayer. 1990. The social consequences of growing up in a poor neighborhood. In *Inner city poverty in the United States,* edited by L. E. Lyman and M. G. H. McGeary. Washington, D.C.: National Academy Press.

Katz, M. B. 1989. *The undeserving poor: From the war on poverty to the war on welfare.* New York: Pantheon Books.

Kelso, W. A. 1994. *Poverty and the underclass: Changing perceptions of the poor in America.* New York: New York University Press.

Kotlowitz, A. 1991. *There are no children here.* New York: Doubleday.

Lane, R. 1995. The perils of school vouchers. In *Rethinking schools: An agenda for change,* edited by D. Levine et al. New York: New Press.

Lareau, A. 1989. *Home advantage: Social class and parental intervention in elementary education.* New York: Folmer Press.

Lewis, H. 1967. Culture, class, and family life among low-income urban Negroes. In *Employment, race, and poverty,* edited by A. Ross and H. Hill. New York: Harcourt, Brace, and World.

Lewis, O. 1950. An anthropological approach to family studies. *American Journal of Sociology* 55, no. 5:469-75.

——. 1959. *Five families: Mexican case studies in the culture of poverty.* New York: Basic Books.

——. 1966. The culture of poverty. *Scientific American* 214, no. 10:19-25.

Liebow, E. 1969. *Talley's corner: A study of Negro streetcorner men.* Boston: Little, Brown.

Lipset, S., and R. Bendix. 1959. *Social mobility in industrial society.* Berkeley: University of California Press.

Mackler, B. 1971. Blacks who are academically successful. *Urban Education* 5:210-37.

Macleod, J. 1987. *Ain't no making it: Aspirations and attainment in a low income neighborhood.* Boulder, Colo.: Westview Press.

Massey, D., and N. Denton. 1993. *American apartheid: Segregation and the making of the underclass.* Cambridge: Harvard University Press.

McAdoo, H. P. and J. L. McAdoo. 1985. *Black children: Social, educational and parental environments.* Beverly Hills, Calif.: Sage.

McLanhan, S., and G. Sandefur. 1994. *Growing up with a single parent: What hurts, what helps.* Cambridge: Harvard University Press.

Murray, C. 1984. *Losing ground: American social policy, 1950-80.* New York: Basic Books.

Ogbu. 1974. *The next generation: An ethnography of education in an urban neighborhood.* New York: Academic Press.

——. 1986a. Class stratification, racial stratification, and schooling. In *Race, class, and schooling: Special studies in comparative education,* no. 17, edited by L. Weis. Buffalo: State University of New York Press.

——. 1986b. The consequences of the American caste system. In *The school achievement of minority children,* edited by U. Neisser. Hillsdale, N.J.: Erlbaum.

Peterson, P. E. 1991. The urban underclass and the poverty paradox. In *The urban underclass,* edited by C. Jencks and P. Peterson. Washington, D.C.: Brookings Institution.

Phares, E. J. 1976. *Locus of control in personality.* Morristown, N.J.: General Learning Press.

Rogoff, B., and W. Gardner. 1984. Adult guidance of everyday cognition. In *Everyday cognition: Its development in social context,* edited by B. Rogoff and J. Love. Cambridge: Harvard University Press.

Sampson, W. A., and P. H. Rossi. 1975. Race and family social standing. *American Sociological Review* 40, no. 2:201–14.

Scott-Jones, D. 1987. Mother as teacher in the families of high and low achieving first graders. *Journal of Negro Education* 56, no. 1:21–34.

Sigel, I. 1985. A conceptual analysis of beliefs. In *Parental belief systems,* edited by I. Sigel. Hillsdale, N.J.: Erlbaum.

Stedman, L. C. 1999. An assesment of the contemporary debate over U.S. achievement. In *Brookings papers on educational policy,* edited by D. Ravitch. Washington, D.C.: Brookings Institution.

Steinberg, L. S., et al. 1992. Impact of parenting practices on adolescent achievement: Authoritative, school achievement, and encouragement to succeed. *Child Development* 63:1266–81.

Vidich, A. J., ed. 1995. *The new middle classes: Life-styles, status claims, and political orientations.* Washington Square: New York University Press.

Wilson, W. J. 1987. *The truly disadvantaged: The inner-city, the underclass, and public policy.* Chicago: University of Chicago Press.

INDEX

ABOUT THE AUTHOR

William A. Sampson grew up in a relatively poor but distinctly middle-class family in Milwaukee, Wisconsin. Both parents constantly stressed achievement, discipline, and education, and he went on to receive degrees from Howard University, the University of Wisconsin at Milwaukee, and finally a Ph.D. in social relations from Johns Hopkins University. Long interested in race, social class, and education, Professor Sampson has put those concerns together in his recent research on the impact of the family on poor black and Latino families.

Sampson is an associate professor at DePaul University in Chicago, where his students have been critical both in his research and in helping to shape his thinking about poor nonwhite families.